About the book

In North America, human beings have become enthralled by the automobile: A quarter of our working lives is spent paying for them; communities fight each other for the right to build more of them; our cities have been torn down, remade and planned with their needs as the overriding concern; wars are fought to keep their fuel tanks filled; songs are written to praise them; cathedrals are built to worship them. In *Stop Signs: Cars and Capitalism on the Road to Economic, Social and Ecological Decay*, authors Yves Engler and Bianca Mugyenyi argue that the automobile's ascendance is inextricably linked to capitalism and involved corporate malfeasance, political intrigue, backroom payoffs, media manipulation, racism, academic corruption, third world coups, secret armies, environmental destruction and war. An anti-car, road-trip story, *Stop Signs* is a unique must-read for all those who wish to escape the clutches of auto domination.

First printing April. 2011
Cover by Working Design
Printed and bound in Canada by Transcontinental Printing
A co-publication of
RED Publishing
2736 Cambridge Street
Vancouver, British Columbia V5K 1L7 and
Fernwood Publishing
32 Oceanvista Lane
Black Point, Nova Scotia B0J 1B0
and 748 Broadway Avenue, Winnipeg, Manitoba, R3G 0X3
www.fernwoodpublishing.ca

Canadian   Patrimoine
Heritage   canadien

Le Conseil des Arts The Canada Council
du Canada   for the Arts

Fernwood Publishing Company Limited gratefully acknowledges the financial support of the Department of Canadian Heritage, the Nova Scotia Department of Tourism and Culture and the Canada Council for the Arts for our publishing program.

Library and Archives Canada Cataloguing in Publication
Engler, Yves, 1979-
Stop signs : cars and capitalism on the road to economic, social and ecological decay / Yves Engler and Bianca Mugyenyi.
Co-published by: Red Publishing.
Includes bibliographical references.
ISBN 978-1-55266-384-4
1. Automobiles--Economic aspects. 2. Automobiles--Social aspects.
3. Automobiles--Environmental aspects. I. Mugyenyi, Bianca, 1980-
II. Title.
HE5611.E55 2010   388.3'42
C2010-902928-3

Contents

This book is dedicated to our fathers, Joshua Mugyenyi and Gary Engler. To Joshua's memory for inspiring his daughter endlessly with his love of knowledge and new places, his sense of fairness and justice, and for teaching her never to honk unless absolutely necessary. To Gary for tirelessly indulging and facilitating his son's all consuming obsessions — from hockey to political activism to writing — for being a coach, and a teammate at the same time.

Preface

"More cars than drivers?" I repeated.

"Yeah," said Yves, "for every person of driving age, there are 1.02 cars."

Later this startling statistic was confirmed when we discovered that for every person with a drivers license there are 1.17 cars. According to the *Globe and Mail*, 246 million registered cars and trucks served 210 million licensed drivers in the USA.[1]

Witnessing the growth of auto travel in my ancestral homeland, Uganda, and reading about China's rapid adoption of the car, our interest in the subject grew. As we waded through stacks of books, journals and newspapers, it became clear that we needed to see for ourselves what the automobile has wrought in its favoured habitat. To see what could happen if Uganda and China followed the U.S. example in car culture it would be necessary for us to journey to that part of the planet where the automobile reigns supreme. We needed to go to the USA. It would be like a field trip to the British Columbia rainforest for graduate students in ecology. We would go from top to bottom, from side to side, to study the land of the car.

It didn't hurt that Yves and I were knee deep into a snowy Montreal winter. We'd had a couple days that were colder than Siberia and believed some time in California, New Orleans, Las Vegas and Miami would thaw us out. Fresh out of university, working a dead end job and mired in existential angst, it was time to bust out of the North Pole. I gave my two weeks notice so we could hit the road, but a few details still needed ironing out. We didn't have a car or valid driver's license between us.

How were we going to discover the truth about automobiles? No vehicle, no licenses, no problem. We'd do this road trip car-less. The bus would be our viewing platform, an elevated perspective from which to survey the land of the automobile.

...

We have tried to take an "ecological" approach to discussing the automobile in its North American context. The private car is a key element of our transportation system, our economy and our environment; it has significant impacts on our health, geography, housing, education and culture. And, all these interact. The automobile is a player in a complex system. It has a place in that system in the same way that an elephant has a place in the complex ecology of the African savannah. To truly understand that place we must look at the system from the perspective of the elephant/automobile and from other points of view, including the overall system. We must understand the car as part of a system in which it survives and thrives. Just as living creatures require and simultaneously create complex habitats in which they interact with other living things, automobiles also require and create their habitats. While human beings may think cars are mere transportation devices — tools at our disposal — in fact they, and us, play a role in a complex transport-economic-social-geographic-environmental-cultural system.

This book is a warning to people who suspect cars might play a significant role in our planet's unfolding environmental disaster: The automobile is much worse than you think. In addition it is a cautionary tale for the majority of our planet's inhabitants. Learn from the "developed world" what good you can, but take heed from what we have done wrong. This book also contains a message for people who believe our current economic system will provide solutions to overcome the environmental destructiveness of the private car: Not bloody likely. Modern capitalism and cars go together like Minneapolis and St. Paul, like rubber and the road. One is very hard to imagine without the other.

Stop Signs

This book is also a road story. Each chapter deals with an aspect of the automobile that is tied to a location we visited, but the book is organized thematically, not by geography. In Part One we describe the effects the car has had on its habitat. In Part Two we discuss why this intrusive species has been so successful.

PART ONE

Homo Automotivis
and its environment

1. Freedom — Fort Lauderdale

The private car is "the last great freedom."
— Ronald Reagan speaking to the Detroit
Economic Club (fresh air was the first)
"The automobile is one of the two most liberating
inventions of the past century, ranking only
behind the microchip." — Wall Street Journal
editorial

I was late. The bus was leaving for New York in half an hour and I still hadn't bought my ticket. I strapped on my backpack, flew out my apartment, and dashed two blocks to the metro. I was lucky. It was rush hour and the trains were back-to-back. Fifteen minutes later I arrived at Berri-UQAM station. I raced through the underground pedestrian tunnel and into the bus station. Panting as I rounded the corner, I spied Yves waving from the bus. I'd made it. Au revoir, Montreal! Like the birds that left us behind, we were heading south.

But, first we had to cross the border. I geared up for the usual harassment.

"Where were you born?"

"Are you carrying dangerous weapons?"

After making it past the suspicious border guards, my mind floated up and away; the engine hummed and scenery rushed past the glass sides of the bus. I leaned my head against the window, the world a sleepy haze of grass, trees, rocks, billboards and highway. From Albany to New York City, through Charlotte and Atlanta, our Greyhound chased the sun.

We were heading for Fort Lauderdale to visit Nina, my best friend, who'd left Montreal to study conflict resolution. As we traveled towards Southern Florida, I reflected on our first phone call after her departure. Nina, always diplomatic, contrasted her experiences in the two cities: "It's so different here…it's hard to describe. I miss the freedom of Montreal."

This struck me as peculiar. She lived just outside Miami, a destination thousands of Canadian "snow birds" spent millions jetting to each year. How could it be anything other than fabulous?

During the last stage of the journey to Fort Lauderdale, I awoke from the sound of my own snoring to find myself seated across the aisle from a friendly new passenger who introduced himself as Earl. Earl was a construction site manager (and Harley Davidson enthusiast) from Tennessee who'd recently moved to Pompano, Florida.

"Are your folks in Montreal, too?" he asked.

"No. My family is back in Uganda."

"Rwanda?"

"No, Uganda."

There was a spark of recognition in his eyes now.

"Ah yes, Idi Amin!"

"That's the place," I sighed, explaining that our family had been exiled from Uganda when I was a baby, but had moved back after the civil war. On mentioning we were heading to Fort Lauderdale with no vehicle to speak of, his eyes narrowed, "You can't *walk* there. If you've got no money, take the transit bus. Good luck to you." As we disembarked, Earl winked at Yves, and muttered something about getting himself some brown sugar.

It was 10:30 P.M when we pulled into the station and public transit was done for the day. We showed Nina's address to an attendant and inquired whether we could foot it.

"Either hail a cab or camp out until morning," she said. Lacking bug spray and marshmallows, we were unprepared for the latter, so we caught a cab and sped down a Florida highway, our driver blasting the air conditioner and Dionne Warwick's greatest hits the entire way. Forty dollars later we stumbled out of the cab into Nina's rental estate.

After an ecstatic reunion, a hot shower and a good night's sleep, I woke up excited about my new surroundings. I began to think more about Earl's warning: "You can't *walk* there." Perhaps it was delirium from the glorious heat, but Yves and I were up for the challenge.

In the afternoon we took the bus to the nearby Davie commercial area, with a plan to look around and return on foot. We began our walk back on a neat little sidewalk just off the mall parking lot. It led us past a mile of strip mall, ending suddenly and suspiciously at the doorstep of a McDonald's. There was no pedestrian path beyond the golden arches and no option but to backtrack and join the highway. There was a sidewalk of sorts on the other side, but we had to cross a six-lane torrent to get there. There wasn't a stoplight or intersection in sight and traffic surged relentlessly. Finally, the traffic broke and we made a run for it. People eyed us from their cars as though we were insane. What was ridiculous was so few pedestrians in such gorgeous weather. And where were the cyclists? The place was flat as a chapatti.

The "sidewalk" was better described as a nature trail. We struggled through a habitat of bushes, bramble and freakishly tall grass, over fences and past occasional parades of small animals. The only thing this path didn't have was people. We were stranded. After what seemed like an eternity, we spotted a traffic light. It turned green and we scooted across the street, frantic, as it turned red again before we'd reached the middle. No wonder potential pedestrians had been put off; the game was rigged.

We made it back, but we'd been put in our place. Earl was right. You can't walk there, and people don't. In a country where you can get to the moon, God help you if you want to cross the street. Fort Lauderdale's splintered land had submitted to the car's insatiable appetite for space and I wondered how all these people would get home if we ever ran out of oil.

...

While trying to get around without a car in southern Florida it occurred to us that from the viewpoint of an evolutionary biologist, one might postulate the emergence of a new species named *Homo Automotivis*, the result of a century of people living with cars and capitalism. This new sort of human, an evolutionary adaptation to a changed environment, has a symbiotic relationship with the automobile: Neither can survive without the other and both define themselves through the other. The symbiosis between *Homo Automotivis* and the car has economic, social, geographical, environmental, cultural and even religious dimensions.

The most convincing sign of the emergence of this new species and its relationship to the car is the incredible amount of time the two spend together. The average American spends 18.5 hours a week in a car, which adds up to about a month a year or one of every six waking hours.[1] This new species and their cars traveled three trillion miles together in 2010.[2] The total number of miles driven on U.S. roads more than quadrupled over the past half century.[3] In the fifties, an American drove an average of 3,029 vehicle miles a year; in the sixties this increased to 3,994; in the seventies it reached 5,440 miles; and in the eighties averaged out at 6,722 miles. By the nineties, Americans drove an average of 8,590 miles per year and by 2003 it escalated to 9,940 miles.[4] Only in the first half of 2008, as gasoline soared to $4 per gallon, did the number of miles driven actually decline. Today drivers average over 10,000 miles a year.

Canadians, the world's second most automotive dependent people, drive 30 percent less than Americans.[5] According to the 2007 Census, 87.7 percent of Americans drove to work in a private vehicle, with 77 percent driving alone.[6] The U.S. Department of Transportation explained, the "private vehicle, especially driven alone to work, is the mode of choice."[7]

Homo Automotivis inhabits a land where housing is designed to maximize the use of the car. As cities seep outwards and destinations disperse, the automobile ascends to the rank of absolute necessity, indispensable even for reaching whatever meagre public transit exists. The process has accelerated over the past six decades and during the housing boom that ended in 2007 developers built further and further from the city, encouraging a lengthy convoy into the suburbs, exurbs and beyond.[i] Nearly two-thirds of the U.S. metropolitan population lives in the suburbs and the fastest growing counties are often located thirty miles or more from urban centres.[8] With less than 50,000 residents, these "micropolitan" areas are not big enough to gain metropolitan status but are "too urban to be rural."[9]

It is increasingly common for commuters to relocate as far as a hundred miles from the city. In an amusing promotional stunt, Midas held a "longest commuter" competition. A lucky contestant won ten thousand dollars in gas money and free maintenance for driving 375 miles (600 kilometres) daily.[10] The not-so-lucky runner up was so disappointed at his loss, he moved another 30 miles from work, topping up his 352 miles.

...

Despite the multiple lane roads crisscrossing Fort Lauderdale and other cities like it, cars often moved slowly or not at all, their human occupants trapped inside. As we progressed from state to state, we noticed that the slower the traffic seemed to move, the more radio shows went beyond run-of-the-mill tips on getting home fast. But, while the announcers were endlessly upbeat, there is nothing fun about gridlock.

On any given day in 2006, major urban U.S. roads were congested an average of 7.1 hours. This was up from 6.2 hours in 1993 and an average of 4.5 hours in 1982.[11] And all signs indicate

---

i One study found that the rapid increase in gasoline prices in the late 1970s led to a much greater reduction in consumption than the increases in the 2000s. The reason is that people live further from their work and it is more difficult to cut out car travel.

that congestion is getting worse. In the thirty biggest cities, the hours lost to traffic jams nearly quintupled between 1980 and 2004.[12] In 2008 almost a third of U.S. drivers said they wanted to work from home to avoid the commute and the previous years had seen a huge growth of commuters who wake up before 5 a.m. to beat the morning rush.[13] A Princeton study questioning participants about a typical day found that commuting was the least popular daily activity ("intimate relations" and "relaxing with friends" were the best part).[14] Commuting — or specifically, buying a big house outside the city — is a prime example of something people think will make them happier despite its proven negative effect.[15]

From lower back pain to sciatica, driving excessively has many other harmful effects.[16] Psychologists report growing complaints about traffic anxiety. "If you're stuck in traffic, there is a feeling of being out of control," said Dr. Laura Pinegar.[17] A 2004 *New England Journal of Medicine* study found that nearly one in 12 heart attacks was linked to traffic (the researchers weren't sure if the main cause was stress or pollution).[18]

Homo Automotivis spends a huge amount of time servicing the auto, driving in search of parking and chauffeuring non-drivers. Both indirectly and directly, the car consumes a considerable share of his day. This means less time for family, less time for leisure and less time for civic engagement.

Then there is the matter of money — acquired through working long hours to satisfy the automotive relationship. It's been calculated that the average person in the U.S. works from January 1 to March 31 to pay for his or her automobile(s). April 1 has been declared auto freedom day; the day people begin earning money for food, board, clothing, education and other necessities of life.[19]

While the convenience of owning a car is often overestimated, the costs of driving are generally underestimated.[20] With insurance, gas, repairs, monthly installments and more, it cost an average of $8,400 a year to own a car in 2010.[21]

Of course, "automobills" depend on the city you live in. In auto-dependent metropolitan areas such as Tampa Bay, Houston, Atlanta, Dallas-Fort Worth and Detroit, residents spend nearly a quarter of household budgets on travel.[22] In the more walk-able, public transit friendly cities of San Francisco, Boston, Portland and New York, residents spend less than 17 percent of household budgets on transportation.[23]

Transportation's proportion of total personal expenditures doubled with the decline of urban rail.[24] In 1935, families spent 10 percent of their budgets on getting around; this rose to 20 percent in 1972 and then plateaued.[25] According to the American Public Transportation Association, individuals who travel without a car can save a whopping $8,368 annually.[26]

Mass transit is not just good for the individual and family budget, it's good for the national budget. In countries such as the Netherlands or Japan, where it's easier to get around by foot, bike or rail, a much smaller proportion of GDP is devoted to transportation.[27] Japan spends nine percent of its GDP on transportation vs. 20 percent in the U.S.[28]

When the automobile is used as the primary mode of mass transit, the poorest are hardest hit. U.S. families in the bottom fifth of income distribution, for instance, spend seven times the percentage of their household income on car insurance compared to families in the top fifth.[29] "Those earning less than $14,000 per year after taxes, spend approximately 40 percent of their take-home pay on transportation. This compares to 22 percent for families earning between $27,177 and $44,461 annually, and 13 percent for families making more than $71,900 per year."[30]

Nearly three-quarters of U.S. households earning less than $15,000 a year own a car and, in an extreme example of auto dependence, tens of thousands of "mobile homeless" live in their vehicles.[31] The poor purchase cars because there is no other option in a society built to serve the needs of the automobile. If you want to work or you want to visit your friends in a city designed by *Homo Automotivis* you need a car. And there is only one way for most people to pay for a car-based lifestyle: work more. More than everybody else, that is. Americans work on average 270 hours more a year than the French and 400 more than the Dutch.[32] [33] Of course people work more to pay for all sorts of things. But, it's one thing to work extra to save for a down payment for a home or to support a new baby; it's quite another to work overtime for a hunk of speeding metal.

Stranger still, after the average time required to buy, maintain and drive a car is divided by the number of miles traveled, estimates place average automobile speeds at some five miles an hour: the pace of a brisk walk. Writing in the early 1970s, Ivan Illich explained: "The typical American male devotes more than 1,600 hours a year to his car. He sits in it while it goes and while it stands idling. He parks it and searches for it. He earns the money to put down on it and to meet the monthly installments. He works to pay for petrol, tolls, insurance, taxes and tickets. He spends four of his sixteen waking hours on the road or gathering his resources for it. And this figure does not take into account the time consumed by other activities dictated by transport: time spent in hospitals, traffic courts and garages; time spent watching automobile commercials or attending consumer education meetings to improve the quality of the next buy. The model American puts in 1,600 hours to get 7,500 miles: less than five miles per hour."[34]

...

While the majority of the U.S. population has access to a vehicle, a significant minority does not. The *Homo Automotivis* democracy denies full participation to as much as a third of its population.[35] While streets once functioned as sites of recreation and social gathering, the dawn of the auto age brought anti-play laws that drove children from the road, the first minority whose freedom was limited by the automobile. (In the early 1900s New

York City police even arrested kids who continued to play on the streets.)[36] Today children are often reliant on elders to get from place to place: school, soccer practice, a friend's home or the arcade. After so many years of dependence, it's no wonder teens lunge desperately for the golden ticket to freedom from parental constraint, the driver's license.

The second minority denied participation in the essential rites of *Homo Automotivis* society are the elderly, stripped of their freedom the day their licenses are revoked. "The hardest thing we do in our practice is actually dealing with driving issues," explained Malcolm Man-Son-Hing, an Ottawa geriatrics doctor.[37] An American Journal of Public Health study found that non-drivers over the age of 70 were four times as likely to end up in long-term care and the health effects on non-driving elderly were particularly severe in areas without adequate public transit.[38] The right to participate in an auto-centric world is also denied to the disabled, many of whom are simply unable to operate a vehicle. Automobile dependence, a lack of curb cuts on sidewalks and oceans of parking between strip malls and bus stops, all serve as barriers to basic mobility for those with physical disabilities. As a result disability advocacy groups have begun to campaign against sprawl.

The best evidence of *Homo Automotivis'* emergence is the popular equation of cars with freedom. But, is a landscape built for cars really a land of freedom? In a city where walking is not an option, biking is dangerous and public transport is inadequate, citizens are handed a life sentence of immobility only to be released with the keys to an automobile.

"The ability to move does not necessarily equate with freedom," writes David Engwicht in *Reclaiming Our Cities and Towns*. "Ask any prisoner. They are free to run marathons around the perimeter of an exercise quadrangle or walk around their cells to their hearts' content. Prison walls do not stop movement per se; they stop access."[39]

At what point do unwanted miles impinge upon freedom? What good is all this motion, if it takes longer to get where you want to go, if the trip is more expensive, if it's more dangerous, if you don't interact with anyone on the way or if there's no longer anywhere interesting to go? What has been lost in the name of the private automobile?

…

A few months after our car-less odyssey, Nina visited me in Montreal. On the day she arrived we wasted no time. I picked her up at the airport, hopping from metro to bus. After dropping her bags at my downtown apartment we wandered a block and a half to my favourite Thai restaurant. Fueled up and ready to hit the town, we walked 25 blocks to the cobblestoned Old Port where we strolled amongst street shows and merchants peddling their wares. Opting out of the walk back, we descended to the underground metro, thundering back downtown. We resurfaced at Guy Street and de Maisonneuve, minutes from the Comedy Nest, where Daliso, a Malawian friend, was performing *Don't Let Them Deport Me* (followed a few months later with the unfortunate *They're Deporting Me Anyway*).

We kept the night going, pushing onwards to St. Laurent, a hub of clubs, bars and lounges. Like the Beastie Boys once said, "You gotta fight for your right to party." When it was time to call it quits, we caught a 24-hour bus, which dropped us a block and a half from my apartment. Safe, sound and satisfied. No need for a car. No need for cable television. Another world is possible. *Homo Automotivis* could be an evolutionary dead end.

2. Get out of the fast lane, moron — St. Louis

I touched my fingers to the glass as our Greyhound flashed past an array of buildings set up like a giant chemistry experiment. Curious looking tubes of concrete crisscrossed every which way, from multi-colored complexes to cylindrical towers. But there were no brightly colored chemicals bubbling to the surface of these vats. They lay idle on the city's edge, thickets of grass had reclaimed the spaces among them.

We were coming into St. Louis, a city that lost 70 percent of its population between 1950 and 2010 (from 856,000 to 319,000).[1] The remnants of its glory days were inked across red brick towers in large uniform letters. Quiet, empty and abandoned, the factories once bustled with people and production.

The bus pulled into a cramped but charming old station. Bone-tired after thirteen hours on board, we strapped on our oversized backpacks and began a slow trek to the downtown core. In the distance we saw steamboats and the ferry to Illinois. The mighty Mississippi was back, now joined by the Missouri. Time worn bridges of steel and iron straddled the asphalt on the downtown edge. A tangle of freeways loomed above, below and to the sides. It was dawn and the streets were empty. We felt small, vulnerable and out of place on terrain meant for automobiles.

As the morning matured, nodding faces and sunshine ushered a pair of obvious travelers into the heart of St. Louis. A few miles on from the highway, we turned onto a small quiet street lined with red brick houses. Nearing the "Huckleberry Finn" youth hostel, we walked past an old Buick when the silence was broken by a sharp cry. Startled, I turned and walked back to verify that this car was indeed yelling at us. Sure enough when I returned it let out another ferocious warning. I marched on in disbelief. One more sign of *Homo Automotivis*. This new species thinks it's perfectly normal to be roared at by a car. (Several weeks earlier in a parking lot at the Houston Galleria, a car rolled by playing thunderously loud music. A rather sensitive vehicle nearby just couldn't take it anymore, adding its shrill voice to the cacophony. Evidently cars can also piss off each other.)

Aside from manufacturers, misanthropes and *Homo Automotivis*, no one could be fond of a car alarm. They're designed to be obnoxious and anxiety inducing, wrecking good moods in their wake and perhaps even our health. As explained in the *New York Times*, "the type of noise produced by a car alarm boosts stress hormones and has been linked to cardiovascular disease, gastrointestinal illnesses, psychological problems and unhealthy fetal development."[2]

Cars are the single largest contributor to the nation's noise level.[3] On the sidewalk, at home, behind the desk, in bed — even infiltrating our dreams — the sound of traffic is relentless. "Many of us hear traffic noise so constantly," writes Katie Alvord, "that we no longer pay conscious attention, yet noise still affects us, even if we are unaware."[4]

Traffic noise can lead to physical and psychological health conditions including disrupted sleep patterns, hearing damage and anxiety. It increases stress hormone levels, heart rate, blood pressure and muscle tension while hampering memory and children's learning.[5] Noise can lead to depression and according to research thousands die prematurely from heart disease triggered by long-term exposure to excessive noise.[6]

The situation seems to be worsening. Costing upwards of a thousand dollars, a new generation of car horns "clock in at more than 120 decibels."[7] Those with less cash to burn can also contribute to the sound and fury of the streets by personalizing their car horns from a vast online selection of downloadable tones or tunes.[8]

Of course *Homo Automotivis* might consider the noise generated by automobiles a problem, but certainly not a crime. You can call the cops about a noisy party down the block, but don't bother notifying the authorities about the guy who blasts his horn every two minutes of his hour-long commute.

Auto noise tends to be concentrated geographically with the most auto dependent populations in the suburbs suffering the least.[9] The adverse effects of noise also disproportionately victimize those with lower incomes as they are more likely to live adjacent to major traffic arteries.[i]

...

It's not just the noise; driving brings out the beast in *Homo Automotivis*, like a lion hunting on the Ugandan savannah. Describing the territorial nature of parking, the *Globe and Mail* reports that, "The typical driver takes 32 seconds to depart from a parking lot when nobody is around — but 39 seconds when somebody else is waiting for the spot."[10] A Dutch study found that 25 percent of drivers displayed aggressive behavior towards pedestrians approaching a crosswalk. The same drivers were then evaluated in a non-driving situation designed to agitate; after two successive wrong numbers, just 11 percent of those reached by phone became aggressive.[11]

...

Growing up, I was anxious to get behind the wheel of a car. I was exhilarated by the thought of my independence, drunk with power and thrilled at this new and dangerous game that I had

---

i Traffic takes up space, both physically and psychologically. A study of 600 people in four New York neighbourhoods reported in the Oct. 6, 2006 New York Times, found that: "Residents of well-trafficked streets were more likely to think ill of where they lived. They were less disposed to letting their children play outdoors. They tended to have fewer friends in the neighborhood, be more likely to stay in their apartments and not hang out on the street to schmooze."

not been allowed to play. During my first lesson, I was determined to conquer the streets of Kampala so I honked my horn at every opportunity. Tempers flared, I had never been cursed at like this before, but at such a great speed, I felt immune. I felt powerful, as if the car had become part of me. Who cared what others thought!

Homo Automotivis' behavior often goes beyond simple anger, morphing into rage. Drivers rage against traffic, roadblocks, potholes, rain, snow, pedestrians and any bicyclist with the nerve to take up part of a lane; the provocation is anything that slows the car. Road ragers curse, exchange obscene gestures and worse. This unmanaged anger is catered to and encouraged with books and websites such as roadrage.com, which sells 8 X 11 cards bearing insults to other drivers ("Get out of the fast lane, moron").

While I have never witnessed a case of sidewalk rage, even the mildest mannered folks seem susceptible to extreme bouts of irrational behavior behind the wheel. I can't help but smile, remembering a weekend drive to the Entebbe zoo many years ago. My father piled my siblings and several toddler cousins into the car one hot Sunday afternoon, but our tranquil ride was interrupted minutes into the journey when an inconsiderate driver cut us off at the clock tower roundabout, provoking a spasmodic fit of fiery language and an exchange of alarming gestures. Three wide-eyed toddlers watched this frenzy from the back seat. My Dad's undiluted emotion turned to muttering and then to silence. It was more curious than anything we saw at the zoo. Even in Uganda there have long been signs of the emerging *Homo Automotivis*.

Of course, locked into motorized machines in militarized lineups and forced to stay on high alert, drivers are bound to lose their marbles. Beyond obvious stressors such as congestion and the desperate search for parking, research has found that driving itself — on roads and in simulators — causes a number of physiological responses including elevated heart rate, increases in serum cortisol and catecholamine levels as well as self-reports of agitation and anxiety.[12]

There are a variety of theories explaining why cars create anti-social behavior. *In Road Rage and Aggressive Driving: Steering Clear of Highway Warfare*, Leon James and Diane Nahl argue this behavior is a territorial defense mechanism. When the "territory of the automobile is invaded, or when some other car tries symbolically to dominate it, the perceived threat is sufficient to evoke almost primeval reactions in even the meekest of motorists."[13] Other scholars emphasize the egoistic roots of antisocial behavior behind the wheel. They argue that the more vehicle owners identify with their car as a reflection of themselves, the more sensitive they are to perceived vehicular insult.[14] For his part, Kevin L. Borg, a car historian at James Madison University, explains: "Human behavior becomes different in a closed vehicle than it is in a social setting ... there is a sense of social isolation."[15] Together with the megalomania induced by the speed and power of an automobile, the car's inaccessibility emboldens the driver who is secure in the unlikelihood of being called to account.

...

Waiting for a bus in St. Louis' university loop we struck up a conversation with a man and woman registering voters. At some point in the discussion, the man asked: "Isn't Canada boring?"

Someone from St. Louis was asking us if Montreal was boring? We were polite as Canadians are supposed to be, but discussed it afterwards. This guy, who was asking us if Canada was boring, lived in a city designed to keep people in at night. No one was in downtown St. Louis that weekend besides the baseball crowd. We even met some out-of-town fans who couldn't find a place to get a burger at 6 p.m. on a Friday night.

This was prime *Homo Automotivis* habitat where even the downtown mall closed down after the cars had gone to bed.

3. Vehicular homicide — Chicago

Amidst symmetrical skyscrapers shimmering in the Chicago sunshine, I made my way towards Arlington House hostel in Lincoln Park. Yves was in southern Ontario for a few days visiting his parents, so I spent the time exchanging stories and ideas with roommates in hostels, bus drivers, tour guides and other strangers. I was experiencing the USA as a friendly, open place, where everyone seemed to have an opinion and I loved it. As a Montrealer, I was not used to strangers striking up conversations with me like this. Chicago seemed more Kampala than Montreal, where one could never be entirely certain whether people were in agreement or simply being agreeable.

Two women shared a room with me in Chicago. Catherine, from Ireland, had left her family and friends to pursue a career as an actress. Victoria, a Chicana from Dallas, was on vacation from a strip bar where she worked as a waitress. As we laid in our bunk beds, I described my car-less journey. Victoria told us that to get her current job, she'd had to lie about owning a vehicle. "I'd be fired if they found out I didn't own one," she said. Still car-less, Victoria had maintained this facade for several months. Just before leaving for her holiday, a colleague spotted her waiting for the bus. Without missing a beat, Victoria smiled and said, "Oh, my car? It's at the garage." We laughed as she told the story, but there was a bitter edge to it. In the land of *Homo Automotivis* one traveled by car, or else.

Chicago was wonderful. I browsed longingly into storefront windows; explored the caverns and other destinations offered by the L-train and stood at the base of the 110-story Sears Tower. The sleek streets were endlessly entertaining. Exiting a corner store with a red, white and blue Popsicle, I stepped onto the pavement of a bustling downtown street. Its sheer width meant that by the time the light changed I was only halfway across. In the past my presence in the middle of the road always managed to convince drivers to stop. (I mean, they have to stop, don't they?) Not in Chicago. When the light changed, there was no hesitation. Cars ripped past in both directions. I stood absolutely still, a human traffic cone. Fear surged through my body, my brain short-circuiting as I experienced the horror of a deer in headlights. I did not want to die with a Popsicle in my hand. Finally, a single car stopped in front of me, forcing those behind to a standstill. I shot forward, a human projectile, grateful to the merciful driver and relieved at my survival. I could've kissed the sidewalk.

I've been in my fair share of car accidents and near misses, the first indelibly etched on my memory. Exiled from Uganda during the civil war of the 1980s, and before our immigration to Canada, my family was living in Manzini, a sleepy town in Swaziland, where my father lectured at the local university and my mother taught at the nearby Nazarene high school. Our tranquil lives were interrupted early one weekday morning. We were about to embark on the daily morning shuttle to pre-school, when my father realized he'd forgotten his bag. He dashed indoors, leaving my younger sister and I inside the vehicle, which was parked on our family's sloping driveway. Overwhelmed by opportunity, I slid into the driver's seat, lifted the brake and squealed with joy as I rolled down the hill in the direction of our open gate. I was oblivious to a gigantic lorry barreling down the adjoining street. My father flew out of the house, managing to stop the descent of the green Peugeot seconds before it hit the street. I failed to grasp that I'd been rescued and was indignant that my first trip behind the wheel ended so abruptly.

Twelve years later I returned to Southern Africa to visit family friends in Zimbabwe. I set off with my host family for Victoria Falls in Zambia. Speeding down the highway in the safety of a red Volvo, we blasted the powerful stereo system, nodding our heads to the Lingala music while I marveled at the smoothness of the roads. I was used to Kampala's endless potholes, which are so ubiquitous they've inspired my sister to make t-shirts with monster-sized potholes swallowing vehicles whole, defining Kampala as the "pothole capital of the world". It turns out we could have used a pothole or two to slow us down. Still enjoying the music, we were slow to notice an enormous trailer, which had turned unexpectedly onto the road several hundred metres in front of us. As it slowly unfolded itself, it blocked every lane of the highway. Our Volvo's brakes were helpless in the face of this obstacle and we careened ahead, turning at the last moment to crash sidelong into the monster vehicle, which sent us flying into a roadside ravine. I recall the accident from that point in slow motion. Glass shattered, metal crumpled around us, blood spattered across the windshield. Finally, the descent of our out-of-control vehicle was slowed by the dry bush land. We remained in our seats for a few moments after the car stopped, unsure whether we had all our fingers and toes. People now surrounded the vehicle. Where they came from and how they were able to get there so fast is a mystery to me. Some gaped, while others helped us from the wreck. We survived. I have a scar on my forehead, which has diminished over the years, roughly forming the outline of a horseshoe. We were lucky. Since then, however, I have been skittish about cars. I know that they're dangerous.

Why are we so cavalier about driving, when it is so obviously dangerous? Are we a society full of adrenaline junkies? Or is this simply one more example of how *Homo Automotivis* has adapted to his environment?

Automobile-related death is so prevalent the word 'accident' first conjures up thoughts of a car crash. They are so common that "accidents feature on the radio as mere hold-ups to the traffic flow."[1]

At the start of the 21st century, car crashes killed more than a million people annually around the world.[i] This number is expected to rise to nearly two million by 2020, making automobiles the world's third biggest killer. In 2007 the International Red Cross estimated that 30 million people had already perished since cars took the road.[2]

While cars claim a disproportionate number of lives in poor countries, where infrastructure and safety standards are weak, the death toll in the USA is also huge. In 2008, 39,800 Americans died at the hands of the automobile.[3] There were also nearly three million non-fatal injuries (hundreds of thousands of these long-term) at an estimated cost of \$200 billion per year.[4]

A hundred years ago, the *North American Review* estimated that the automobile led to more deaths in the first six months of 1906 than the entire Spanish-American War (1898-1902).[5] By 1923, a hundred thousand Americans had met their death at the hands of the automobile and another 23,000 died the next year.[6] [7] In 1926, auto accidents were the fifth leading cause of death in the U.S. and by 1950 they were the fourth biggest killer.[8] And the car's victims are young, relative to other causes of mortality. As a result, the number of years lost in life expectancy from car deaths equals or exceeds those caused by cardiovascular disease or cancer.[9]

Every year in the U.S. alone some 700 hundred cyclists and 6,000 pedestrians die at the hands of the automobile and another 110,000 are injured.[ii] [10] [11]

Road deaths are so common in the USA they've spawned new cultural practices. Each year an estimated 4,000 to 8,000 roadside memorials are erected to car victims. The book *Crosses Across America* documents the rise of these monuments

---

i *In many places automobile fatalities were mostly pedestrians and cyclists: 89% in Addis Ababa, 85% in New Delhi and 64% in Nairobi.*

ii *The pedestrian fatality rate hit its peak at 15,000 in 1934.*

to the recklessness of automobility. "Many mourners are too overwhelmed to buy materials to make their own crosses," said Jacquelyn Quiram, justifying her business, roadsidememorials. com, where solid oak crosses can be purchased for just under a hundred dollars apiece. Roadside memorials are so widespread that they've been deemed a danger by numerous states, many of which now regulate their location and duration.[12]

While government busies itself regulating roadside memorials, it seems unprepared to challenge the automotive industry's cash cow: the SUV.

Of all vehicles, SUVs are the most likely to kill pedestrians. This prompted the *British Medical Journal* to call for warnings on SUVs to "advise potential purchasers of the increased risk of severe injury and death to pedestrians associated with these vehicles."[13] SUV height increases the likelihood of reversing over small children. Between 2002 and 2006, 474 U.S. children died after being backed over by a vehicle, up from 138 in the previous four years. This increase was largely attributed to the rise of the SUV.[iii] [14]

Everywhere the SUV roams, people are endangered.[iv] SUV drivers are more aggressive and yet less able to accurately judge speed. It is also harder for car drivers to see around an SUV. When an SUV hits another vehicle, it is nearly three times as likely to kill or maim the driver in the other vehicle.[15] On colliding with an SUV, a smaller car will often go under the high bumper, increasing the occupant's risk of death.[16] SUVs are celebrated as rugged. Like most cars, they are marketed for their speed and

---

iii Backovers injured over 7,000 U.S. pedestrians in 2007.

iv While it is small comfort for anyone whose physical space has been invaded by the endless disaster that is the SUV, it may tickle you to know that according to industry research, the owners of these notorious polluters are often insecure, vain, self-centered and self-absorbed. They are also more frequently nervous about their marriage and lack confidence in their driving skills.

air of danger. A columnist in Canada's *National Post* explained: "Naming a product after a potentially deadly catastrophe, Gunplay or the Devil, would be an invitation to a PR nightmare in any other sector, but this is the car industry, where fast, dangerous and irrational sells. Just look at the number of cars named after predators: Cougar, Jaguar, Barracuda, Viper. Or menacing wind patterns, such as Maserati's Kubang and Ford's Zephyr."[17] From the Jeep Hurricane to Chrysler's Crossfire to Lamborghini's Diablo, the list is endless. Automakers promote speed and danger, ignoring the fact that drivers who perceive their cars as being high performing are significantly more likely to take risks on the road.[18]

No amount of advertising sheen can gloss over the reality that speed kills. For every 6.25 miles (10 kilometres) per hour reduction in the speed limit, death and injury are reduced by 15 percent.[19] "A car traveling at 35 mph takes 21 feet longer to stop than when it is traveling at 30 mph," explains Carl Honoré. "A pedestrian hit by a car doing 20 mph stands a 5% chance of dying; at 30 mph that figure jumps to 45%; at 40 mph it is 85%."[20]

But is it speed that kills or *Homo Automotivis* behind the wheel of his car? The Japanese bullet train, the Shinkansen, is one of the world's fastest modes of land transportation. Yet it has not seen a single fatality since its inception in the 1960s.[21] For every mile of travel, the car is dozens of times more likely to cause death and injury than a mile of travel on the train, bus or airplane. The number of deaths per 100 million miles traveled by car is 0.79, by commuter railroad 0.02, and by transit bus 0.01.[22] Automobile mileage makes up half of the total miles traveled by all modes, but cars are responsible for up to 94 percent of all transportation fatalities.[23]

...

Notwithstanding media images of scary young black men on tough, run-down streets, living in U.S. suburbia is more dangerous than living in the inner city. According to a 15-year

University of Virginia study, residents of inner cities including Baltimore, Chicago, Houston and Philadelphia were up to 50 percent less likely to be killed by either a murderous stranger or an automobile accident.[24]

Urban Sprawl and Public Health explains: "In each metropolitan area studied, the risk of dying in traffic in the suburbs was far higher than the risk of being murdered by a stranger in the central city (even in central cities the traffic fatality rate was generally higher than the stranger-homicide rate.)"[25] In summary, "homicides", writes Professor William H. Lucy, "are not nearly so great a danger as traffic fatalities."[26]

A common reason parents give for moving to the suburbs is to find a safe environment for their children. Yet from the age of 1 to 24 years old, the biggest killer is automobile accidents, with car-dominated suburbs suffering the highest traffic fatalities.[27] Suburbanites drive more and their sprawling landscape contains the most dangerous roads: high speeds, multiple lanes, no sidewalks and long distances between intersections or crosswalks.[28] Traffic fatality rates in the most sprawling counties are nearly 10 times higher than in the most compact counties.[29]

Many studies show that it's safer to walk as pedestrian density increases.[30] Likewise, more bikes on the road lowers the injury rate for cyclists as motorists watch out for pedal-powered transit.[31 32] Countries with greater numbers of cyclists suffer significantly fewer bike fatalities. "Per kilometre cycled, American cyclists are twice as likely to get killed (eight times as likely to be injured) as German cyclists, and over three times (30 times) as likely to get killed (injured) as Dutch cyclists."[33]

Increased cycling and walking also reduce total transport fatalities, as there are fewer drivers on the road. For the same reason, transportation safety is heightened in places with significant rail transit. Simply put, travel is safer in cities designed for walking, biking and public transport.

...

Chicago's meatpacking district, made famous in Upton Sinclair's novel, *The Jungle*, was an unlikely source of inspiration for the Ford Motor Corporation. "The sight of dead animals being disassembled, chopped up and ground into meat on a Chicago packing plant's moving belt gave Henry Ford the billion-dollar notion of the assembly line."[34] Chicago's newer meat packing district covers a much larger area: An open-air highway slaughterhouse where millions of anonymous victims are permanently silenced. U.S. automobiles flatten as many as a million animals per day; cats and dogs as well as gophers, frogs, squirrels, skunks (these myopic little critters see barely three metres ahead), birds, hedgehogs and the like meet an untimely death as highway road kill.[35] [36] Deer alone are hit more than 4,000 times per day by cars, SUVs, and other U.S. vehicles.[v] [37] The Inland Northwest Wildlife Council of Spokane, Washington collects about 5,000 pounds of meat each year from road kill (mostly moose, elk and deer), which they donate to the local Union Gospel Mission.[38] "For some people," said Frasier Shilling of wildlifecrossing.net, "the only contact they have with wild animals is when they run them over."[39]

Perhaps PETA should consider *Homo Automotivis* and cars for their next campaign.

---

[v] *In 1995 one in six Wisconsin accidents involved a deer.*

4. Vroom, vroom, cough, cough — El Paso

The bus driver shifted uneasily in her seat. A few minutes later the bus broke down. Apparently it had overheated. When it became clear the clunker wasn't going to budge another millimetre, our driver phoned for help. Forty-five minutes later a minivan chugged towards us through the quivering afternoon heat. Fewer than a dozen passengers, we tumbled in without a squeeze. Our new driver complained bitterly as we returned to the station. We weren't the first group of passengers collected from the highway that day. Frustrated by El Paso transit's bad rap, he grumbled that the buses were only meant to last 12 years, which had long passed.

Indeed, it was frustrating. Our plan to see El Paso and then make it to Mexico for cheaper lodgings was shot. We were well off schedule and the public buses would stop running in a few hours.

As the minivan puffed its way back to the depot, we passed a playground. It was surrounded by prime *Homo Automotivis* habitat. Caught within a web of highway, thousands of cars crossed on every side and even above. The playground was protected by 20 feet of wire fence, but the planner failed to grasp that nothing short of gas masks would keep these kids safe. Oblivious and likely without alternatives, the kids ran, swung and hurled themselves across monkey bars. Sandwiched between speeding automobiles, it was a surreal image of societal neglect: Children gathered together to breath the poison from busy roads.

The waste products of the automobile are causing no less than a public health crisis. Harvard University researchers determined that respiratory illness attributable to automobile toxins kill 30,000 people every year in the U.S. and are responsible for an additional 120,000 premature deaths.[1] The exhalations of the automobile breathe life into an array of disease with children as well as the elderly, more penalized, even though they are less likely to own a car.[2]

From cancer to asthma, to decreased lung growth in children, the youngest members of society are the most vulnerable. Perhaps *Homo Automotivis* has made a collective decision that getting used to the automobile is a priority of childrearing. Right from the womb babies are vulnerable to the car's toxic vapors. "Mothers living near highways are more likely to give birth to preterm or low birth weight babies."[3] Children exposed in-utero to high levels of urban air pollutants have significantly reduced birth weights and reduced head circumference.[4] In developing fetuses, air pollution from traffic appears to cause genetic changes — the kind linked to cancer.[5]

Babies in strollers and toddlers, new on their feet, spend their days at ground level with automobile exhaust pipes. Automobile exhaust creates a toxic environment by releasing the gaseous precursors to ozone. During times of high ozone children playing outdoors face a greater risk of developing asthma. School absenteeism, respiratory symptoms, medication use, emergency department visits and hospitalizations all increase on days of ozone level peaks.[6] [7] Stifled and incapacitated, the lungs of over five million American children are asthma afflicted.[8] One study determined that those who lived within 250 feet of a major road were 50 percent more likely to develop asthma within the year.[9]

Children and teenagers raised in heavy air pollution are less likely to reach old age. They are more likely to have reduced lung capacity, increasing their susceptibility to illness and premature death as adults.[10] [11] A 13-year long study that followed 3,600 children in central and southern California showed that the damage from living within 500 yards of a freeway was equivalent to residing in communities with the highest individual pollution levels.[12]

An *American Journal of Epidemiology* study found that children living in neighbourhoods with significant traffic pollution scored worse on intelligence and memory tests than children who breathe cleaner air.[13] A Denver study showed that children living adjacent to heavily trafficked streets were at greater risk of developing childhood leukemia and other cancers. The researchers speculated that the children were exposed to benzene and other carcinogens via inhalation as well as through exposure to soil contaminated by vehicle emissions.[14]

The health hazards associated with the car are not confined to the pollution spewed from tailpipes. Children living near auto body shops and gas stations, for instance, have dramatically higher rates of leukemia.[15] Still today, lead poisoning remains a concern. Although leaded gasoline was phased out, car batteries remain a major source of waste lead, a highly toxic metal that is also of particular danger to growing children.[i][16]

Even tires pose a health threat, in the form of particulate matter. Tires lose about a pound of rubber each year, with these minuscule grains escaping into the atmosphere. The particles are small enough to embed themselves into the deepest part of the human lung.[17] These tiny fragments fly under the radar, but their impact is considerable. Before a tire ever hits the road, the rubber is treated with an extensive range of chemicals: xylene, benzene, petroleum naphtha, chlorinated solvents, polycyclic aromatic hydrocarbons, anthracene, phenanthrene, phenols, amines, oil, acids and alkalis, polychlorinated biphenyls, halogenated cyanoalkanes, processing aids, plasticizers and more.[18] This deadly combination of known carcinogens, neurotoxins, heavy metals and other poisons gnaw at healthy human cells, agitating them into abnormality.[19]

---

i An Environmental Research study linked the elimination of lead in paint and gasoline to a major reduction in violent crime in the mid 1990s.

Particulate matter poses a variety of health threats, including ischemic heart disease, congestive heart failure, stroke, impaired breathing, damage to lung tissue, cancer and premature death.[20] Inhaling greater amounts of particulate matter per pound of body weight, children and babies are more susceptible.[21] Through both tire dust and combustion, cars generate copious amounts of particulate pollution. Exposure to all kinds of particulate pollution causes an estimated 60,000 premature deaths a year.[22] *Urban Sprawl and Public Health* argues that "high levels of PM [particulate matter] exposure are estimated to shorten average life expectancy by as much as one or two years."[23]

Then there are the tailpipe gases, which are invisible, but their effects are real. Ozone, the major component of smog, precipitates choking and stinging eyes, damages lung tissue and aggravates numerous respiratory diseases. As of November 2009, about 40 percent of the U.S. population lived in metropolitan areas violating the Environmental Protection Agency's ozone safety standards.[24]

"Clogged arteries can clog your arteries," read a *Vancouver Sun* headline.[25] A study found that the atherosclerosis risk associated with living near a busy street is probably greater than the risk associated with second hand smoke exposure.[26] Another study published in the *New England Journal of Medicine* found that people susceptible to heart disease were three times as likely to suffer a heart attack within an hour of exposure to significant traffic pollution.[27]

We usually associate toxic chemicals with plants and factories. "But it turns out that over half of the cancer incidence is caused by air pollution coming from cars."[28] From benzene to formaldehyde, motor vehicles emit a variety of carcinogenic and toxic air pollutants.[29] The statistics are grim. As much as 80 percent of the cancer-causing substances inhaled by New Yorkers come from tailpipe emissions.[30] In San Bernardino and Riverside

California, breathing the summer air has been likened to smoking a pack a day.[31]

...

While neither cancer nor heart failure are contagious in the strict sense of the word, our air is shared so neighbours can and do pass on fatal diseases. Living in downtown Montreal without a car, we are exposed daily (even indoors) to a plethora of car-generated toxins. *Urban Sprawl and Public Health* argues that, "more dense living that doesn't eliminate cars could increase exposure to locally scaled pollutants such as particulate matter and air toxins."[32] The suburban commuter exports his waste into the downtown core, returning daily to the (relatively) fresh air of the outskirts.

The children we passed on the highway in El Paso were fenced in, but on our way into Ciudad Juarez we encountered the opposite: children fenced out. Crossing into Mexico, Canadian documents in hand, we passed a group of children working in the sweltering heat. Arms outstretched, they sold candies and begged on the edge of the USA, a place most of them would see daily, but never set foot in.

But borders are deceiving: There is no barrier between the air coming out of an exhaust pipe and the air being filtered through our lungs; no barrier between U.S. and Mexican air, no barrier between pollutants generated by automobiles that "live" in the suburbs and car-less inhabitants downtown.

5. Loosen your seatbelts —
San Antonio

Downtown San Antonio was thoroughly charming and in hindsight we should never have left its three-mile radius. Tiny birds danced around ornate benches and old-fashioned trolleys rambled cheerfully along narrow streets. It was laid back, walk-able and convenient. The Alamo is the soul of downtown; a dreamlike enclave of jade fountains, old gardens and low archways. Constructed by the Spanish in the 18th century to aid colonial expansion, it was made famous in the mid-19th century as a battleground between Texan and Mexican troops. Not far from this ruin, we arrived at the River Walk or Paseo Del Rio. Below the city, a canal flowed alongside restaurants and boutiques. Lizards scuttled quietly, boats sailed by and we were told that on occasion a noisy cattle crossing caused a spectacle. (I made a note to tell my mother, a rancher who rears long-horned Ankole cows, about this strange American custom.) Families strolled, couples embraced. Cars were nowhere to be seen. A bustling oasis had been reclaimed from *Homo Automotivis*.

Despite its beauty, highway planners once attempted to build an expressway through San Antonio's historic city centre — a plan mercifully thwarted by outraged citizens.[1] Not so outraged however that the rest of the city was saved from cars. In fact, it turns out that the lively centre is an anomaly in a city spread out to nowhere.

If it hadn't been for our book habit, we may never have noticed that the interesting, accessible city centre was utterly unrepresentative of San Antonio. With no bookstore to be found, we left downtown. Ignorant and naive, we climbed aboard a city bus and forty-minutes later were ejected at a Wal-Mart terminus. Assured that the connecting bus would pass "near" the bookstore, we climbed aboard the next bus, arriving at what could loosely be defined as a destination. With more than a little hesitation we watched the bus depart. The air was thick with heat and the only sign of life (besides cars hurtling down the highway) was a 7-11 "convenience" store. But this place could only be described as "convenient" for passing automobilists.

We beat a path down a grassy trail, up sharp hills and through the relentless heat. Sweating and exhausted, I stumbled on the uneven pathway, plummeting into an embrace with the undergrowth; I was bruised and indignant. We had not signed up for a safari. We'd been in the bush for nearly half an hour with no sign of a bookstore, when a garish forest of brightly colored signs appeared in the distance. Was this a mirage? Through blurry eyes I discerned an oasis of commerce and in the middle of it all stood a Barnes and Nobles. Yves and I all but skipped with delight as we entered the air-conditioned building, sank into comfortable chairs; stacks of books, magazines and newspapers piled high.

Like all good things, this visit to the land of ideas came to an end. A phone call to the transit authority determined that their lackluster service was through for the day. It was the middle of the week. The sun was still shining brilliantly. There was no excuse for this nonsense. We inhaled, exhaled, gritted our teeth and caught a cab back to Wal-Mart. Later that evening, we retreated back into the arteries of San Antonio for a super-sized meal on the River Walk.

...

San Antonio is the obesity capital of the most overweight nation in the world. And it's not just all the great Mexican restaurants. Food is only part of the obesity equation. Car dominance translates into less walking. Less walking means less exercise, a central element of the obesity epidemic. For every hour walked per week, the risk of obesity drops five percent.[2]

One might say sprawl produces sprawling people. A 2003 study determined that residents of the 25 most sprawling U.S. counties were an average of six pounds heavier than those in the 25 most compact counties.[3] The *American Journal of Preventive Medicine* found that "an extra thirty minutes in the car each day translates into a three percent greater chance of being obese."[4] Apparently, cars can make you fat. A study titled, A Silver Lining? The Connection Between Gasoline Prices and Obesity attributes 13 percent of the jump in U.S. obesity between 1979 and 2004 to a drop in gas prices (and subsequent increase in driving).[5]

Muscles and joint difficulties, hypertension, diabetes, heart disease and cancers are all linked to excessive weight. A *Homo Automotivis* irony: General Motors carried out a two-year study of nearly 200,000 employees which found that overweight and obese individuals incurred up to $1,500 more in annual medical costs than their slimmer employees.[i] Some health analysts even predict that rising obesity will lead to a decline in the current generation's life expectancy.[6]

There is good reason to believe that for reasons of class and aesthetic bias, obesity's impact on health has been overstated. It is true that the only thing the poor consume more of than the wealthy is food. There is no disputing, however, that exercise (or lack thereof) is a major health indicator. The National Coalition for Promoting Physical Activity claims thousands of Americans die annually from health conditions and diseases related to a sedentary lifestyle.

Exercise protects against innumerable ailments from osteoporosis to depression; it boosts cognitive functioning and can even help to ward off Alzheimer's disease.[7][8] Under the headline, "L'exercice, le champion de la prévention contre le cancer," Montreal's *La Presse* reported that over 50 separate studies found

---

i It was not reported whether GM's study considered the role of car dependence in rising obesity.

that those who exercised regularly were less likely to get cancer.[9] Another study found that women who walked a minimum of 10 blocks a day were 33 percent less likely to develop cardiovascular disease.[10] A November 2010 study reported that people with Alzheimer's who walked five miles a week slowed cognitive decline while another study concluded that people aged 70 to 82 years who engaged in physical activity were far more likely to stay alive.[11] [12] It's possible that the only major downside to exercise — especially outdoors — may be taking in extra deep breaths of automobile-generated air pollution.[ii]

Despite its benefits, exercise (particularly walking) has decreased. In 2000, only 26.2 percent of U.S. adults met recommended levels of physical activity (defined as thirty minutes of any physical activity for five days per week or vigorous activity for twenty minutes three days a week).[13] The typical U.S. resident walked three miles a day a century ago; today the average is less than a quarter mile.[14] The major reason for the reduction in walking is the built environment. One study found that "people who lived in the most walk-able neighbourhoods were 2.4 times more likely to walk for thirty minutes or more [a day] than those who lived in the least walk-able communities."[15] Transit also helps. A July 2010 study of a new light rail in Charlotte, North Carolina found that those who stopped driving and started walking to the light rail, walked 1.2 miles over their two commutes and lost an average of 6.45 pounds.[16]

Sprawl and the suburban landscape are built to serve the needs of *Homo Automotivis*, with sidewalks non-existent or disconnected, crosswalks poorly marked or absent, and the velocity and volume of vehicular traffic overwhelming. Walking and biking have become impractical, even dangerous.

There is another reason people have stopped walking:

---

ii *Because of exertion cyclists ingest nano particles, which accumulate in organs and cause inflammatory reactions, five times faster than pedestrians or drivers.*

Cars have made us lazy. The more we use them the more we cannot fathom traveling without them. One survey suggests the extent of psychological dependence is extreme. An average American is only willing to walk about a quarter mile and in some instances (such as errands) only 400 feet.[17] Otherwise, *Homo Automotivis* takes the car. The true extent of auto-dependence is revealed by drivers willing to wait five minutes for the closest parking spot to where they are going rather than park a block away and walk. The car has produced a state of mind where walking a few extra feet is a defeat.

Even the most rambunctious among us have stopped moving: 85 percent of American children do not walk to school regularly.[18] This is undoubtedly influenced by distance. In 1969, only a third of all children lived three or more miles from school; today the figure has risen to half. But it is not only children living far from school who aren't walking. In 1969, 87 percent of students living within a mile of school walked, today only a third make the same trek.[19] It's no surprise then that a quarter of all morning road journeys are devoted to driving children to school.[20] Traffic jams at sprawl-driven mega schools are increasingly common and sometimes require police direction.[21]

It is less that children cannot walk to school and more that *Homo Automotivis* parents, fearing for their children's safety, prefer to drive them. The most commonly cited fear? Not bullying or kidnapping. The major reason cited by parents for restricting unaccompanied travel: traffic danger.[22] When parents use cars to protect their children from other cars, it results in notoriously dangerous schoolyard pickup areas.[iii]

...

Cars are closely associated with another factor in the rising obesity epidemic. At the heart of Ford's revolution in

---

iii Parents are right to be concerned about cars. The road is a dangerous place and the more traffic children encounter on their way to school — measured by the number of intersections they cross — the higher their risk of being hit by a car.

industrial production was the assembly line. With Ford's new system, manual labour remained stationary and repetitive. Work moved while the worker stood still. "Save ten steps a day for each of 12,000 employees," proclaimed Henry Ford, "and you will have saved fifty miles of wasted motion and misspent energy."[23] In Ford's mind, progress at the workplace meant eliminating all unnecessary movement.[24]

The assembly line also eliminated all unnecessary thought. Ford had no use for experience in the working ranks, preferring those with less to unlearn.[25] The assembly line destroyed labour as a source of identity and self-worth. In *Wheels for the World,* Douglas Brinkley explains that by the late 1970s, "building cars had reached a kind of perfection as a dehumanizing institution."[iv] [26]

Fordism may not have been as unhealthy if reducing workplace energy output led to more leisure time. Yet Americans work almost as much today as in the 1920s, mostly to pay for their cars. Many working people have less time for leisure and after a long day's work, often turn to TV — an activity inversely linked to exercise. Busy parents, especially the working poor, frequently use television as a babysitter, creating an environment where naturally energetic children are rendered boob tube zombies.

...

Stress is also a significant factor in the obesity epidemic and a wide body of research cites automobile driving as a source of everyday stress, particularly in long commutes and heavy traffic.[27] A study of 600 nurses found that for equal commuting times, those who drove had significantly higher signs of stress than those who took public transit.[28] "Automobile commuting", concludes *Urban*

---

iv *Repetitive work is generally disempowering and workers who don't feel in control of their work environment usually have higher job stress levels. "It turns out that a quarter to a third of workers have high job stress and are drained and used up at the end of the day," said Linda Rosenstock, the former Director of the National Institute for Occupational Safety and Health.*

Sprawl and Public Health, "is more stressful for more people than these other forms of travel."[29] Additionally, long sedentary drives mean less time for stress-busting exercise. And so the vicious cycle ensues.

We hardly need scientists to tell us that food is comforting, yet there are increasing reports on the link between stress and the impulse to eat. Food with lots of sugar and fat appears to calm the body's response to chronic stress.[30] What's more, there is also research to show that stress hormones encourage the formation of fat cells, particularly the unhealthiest kind.[31] No wonder all this driving is having an effect on the waistline.

If he weren't a *Homo Automotivis* the U.S. Surgeon-General might consider slapping this warning on the hood of every car: May cause all manner of diseases, violent rage, climate change and obesity.

6. Goodbye downtown — Mobile

This was Mobile, Alabama? On the town's edge, beside a freeway and an abandoned store, we pulled into a bus station. We needed to stay positive. We were assured there was "somewhere" nearby but our prospects of finding it didn't seem good. Public transit was done for the day — it was 6:30 on a Saturday evening — only the private automobile could get us to where we wanted to go, which was anywhere but here. Looking confused and downtrodden, a bus driver took pity on us and offered advice about a Greyhound special at a hotel. Although it was a fair distance away, like many businesses in an auto-dependent economy, it delivered — us.

Before long we were in a minivan talking to a young hotel driver named Leanne who was new to her job and eager to impress us with the sights and sounds of her hometown. As we rolled down the highway Leanne raved about the hotel's location: "There's a Pizza Hut, a Dominos, a McDonald's, a gentleman's club and a 24 hour Wal-Mart — it never closes." When Yves told Leanne he'd never seen the inside of a Wal-Mart she was visibly shaken, but recovered quickly.

"Oh, it's great! You can spend hours in there. I don't usually do this, but I'll take you there when you settle in." Yves politely declined her offer. After 20 hours on the bus, Wal-Mart wonderland would have to wait for another day. Instead, we opted for a stroll on the highway and pizza to go.

The next morning we got a lift back to the bus station and made our way into the city centre. There was a powerful old-world feel about downtown Mobile. Its colonial streets, a blend of French, Spanish and British influences, were filled with grand, historic architecture. Little restaurants, cafes and boutiques gathered around a central park where we sat down at a bench.

A street preacher in a three-piece suit paced around the central fountain, waving his bible and screaming about the wrath of God.

We pushed forward through the city and eventually arrived at a bus stop (on what was, it seemed, the only line), where a middle-aged woman in a large yellow hat soon joined us. Curious, she introduced herself as Anita and asked where we were from and what we thought of Mobile. On mentioning my admiration for the massive residential manors she was quick to remind me that these stately houses were built on the back of black slaves. Literally. As we chatted some more, Anita voiced irritation at Mobile's secondary role in the civil rights movement. "Montgomery's got a civil rights museum. What do we have? There's no reason to come to Mobile." We boarded the bus where a ginger-haired bohemian holding a large book in his skinny lap joined the conversation. He nodded his head with increasing vigor as Anita's passion grew. She concluded it was time to leave Mobile for Portland. Anita had never been to Oregon, but seemed confident it had more to offer than Mobile.

We waved goodbye to our Mobilian acquaintances and disembarked across from our destination. Later in the day, as we wandered further we realized that the downtown area we had grown fond of was not all gothic fountains and charm. Wooden slabs boarded up rows of empty commercial spaces; a long line stretched out of an employment centre. Downtown Mobile had hit hard times. It occurred to us that Leanne's Wal-Mart hadn't helped the situation. The world's biggest retailer and *Homo Automotivis'* favourite store, has undermined historic city centres across North America.

It is impossible to imagine Wal-Mart without the car. *Advertising Age* described the company's intense dependence on automobility: "When gas prices dropped sharply in late 2007, Wall Mart started posting its best same-store sales results in years. The rebound in gas prices was just as tough on Walmart as the drop was favourable. The retailer's year-over-year customer traffic turned negative last year just as gas prices shot past their 2008 levels."[1]

Wal-Mart's land use is appalling.[i] To set up its gigantic stores, Wal-Mart buys cheap land next to thoroughfares on the outskirts of cities. A survey of four "big box" retailers in Lancaster, Pennsylvania found that these projects generated as many as 60,000 additional automobile trips per day.[2] You can't get there any other way.

A week later in El Paso, we checked out Wal-Mart's even bigger brother, Sam's Club. Roaming the aisles, we paused in front of a five-pound apple pie.[ii] I couldn't imagine anyone buying that and walking it home. But with a buggy and then a car you don't have to actually carry anything. From cases of canned corn to five-pound pies, the "warehouse" store requires an automobile, preferably a big one.

Wal-Mart has other reasons for setting up shop on the highway. The company's vehicles travel one billion miles a year and Wal-Mart maintains an intense interest in highway policy.[3] The company has lobbied for truck-only lanes and led a push in 2006 to extend the trucking workday up to 16 hours.[4] [5]

According to the *Economist*, "one reason that Wal-Mart became a cost-cutting behemoth was because it exploited the logistical advantages of the new [interstate highway] system faster than its competitors did."[6] With masses of truckers on publicly subsidized roads, Wal-Mart effectively stores goods en route. On-demand delivery eliminates the middleman by delivering goods straight to the retailer. With moving goods literally stored on the roads, wholesale costs are socialized. Instead of individual corporations, society pays. Inventory systems like Wal-Mart's

---

i Of a couple thousand U.S. outlets, only 20 had a second floor in 2006.
ii A January 2011 study found that each new Walmart super centre per 100,000 residents led to an average weight gain of 1.5 pounds per person and increased the obesity rate by 2.3 percentage points.

require more regular shipments of smaller product quantities rather than occasional larger shipments. The rise of on-demand (or "just in time") delivery over the past 30 years has been a major boon for long-haul trucking. This has been at the expense of rail, which is three times as fuel efficient and safer.[7]

Beyond benefiting from socially built road networks, Wal-Mart is a major welfare recipient. According to a 2004 study by Good Jobs First titled, *Shopping for Subsidies: How Wal-Mart Uses Taxpayer Money to Finance Its Never-Ending Growth*, Wal-Mart Stores Inc. received more than $1 billion in economic development subsidies from state and local governments and that's likely just the tip of the public trough at which the company feeds. Good Jobs First concludes that while public sources revealed 160 subsidized Wal-Marts, "more than 1,000 Wal-Mart stores may have been subsidized."[8] Not bad for a company with annual revenue of $250 billion.

Wal-Mart responds to charges of corporate welfare by arguing they collect and pay billions in sales taxes, local property taxes and corporate taxes all the while creating jobs. Superficially, Wal-Mart's response seems reasonable: Government subsidies for Wal-Mart generated spin-offs. But it's not that straight forward. Wal-Mart, for instance, uses its massive legal budget to challenge county property tax evaluations.[9] They also employed accountants to devise complex tax avoidance strategies that allowed Wal-Mart to pay half the average state corporate tax rate between 1997 and 2007. [10]

The boarded up stores studding downtown Mobile once paid taxes and provided jobs. No longer. The near impossibility of competing with Wal-Mart means widespread store closures that sap the life out of the city centre. Abandoned by car-dependent shoppers the closures go way beyond simply being unsightly, they come with massive social costs. Public schools, public transit and other social services suffer when property taxes from local businesses disappear. Near-by residential neighbourhoods are destabilized. As local jobs disappear, crime rates rise. Even as sources of income for local government drop, pressure to spend more on policing rises. For many youth, a "brush with the law" is more common than a part-time job at the local quickie mart. The combination of big box stores and auto dependency is spurring a vicious downward spiral.

What's worse, downtown is the one place people don't need cars. There is a symbiotic relationship between downtown shopping and walking, biking and public transit. A study in San Diego showed that the major downtown shopping centre attracted three-fifths of its clientele from public transit and walking while "a comparable suburban centre attracts only five percent from non-driving modes."[11]

Downtown Mobile doesn't have a monopoly on abandoned stores. The negative effects of big box stores have even reached suburban neighbourhoods. Adjacent to Mobile's Greyhound station a large retail store had gone out of business. There was a visceral emptiness; the closure had the impact of a half-dozen abandoned downtown shops. It can be difficult to find tenants for large retail spaces, and according to Suzanne Chen of Retail Realty group, "Sometimes they [Wal-Mart] would rather sit with a vacant building than budge on letting a competitor in it."[12] As a result, hundreds of empty former big box stores litter the suburban and rural landscape, with Wal-Mart alone holding more than 150 vacant stores.[13] Many of the company's former stores stay empty for ten years, with pedestrians and the community left bearing hollow weight. These spaces are often left vacant because they are considered too small. Incredibly, nothing less than a 17 football-field-sized super-centre will satisfy the needs of *Homo Automotivis'* Sprawl-Mart.

7. Billboards — Everywhere

Somewhere in Alabama, far from any metropolis, we were rolling along a scenic country road, when suddenly, the billboards returned. Tall, loud and ugly, these odes to *Homo Automotivis*' consumerism followed us from cities, to towns, to the middle of nowhere. In fact the places they aren't stand out. Yet, without cars, what would be the point?

Outdoor advertising is nearly impossible to avoid and constitutes one of three primary means of communication (alongside TV and radio) for *Homo Automotivis*. Clear Channel Outdoor boasts that it "is great, because you can't turn it off, throw it away or click on the next page."[1] Roughly $7 billion is spent annually on half a million billboards stacked across the USA.

My clearest memory of Tallahassee was a dizzying road into the Greyhound station, where the billboards were packed tighter than an LA freeway at rush hour. I had never seen so many billboards in one place. Yves and I picked up matching neck and eyestrains just looking out the window. Hundreds of enormous signs urged us to want, crave and buy. Loud, rectangular "litter on sticks" billboards towered over us on an intimidating scale, their clashing colors trashing the landscape. It's an aesthetic that can only be appreciated by someone traveling in a fast car.

The modern billboard was a direct response to automobility. A 1923 issue of *Poster* — an outdoor advertising trade magazine— noted that "no other one factor has been so largely responsible for the remarkable growth of poster advertising during the past decade as has the motor car."[2]

Before the advent of the automobile, billboards (or billposters as they were then called) were far smaller. And as road travel got faster, messaging got simpler. Describing the new face of advertising in *Buyways: Billboards, Automobiles and the American Landscape*, Catherine Gudis explains that, "Heavy text was out and logos were in."[3] Billboard designers assumed driver distraction, necessitating a simple, quick and obvious message. Subtlety was out; loud and bold were in.

At the same time storefronts increasingly became "living billboards".[4] The attention of speeding motorists was sought through the electric glow of neon. "Circular Meccas of neon," was the description historian Michael Witzel gave to the early California drive-in restaurants that epitomized the logo building.[5]

This was just the beginning. The auto influenced "aesthetic of speed" extended beyond the billboard and storefront to the TV set and newspaper.[6] Gudis argues that the impact of this aesthetic has "infused not just our physical environments, but the very ways in which we see, understand, and picture the world around us."[7] Simplicity and lack of subtlety are hallmarks of many modernist artists from Constructivists to the Suprematists.[8] Lone circles and black squares as art? Blame the car.

Outdoor advertisers and billboard apologists claim they are the art galleries of the masses. Others take a harsher view.[9] Describing the "arrogance and power" of billboards, John Miller, founder of Scenic America, writes: "When we tell advertisers it's OK to turn our communities into round-the-clock outdoor commercials, we are telling litterers and defacers that trashing aesthetics and ignoring our right to privacy is acceptable. Litterers and defacers, and many of the rest of us, realize there is little difference between the crass intrusiveness of a billboard and that of deliberately dumped garbage or scrawling on a wall."[10]

Responding to early criticism of billboards, advertisers claimed they united the nation through shared images of consumer goods and ideas.[11] The billboard's effect, however, was more 'homogeneity' than 'unity'. They were central to the first national advertising campaigns, in which outdoor advertisers trained the masses to "discard their class and regional distinctions in favour of the mobility, domesticated privacy and individualism promised by mass consumption."[12] More than shattering regional and class barriers, billboards accelerated the emergence of a consumer culture. From coast to coast, every American on four wheels was part of a newly expanded market for mass production.

The automobile and the billboard are evident elements in the grand symbiotic relationship that created *Homo Automotivis*. While cars provide an audience for outdoor advertising, billboards provide a stage to promote the wares and culture of mobility.[13] As far back as the early 1900s, billboards advertised the automobile's associated industries. Motels, fast food restaurants and gas stations were most heavily dependent on billboards, putting their brands in the most opportune place: the roadside. On the backdrop of the natural wonder, a 1924 Supreme Auto Oil ad illustrated the relationship between the billboard and car with the declaration, "Go see the Grand Canyon in your car." Billboards helped advance the automobile as a symbol of prosperity and the key to unlocking the freedom and adventure of the open road.

8. Parking is a losing game — Atlantic City

> *"**Question**: Two of my neighbours are in cahoots. When one pulls his car out of a spot, the other is always parked directly in front or behind and moves his car just enough to take up two spaces, so no other car can squeeze in. When the first car returns, the other moves back, restoring parking spots for both. Is it ethical for them to save spaces for each other, instead of leaving one for another parking deprived New Yorker?*
>
> *"**Answer**: If either of them were ethical, they wouldn't use private cars in Manhattan, a city with excellent public transportation. Why should the non-car-owning majority allow the car-owning minority to store their private property, i.e. cars, on public property at no charge? Why should my every walk to the store be akin to a stroll through a parking lot? Why should that majority be subject to the many costs and risks to health and safety attendant on the private car?"[1]*

I'm a ruthless monopoly player, but my sneaky little brother outdoes me every time, lining his pockets with $500 notes before the game even begins. After many two-dimensional trips through Atlantic City on family game night, I was excited to see the real thing.

In transit between Philly and New York, we had six hours in the city, which turned out to be more than enough time for Yves to lose a small fortune. (I don't know if there was some kind of conspiracy, but the Greyhound went straight to the casinos.) I pulled my light-pocketed partner from the windowless halls of a Trumped-up gambling palace into the sunshine and onto the boardwalk where we wandered for the remainder of our time. There was a sandy beach to one side, warm wood beneath our feet, throngs of strolling pedestrians in all directions and, oh yes, no cars in sight. I understood why it was the choicest piece of real estate on the Monopoly board.

But Monopoly's correspondence to the real Atlantic City only went so far. Take "Free Parking", for instance. In Monopoly this comes around once every 40 spaces. Yet on the casino side of the boardwalk, a football field away from the Atlantic Ocean, we couldn't have walked 40 paces without stumbling onto a place to park. In fact, Atlantic City devotes much more space to parking than gambling. For example, the four casinos at Bally's Park Place take up 220,000 square feet, but the complex's 4,000 car garage is over 1.25 million square feet. The Borgata, across town from the boardwalk, provides 161,000 sq feet to shoot some crap or play the slots, but well over two million square feet to rest 7,100 cars.[i] The original 5,000-car garage cost $100 million of the Borgata's $1 billion price tag — roughly $20,000 per parking space.[ii] Storing the automobile in its resting state is anything but cheap.

Beyond the seemingly endless quest for an empty spot, parking is rarely discussed, yet it greatly shapes *Homo*

---

i Gaming areas figures were taken from the casino web sites. We have used a conservative 300 square feet of space per parking spot — the literature says the average is 345 square feet when one includes the actual parking space, the driveways and entrance roads etc.

ii This was on top of the $330 million spent by government on a 2.5-mile tunnel to connect the Borgata resort area - opened in 2003 - to the Atlantic City Expressway.

Automotivis' urban environment. In Monopoly, parking is fairly benign; a minor inconvenience when amassing property early in the game, a reprieve from paying rent later on, or an opportunity for a cash grab. In the real world, parking is more troublesome. Cars are parked 95 percent of the time, creating a huge storage problem.[2] Some architects have gone as far as describing parking requirements as "the single greatest killer of urbanism in the United States today."[3]

The car has an insatiable appetite for space. Requiring 300 square feet for home storage, 300 square feet for storage at destination, 600 square feet while traveling and another 200 square feet for repairs, servicing or sale, an automobile occupies about 1,400 square feet altogether — more space than most apartments.[4]

"When a pedestrian puts on his car," the authors of a book about parking say, "he or she increases [their] bulk by about thirty times."[5] Compared to a bicycle, a car needs nearly twenty times more space to park.[6] Some say that only one third of an average street is needed for pedestrians, ambulances, transit vehicles and utility lines. The rest of the road exists to service personal cars — mostly while they are stationary.[7] Roads, garages, fuel stations, parking and other vehicle supports make up between one-third and one-half of the total space offered by American cities — and as much as two-thirds in car-saturated towns.[8]

The loss of space to parked cars is incredible. About 4,950 square miles in total are devoted to parking in the USA.[9] [10] Home storage for U.S. automobiles alone takes up 688,000 acres (1,100 sq miles) of land.[11] Yet, apparently this is not enough. Enter the home car stacker — a bunk bed for automobiles — an increasingly common contraption found in family garages. At four grand apiece, these stackers are pricey, but motorists have no option but to provide their third (or fourth) car purchased a place to rest.[iii]

---

iii Some luxury towers feature an elevator that lifts cars to the apartment owner's floor so they can have the car next to them.

As we drive down a path of total auto domination, two or three storey family garages could become the norm: The first level for Johnny and Sue's cars, the second level for Mom and Dad's and the third level for the old clunker or the vintage collector item. What's certain is that the requirements of automobile storage have profoundly altered housing architecture. Before the rise of automobility it was the norm for single-family homes to be built with a front porch. Most U.S. houses built over the past half century, however, have replaced this with a front garage. More than an aesthetic outrage, this shift in architecture has had a significant impact on social life, which has relocated from the semi-public front porch to the backyard. The social activity of the auto-centred house is now far removed from life on the street. This shift towards enclosed, private space has reduced community interaction undermining the traditional uses of streets as meeting grounds, playgrounds and sites for civic engagement.

Traveling by bus across the USA, we repeatedly witnessed the triumph of the automobile over human beings. Every search for a bookstore led to the edge of some strip mall, typically blocks from the entrance to the shopping area. Regularly, our first thousand steps were a march through row after row of automobiles. In El Paso, between a Wal-Mart and Sam's Club, we watched employees struggling to gather shopping carts on an immense parking lot. I imagined them as the suburban U.S. equivalent to Ankole herdsmen shepherding animals across once dangerous plains. The vulnerable cattle are left to graze during the day but must be rounded up before nightfall. But at Wal-Mart, the fears are less about preying hyenas, than about bands of bored teens battering carts in bumper car games or the homeless capturing shopping carts as beasts of burden.

Like nomadic herdsmen, cars require immense amounts of grazing area. It is not uncommon for suburban parking to consume two to three times more space than the buildings they serve. Ironically, these paved expanses negate the advantages of suburban dispersal, particularly access to green space.[12] We could probably dig up an asphalt industry rep willing to proclaim the majestic beauty of endless parking ("the perfect symmetry of the white lines contrasting the jet black of freshly laid asphalt...") but for most, parking is an eyesore. Whether on the exurban fringe or downtown, parking blight is a plague upon the land.

Parking space and office space are like the yin and yang of commerce. Counting roadways, aisles and access paths, it is common for employers to put aside at least 300 square feet for every car.[13] This is bigger than many actual offices and about the size of five typical (6' X 8') cubicles. One Los Angeles office building soars confidently 21 floors into the sky, but rests upon fifteen levels of parking.[14]

On our visit to the City of Angels, we entered a mall near the Walk of Fame that devoted its first half dozen floors to parking. Even after riding five flights of escalators to get a smoothie, we conceded it was better than Houston, Cleveland, St. Louis or Kansas City, where parking spread out as far as the eye could see. In those cities, central districts were disjointed and fragmented, creating an impression of being unfinished — impressive buildings diminished by their parking lot frames.

"Perhaps nothing has made American cities less memorable," write John Jakle and Keith Sculle in *Lots of Parking*.[15] "Parking lots have eaten away cities in the United States like moths devouring a lace wedding gown," chimes in Mark Childs.[16] Vivid imagery but history reinforces the argument. In the first half of the century, many charming centres were stripped of their character as historic buildings were razed to make way for surface parking.[17] Ironically, this kind of destruction was often carried out under the guise of urban renewal (begging the question, what would it look like if they were *trying* to make it ugly?). In 1910, for instance, Detroit's Cadillac Square met its end and became a giant parking lot.[18] "All across the United States", write Jakle and Sculle, "especially in county seat towns with court house squares, public space was systematically diverted to parking, thus eroding traditional open space in favour of auto storage."[19]

Demolishing downtown buildings had several effects. The first was more parking, which facilitated driving. The second was a ruined landscape and a vicious cycle whereby growing numbers of automobiles resulted in yet more demolition. This further reduced the pleasure of walking downtown, which in turn reduced property values. As the value of property declined, it became even easier to raze buildings for parking. This auto/parking cycle stripped centres of their appeal, leaving lots of space for parking.[20]

No great city has an abundance of parking. At least, that was the conclusion of *Better Neighbourhoods*, a study by the San Francisco planning department, which described places like Joe DiMaggio's childhood neighbourhood of North Beach as a dying breed: "If we had to rebuild a place like North Beach under today's parking requirements, as much as a third of the space where people live would be given up for parking. We would lose much of the street-life — the shops and cafes, the vendors and the stoops — that make areas like North Beach vibrant and interesting. We don't build places like these today because we require so much parking. There are plenty of examples of the kinds of buildings our parking requirements result in. We just need to imagine a city composed entirely of these buildings, and ask ourselves if this is the kind of city we want in the future."[21]

Contrary to orthodox planning, great streets do well without "enough" parking.[22] In the vibrant central district of Carmel, California for instance, off-street parking is prohibited.[23] Similarly, Boston, New York and San Francisco limit parking downtown (though they require it everywhere else).[24]

In 1923, Columbus, Ohio, became the first city to make off-street parking mandatory for all new apartment buildings.[25]

Twenty-five years later, 185 cities had introduced parking requirements for land uses ranging from hospitals and theatres to office buildings and houses.[26] "By 1960," Jakle and Sculle explain, "nearly every large American city included parking requirements in its zoning program not just for tall buildings but for all buildings."[27] Even Houston — a city without zoning — requires off-street parking for every imaginable land use (restaurants, shops, apartments and more).[28]

In many West Coast counties, five parking spaces — about 1,500 square feet — are required for every 1,000 square feet of shop or restaurant floor space.[29] With 30,000 members from urban development industries, real estate, government and academia (providing "leadership in the responsible use of land") the Urban Land Institute (ULI) calls for four parking spaces per 1,000 square feet of net rentable office space. Their recommendation works out to 1,200 square feet of parking for every 1,000 feet of office.[30] The Community Builders Council of the Urban Land Institute prescribes a minimum of two square feet of parking space for every square foot of store space.[31]

In one especially arduous stipulation, Montgomery County, Maryland, required funeral parlors to provide 83 parking spaces (24,900 square feet) per 1,000 square feet of floor area.[32] Perhaps that explains the high cost of dying.

In *Divorce Your Car*, Katie Alvord reflects upon the priorities of a California city that required 2.8 public library books per thousand residents and 2.2 parking spaces for every housing unit; a 4,000 unit development with an average of 2.7 people per unit would need 30 new library books and 8,800 parking spaces (2,640,000 square feet).[33] This could be why more people seem to know the make and model of a car than the capital of the neighbouring state.

Unlike most zoning ordinances that simply prohibit something, parking requirements are proscriptive: They tell developers exactly what to do.[34] No city bans the construction of apartments with one bedroom or bathroom. Many, however, ban the construction of apartments with only one parking spot.[35] Converting buildings to different uses is difficult in places with supercharged parking requirements. In many cities, a new business simply cannot move into a building that formerly housed an operation with lower parking requirements without adding more spaces (or obtaining a variance).[36]

Extensive parking requirements have reduced many architects to designing buildings around parking laws. "Form follows parking requirements," laments parking guru, Donald Shoup.[37] This was already the case in 1948 Los Angeles, when the *Journal of American Institute of Planners* noted that, "in many cases, the number of garage spaces actually control the number of dwelling units which could be accommodated on a lot."[38]

Since all units, irrespective of size, are generally required to have a parking spot, apartments have become larger and more expensive.[39] The financial and logistical burden created by parking requirements restricts the rooming supply. "Zoning requires a home for every car, but ignores homeless people," writes Shoup. "By increasing the cost of housing, parking requirements make the real homelessness problem even worse."[iv] [40]

...

Most significantly, parking requirements have spurred private car travel through free parking.[41] Parking and car travel are mutually reinforcing; more parking means more car travel and more car travel means increased demand for yet more parking. Additionally, mandatory parking is almost always "free" (the law

---

iv *"Next they're going blame the misery of the Great Depression on cars," some auto-apologista may scoff. We will not disappoint. Many have argued that the car industry — the major growth sector in the 1920s — played a part in triggering the Depression. Between 1920 and October 1929, motor vehicle registrations increased from 10 million to 26.7 million and most of these vehicles were purchased on credit and the Depression was largely triggered by excessive credit.*

sometimes stipulates that it must be). In Los Angeles, for example, commercial and office spaces must provide at least three free parking spaces for every 1,000 square feet.[42] Even when zoning laws don't mandate free parking, the saturated "market" creates an expectation that parking will be free. Would there be any need for parking requirements if people were willing to pay? Wouldn't profit-oriented businesses sell as much parking as they could charge for? Yet, drivers park free for 99 percent of all car trips.[43] "It is no doubt ironic," quipped German auto historian, Wolfgang Zuckermann, "that the motorcar, superstar of the capitalist system, expects to live rent-free."[44]

The push for subsidized parking began in the 1910s and 20s. Cities across the USA began devoting tens of millions of dollars to widen streets and cut down trees to increase parking space.[45] Today it would be hard to find a street without space for curb parking, which Donald Shoup argues, "may be the most costly subsidy Americans cities provide for most of their citizens."[v] [46]

Municipal support extends well beyond curbside parking. By 1942, one in five U.S. cities with populations over ten thousand controlled at least one city centre parking lot (in half of these cities, land was purchased or leased with the express goal of providing parking.)[47] In the land of free enterprise, two-thirds of downtown off-street parking was municipally owned by 1972.[48] Today, about half of the 16,000 surface pay lots are publicly owned.[49]

Traveling car-less through the U.S., a particularly ironic subsidy stood out: Mass transit lines across the country provided free parking. San Francisco's Bay Area Rapid Transit (BART) alone has a total of 46,000 parking spaces, each of which cost about a dollar a day to operate — $17 million a year.[50] Somewhere along the line, it was decided that meager public transit coffers should subsidize public parking (usually for wealthier suburbanites).

v In Montreal and elsewhere only a motorized vehicle is allowed to occupy a parking space unless the city has granted a special permit.

Another place tax dollars subsidize parking is the workplace. Taking advantage of a tax benefit (generally unavailable otherwise) employers can deduct the cost of free parking for their workers.[51] (The tax code allows companies to spend up to $175 per month on parking for each employee, but only $65 per month on mass transit.)[52] Employer parking subsidies mean 90 percent of those who drive to work park free, costing taxpayers roughly $50 billion annually.[vi][53]

In Atlantic City, all overnight visitors and club members park for free, while others pay nominal amounts. How much of the $150 Yves lost at blackjack went to the casino's parking lots? Without the cost of parking, those free drinks may have come quicker (and an inebriated Yves would have kept playing and won it all back!) The point is that the cost of "free" parking is almost always hidden. Be it a Trump casino, Wal-Mart, McDonalds or 7-11, the free parking that lurks in the backyard of almost all private enterprise is buried in product prices. "Seemingly, everyone but the motorist pays for parking," lament Jakle and Sculle.[54]

The cost of "free" parking is astronomical. In 2002, for instance, the total subsidy for off-street parking in the USA was between $127 billion and $374 billion.[vii][55] Shoup argues that, "The cost of all parking spaces in the U.S. exceeds the value of all cars and may even exceed the value of all roads."[56]

Atlantic City was once famous for its "jitneys" that provided cheap rides around town. When Monopoly was still called The Landlord's Game, it had a space called "Labour Upon Mother Earth Produces Wages", which was later changed to "Go".

vi *Some employers allocate spots based upon social positions, giving the closest spots to office entrances to senior management or the top salesperson. Dave Beckham, the top sales executive at San Diego based Five Point Capital inc., told the Sept. 4, 2007 Wall Street Journal "I like knowing that everyone sees my car and that it's there for a reason."*

vii *The numbers vary widely since it's difficult to calculate the exact amount paid for parking by every institution in the country.*

The opposite corner was also changed from its original title of "Public Park" to "Free Parking".[57] Nineteen spaces later, past two railroads and a jailhouse, to the right of "Boardwalk" lies "Park Place". This fancy property wasn't named after a paved lot, rather an area with lawn, trees or shrubs. Across North America, there is nothing that has negated the idea of the park more than parking.[58]

9. People are obstacles to progress — Atlanta

While I fell asleep at the mere sound of an engine, Yves stayed awake and restless from city to city. A couple hours north of Atlanta, I woke up to find the seat next to me empty. Yves was not on the bus.

"I think we left him at the gas station a couple minutes ago," said a fellow rider.

I walked up to the front to tell the driver we couldn't leave Yves in rural Georgia. The driver made an announcement about our missing passenger and we returned to the gas station, where Yves was waiting with three newspapers tucked under his arm. From that point on we were less than popular and I was looking forward to reaching our destination.

Dazed and confused after thirty-two hours on the road, we staggered into the chilly darkness of the evening. We arrived in Atlanta on a Sunday. Yves' buddy Mike had joined us and was continuing on that night for northern Mexico, where he would hitchhike his way southwards. We pulled in just off downtown. Barely a soul could be seen on a street rife with empty parking. As we left the station, we were warned not to venture too far. But we needed to get to the Five Points transit station, so we set off regardless, burly friend in tow.

Vacant lots surrounded us immediately. After three blocks, Mike stopped abruptly and hugged us goodbye. This avid traveler had lost interest in seeing more of the city, appearing more concerned about his solo return to the station.

We ventured a little further, until a police car glided along side us. We were initially alarmed by their interest. The officers voiced concerned about our safety, offering us out-of-towners a lift to a safer part of town.

"Why is it so dead?" asked Yves.

"Parking for the stadiums," replied the officer behind the wheel.

…

The next morning, Yves and I trooped over to Martin Luther King's childhood neighbourhood, Sweet Auburn. Stopping to rest on a bench in a small park, we were soon approached by two enterprising park residents, who offered an unofficial tour in exchange for lunch. It sounded like a fair deal and we took them up on it.

They told us Sweet Auburn had seen better days. A wall divided the neighbourhood in two. An immense highway underpass separated it from downtown, decreasing the property value and standard of living. It was an eyesore. Noisy and dangerous, the underpass introduced smoke, dirt and air pollution into the community. Sweet Auburn was yet another thriving neighbourhood devastated by highway construction. For *Homo Automotivis* it makes perfect sense to disrupt, divide and destroy communities to get cars to their destinations a few minutes faster.

To make way for the interstate in the 1950s and 1960s, highway agencies demolished 335,000 urban dwellings.[1] The state rarely compensated displaced families after razing their homes.[2] Sometimes the architects of destruction spoke frankly about the problems they faced. "The most serious obstacles in our road-building program are not money, not engineering problems, nor cruel terrain — but people," explained James Morton, Special Assistant to the U.S. Secretary of Commerce in 1964.[3]

Deciding where to build a highway is inherently political. And race often underlay the choice. "A great body of work shows that urban freeways destroyed the hearts of African-American communities in the South Bronx, Nashville, Austin, Los Angeles,

Durham, and nearly every medium to large American city," explains *Once There Were Greenfields*.[4] In West End Boston, for instance, highway building drove out thirty thousand, predominantly African American, residents in the 1960s.[5]

Urban planners and politicians encounter less political opposition when building highways in marginalized, vulnerable communities. What's more, in some cases, highway building may have been used to impede ascending black communities. Historical records show that Atlanta planned a 51-metre-wide parkway to serve as a barrier between black and white neighbourhoods in 1917.[6] Again in 1941, the Atlanta City Planning Commission proposed a greenbelt parkway to halt expansion of a black neighbourhood.[7] Further west, in Nashville, Tennessee, the construction of Interstate 40 was initially planned through a white neighbourhood. However, in a racially charged move the route was redrawn to pass through the flourishing Jefferson Street corridor.[8] The corridor was "home to roughly 80% of Nashville's African-American owned businesses", explains *Once There Were Greenfields*. "Not only did the construction of the I-40 destroy this commercial district; it also demolished 650 homes and 27 apartment buildings."[9]

Bulldozing African-American houses for highways gave rise to the catchphrase "white roads through black bedrooms." The phrase was coined to highlight frustration with the injustice of racially charged highway planning.

In addition to protesting highway construction, numerous civil rights organizations opposed the urban "renewal" taking place alongside it. They claimed that urban renewal (also referred to as "Negro removal") was used to purposefully break up, divide and destroy neighbourhoods with the goal of weakening the political clout of blacks and other minority groups.[10] The outrage caused by racially charged city planning was not short lived.

When racial conflicts engulfed inner cities in the late 1960s, urban renewal and freeway construction were two of the major grievances.[11] From Watts to Newark, a major precursor to the riots was highway building.[12] Of the numerous uprisings across the USA, the worst manifestation of racial unrest took place in Detroit in July 1967. Sparked by frustration with a racist police force, the violence raged for four days and three nights.[i] A *Detroit News* survey revealed that, after police harassment, urban planning was the most cited reason for racial tension leading to the riots. Prior to the unrest, a government demolition derby ripped up "Paradise Valley," the heart of Detroit's black community, to make way for Interstate 75. Michigan's Governor George Romney conceded, "What triggered the riot in my opinion, to a considerable extent was that between urban renewal and expressways, poor black people were bulldozed out of their homes. They had no place to go in the suburbs because of suburban restrictions."[13]

"White flight" was a much-discussed outcome of the racial uprising. The newly constructed Interstate provided an easy route to the suburbs. Detroit's white population diminished from 1,500,000 in the 1950s, to 220,000 in 2005.[ii] [14] The desire to avoid living with or near blacks, especially after the 1960s riots, stimulated suburban expansion. Highway construction aggravated racial tension while simultaneously subsidizing an exit to the suburbs. When black communities cried foul against urban planning injustices, white residents had one more reason to leave the city. This spatial segregation accelerated the ascendance of the car, the primary instrument of white flight. The circle was complete.

Although largely understood as a phenomenon of the late 1960s, the white exodus from the city began decades earlier.

---

i Over seven thousand were arrested and 43 left dead; all but 10 who perished were black, slain mostly by the police and National Guard. Evidence suggests that the Motel Algiers housed one of the most heinous incidents of the riot: the National Guard execution of three unarmed African Americans.
ii 82% of Detroit's residents are black.

The most famous example is the meticulously planned suburb of Levittown, Long Island. In 1953 it had a population of 70,000 — all of whom were white.[15]

As far back as 1930, census data reveals that southern cities were increasingly segregated.[16] A case study of Atlanta between 1900 and 1935 concluded that since white people "could generally better afford the price of an automobile, it gave them a novel advantage over black Atlantans; greater mobility and an opportunity to act out their racist views by moving away to planned suburban neighbourhoods on the north side" of the city.[17] By 1930, Atlanta's central Ward 1 neighbourhood was 96 percent black up from 57 percent in 1900.[18] "By 1930," Howard Preston asserted, "if racism could be measured in miles and minutes, blacks and whites were more segregated in the city of Atlanta than ever before."[19]

...

Another outcome of "white roads though black bedrooms" was white pollution in black lungs. In *Highway Robbery*, Robert Bullard explains: "African-Americans and Latinos are disproportionately exposed to harmful air pollutants, partly as a result of the Interstate Era when urban freeways were often routed through communities of color in cities across the country."[20] A third of white Americans reside in areas that fall below national air quality standards for two pollutants or more. Fifty percent of African-Americans and 60 percent of Latinos, however, live in these high pollution zones.[21] Exposure to pollution in these communities has led to higher rates of asthma and cancer.[22] While they comprise 12 percent of the population, for instance, African Americans make up 24 percent of asthma deaths.[23]

Spatial separation strengthens the disadvantages of race and class in other ways. The movement of better off whites from the city diminishes the property taxes required for social services such as schools, community centres and other public services.

For those left in these urban centres, economic opportunities become harder to reach. The Detroit metropolitan area (followed by Atlanta) had the highest percentage of its office space located outside the city. Coincidentally, in the five most office sprawled cities (Washington, Miami, Philadelphia, Detroit and Atlanta) people of color comprise the majority population.[24]

Relocating offices to the suburbs is particularly disadvantageous to the car-less who often cannot reach these jobs by public transit. People of color are hardest hit since they are less likely to own a car and twice as likely to utilize non-automotive modes of transport to get to work.[25] Across the USA, 24 percent of black households are car-less compared to seven percent of white households.[26] Atlanta's figures mirror the national average.

African American Atlantans are much more likely to use mass transit; 28.2 percent of black males and 35 percent of black females take the Metropolitan Atlanta Rapid Transit Authority (MARTA) to work compared with only 4.4 percent of white men and 6.7 percent of white women.[iii] [27] Robert Bullard notes that some white Atlantans jokingly refer to the MARTA as, "Moving Africans Rapidly Through Atlanta."[28] ("Nigger bus" is another derogatory phrase used to describe public transit.)

MARTA is associated with African Americans, eliciting negative attitudes among many suburban Atlantans; resistance to "urban" infiltration constrained MARTA to serving two of the Atlanta region's ten counties.[29] When Cobb County voted against joining MARTA, for instance, the unofficial slogan was "Stop Atlanta."[30] As a result MARTA has lines that bypass wealthy suburban areas or terminate at their boundaries.

We had our own experience with what appeared to be race-inspired transit planning. In the suburbs of New Orleans

---

iii According to Highway Robbery, despite the demography of its patronage, MARTA prioritized a costly rail system for the predominantly white northern suburbs and a network of cheap buses for black areas.

buses ended their routes abruptly at the edge of municipalities as if the asphalt itself had run out. Even less subtle, some highways are made to block buses. In New York, for instance, overpasses on the Jones Beach Parkway from Manhattan to Long Island were built deliberately low to stop busses from passing beneath and reaching the beaches.[31] [32]

...

At the Martin Luther King museum we witnessed Atlanta's long and rich civil rights history; evidence that collective struggle can be victorious, even in the face of incredible oppression. While car companies no longer restrict their wares from being sold to African Americans, transportation racism is still alive. [iv] [33] As Martin Luther King once said, "Urban transit systems in most American cities have become a genuine civil rights issue."[34]

---

iv *According to the Dec. 16, 2006 Washington Post, Daimler-Chrysler settled a class action suit brought against it by black customers regarding lending policies in 2003. According to the May 10, 2007 Washington Post, Blacks paid a median interest rate of 7% on new car purchases, compared to 5% for whites and 5.5% for Hispanics. On used cars, it was 9.5% for blacks and 9% for Hispanics, compared to 7.5% for whites.*

10. The state religion — Salt Lake City

Somewhere between San Francisco and Utah I fell asleep and awoke to a dazzling white plain that stretched into the horizon. The fierce light reflecting off the salt lake was unearthly. But at our lodgings on West North Temple Street, not even the astonishing beauty of a city ringed with mountains could mask the soulless sprawl that covered the terrain with billboards, fast food chains and auto repair shops. As my eyes wandered towards the sky my view was obstructed by an enormous billboard, empty, save the statement: "Sixteen million cars pass this sign every year. Rent it."

The streets were the cleanest I'd ever seen. Perhaps this was because nobody walked them. It was Saturday afternoon. We'd been sitting at a bus stop for three-quarters of an hour, and not one pedestrian or transit vehicle had passed by. A growing anxiety from the apocalyptic emptiness was relieved when the city bus finally appeared. It delivered us to the downtown commercial area where a shopping plaza overflowed with energetic citizens. Later that day, we discovered the bus stop was a mere 45-minute walk from the downtown mall.

Getting around downtown Salt Lake City was once again difficult. Crossing up to 10 lanes at a time, we dodged and dashed our way across downtown streets. From massive parking lots to biased-against-pedestrian traffic lights, the usual symptoms of rule by automobile were everywhere. We did, however, discover a pedestrian overpass at one junction, where we made a long march across an iron loop that wound in on itself. We were happy to avoid cars, so I won't dwell on how pedestrians had to walk twice the distance to avoid inconveniencing a little used road.

As messy as car-less travel was in Salt Lake City, we always knew where we were. The streets were labeled North, South, East or West Temple and at the centre of it all was a (surprise!) big temple. Naturally, this was the first attraction we sought out. On arriving at Temple Square we were immediately approached by two smiling young women wearing nametags. The flags on their tags informed us that Sister Olga was from Germany and Sister Marie was French.

"Can we give you a tour of the square?" said Marie.

"Yes, please," I said.

Yves declined and wandered off on his own, leaving me outnumbered.

Marie and Olga began with an abridged history of the Church of Latter Day Saints, describing how members fled to Utah in the mid-nineteenth century to escape religious persecution, establishing Salt Lake City in a previously infertile valley. Our first stop was the famed Mormon tabernacle choir's performance hall. Fashioned out of painted wood, the faux marble pillars and faux brass tubes of the organ held their original places in the hall. Interesting. When we reached the mouth of the Temple, the sisters stood back in silent awe. It had taken 40 long years to build the ivory structure that towered over us, but after standing around for a bit, I realized we weren't going inside. I wasn't allowed in. Nor were the sisters. Actually, almost no one was. What a letdown. After several more impressive buildings, a discussion about the intricacies of my hairstyle and a 20-foot Jesus statue, I bid farewell to Marie and Olga. (It was not the last I would hear from them. Weeks later, they e-mailed me in Montreal and sent two Montreal-based sisters to my apartment for a visit in my kitchen. If only anti-car activists were that well organized.)

For Mormons, Salt Lake City is a sacred place. But through the eyes of an archaeologist working centuries into the future, it might seem like the automobile was worshipped above all else. The one true religion of *Homo Automotivis* — the worship of cars — is nowhere more evident than Salt Lake City despite its Mormon roots. The streets had been given up by pedestrians as an offering to automobility. The volume of space reserved for the car in the city certainly overwhelmed the Temple and its square. The architecture, planning, services and economic activity of the city, lead one to believe the car is esteemed above all else.

If that seems like an exaggeration, the link between religion and the automobile must at least be admitted. With the majority of mega churches built in the suburbs, exurbs and beyond, organized religion is virtually inaccessible without a car. Perhaps this explains why numerous religious leaders convened in Washington in early 2006, falling to their knees to seek God's help in reducing the spiraling cost of gasoline.[1]

…

Most commentators on the USA mention the power of religion. Few have noted that more people worship the automobile than go to church. But, as far back as 1910, Rev. I.T. Lansing of Scranton, Pennsylvania complained that Americans spend more money on cars than "church work" and in 1964 Lewis Mumford lamented the "religion of the motorcar."[2][3]

The *Homo Automotivis* worship of cars, lets call it Automotivism, is catholic in its all-encompassing nature. While in the European Middle Ages life revolved around the church, with most important events celebrated there, today the car has become a sacred place. Devotees give up much of their lives to its worship.

In 1960s USA nearly 40 percent of marriage proposals took place in the front or back of an automobile and with the opening of the first drive-in church over 50 years ago, an Automotivist could even get married in a car.[4] In fact, a true devotee can spend a major portion of her day communing with the deity at drive-thru banks, mini-marts, liquor stores and even drive thru libraries and vaccine clinics. There are Town Hall drive-thru windows for paying taxes, fines, utility bills and municipal service fees as well as drive-thru voting in Orange County. Automotivists can get evergreen seedlings at a drive-thru nursery or pay their last respects at a drive-thru mortuary. There is even a drive-thru strip club with viewing windows at $5 a minute on Route 22. Cars serve as offices, as dining areas and even as homes — tens of thousands of America's "mobile homeless" live in their cars. There are more than twice as many Google hits for "car" than "god". They even outnumber "sex." According to a study by Progressive Insurance, 45 percent of married men and women declared the car to be the most important thing in their life.[5]

A December 2006 poll found that almost four out of 10 Americans considered their car to have a personality of its own.[6] Many people name their cars. Some show their respects by having them tattooed on their bodies or being buried with them. One man even tried to marry his 1996 Mustang GT. "In California they are doing same-sex marriages," he said. "So we are here in Tennessee. Why can't we do the good ol' boy thing and marry our cars and trucks?"[i][7]

"The American," William Faulkner once wrote, "really loves nothing but his automobile."[8] One thing is certain, when it comes to the car there is no lack of devotion. Our modern day hymns have drawn endless inspiration from the car. The first ode was set to music in 1899 with the release of "love in an automobile," followed by 120 automobile-themed tunes produced between 1905 and 1908.[9]

At the dawn of the rock and roll era, records linked the car with freedom and escape from the restrictions at home, with teens bopping to refrains like "She's gonna have fun, fun fun 'til her Daddy takes the T-Bird away." Throw an automobile into the lyrics and you're that much closer to a hit. In the first eight months

---

i Mechaphiles are individuals sexually obsessed with cars. A man from Washington state, Edward Smith, claims to have had "sex" with 1,000 cars.

of 2004, 59 different car brands were mentioned a total of 645 times in songs that made it onto the Billboard Top-20.[10]

The car made an easy crossover from radio to the silver screen, with car flicks constituting an entire genre. Car-film mania was kick-started by Thomas Edison in 1900 with his film short *Automobile Parade*. From the *Gumball Rally* to *Mad Max* through to *Herbie Reloaded*, the movies have come *Fast and Furious*.[11]

It is not unusual to find cars brought to life with a heart and soul. *Susie the Little Blue Coupe*, *My Mother the Car*, and *Chitty Chitty Bang Bang* were among the first cartoon, television series and feature films to anthropomorphize the car. Who could forget 1983's *Night Rider*, featuring a computerized car clearly smarter than its driver. In Disney's *Cars*, the characters have windshields for eyes and radiator grills for mouths. From Lightning McQueen, a feisty competitor at the Piston Cup races, to the television commentators and noisemakers in the crowd, everyone is a car.

Browsing the shelves at Barnes and Noble, we saw more magazines about cars than current affairs and politics put together. And those other religions barely registered on the shelves. The sacred texts of Automotivism like *Car & Driver*, *Road & Track* and *Motor Trend* are found everywhere. There is even evidence of a mature religion with the emergence of sects that cater to all sorts of gear heads and car nuts. For example there is *Box and Bubble* (devoted to "tricked-out" older cars) and *Scraper Magazine* (a tribute to the DIY enhancements of the scraper movement).

Across the country, thousands make pilgrimages to auto events. Held once a year on the third Saturday of August, the Woodward Dream Cruise is the Mecca of classic car festivals. It attracts nearly two million people and 40,000 (muscle, collector and other special interest) vehicles — enough to pack a 10-lane avenue in urban Detroit for 16 miles.[12]

Shrines dot the landscape. In 1953, there were 41 publicly accessible antique car collections or museums.[13] Today, hundreds of these memorials pay tribute to the automobile. In 2005, five cities competed to host the NASCAR Hall of Fame, offering significant subsidies to attract the economic spin-offs sure to ensue from throngs of pilgrims flooding this car-racing sanctuary.[14]

NASCAR is the second most watched U.S. "sport", with a multi billion dollar TV deal and licensed product sales worth $2 billion annually.[15] Its following is so intense that million-dollar condos have sprouted around NASCAR stadiums (the view from the balcony is no doubt good, but each stadium hosts only a few races a year). Spreading into other mediums, NASCAR 3-D was the most popular Imax film of all time and the NASCAR series is a top selling computer game (together with Grand Theft Auto, Hot Pursuit and OutRun).[16]

Finally, Automotivists are coveted by political parties more than followers of any other religion. About 45 percent of U.S. male voters and 37 percent of women are members of the NASCAR sect and regularly attend races or worship by TV. The so-called "NASCAR Dads" were the most sought after voting category in the 2004 presidential elections (and yes, Bush Jr. won them over).[17]

In *Without Wheels*, Terence Bendixon describes the heights to which the car has risen: "It has become a religion. It has articles of faith — the motorist's right to the freedom of the road; it has a priesthood — the highway and traffic engineers; it has an array of costly tabernacles that have already been described in terms previously reserved for cathedrals ... and it has a vast, unthinking following. Motorization is indeed a religion with an impressive record, but like others before it, it has grown greedy, corrupt and careless. A reformation is due."[18]

11. Autoeroticism — Miami

We were staying "just 20 minutes from Miami," but it took an hour to get to Fort Lauderdale's inter-city transit. When we finally arrived in downtown Miami, we took a free sky-shuttle, peering down through glass walls at a bright city bustling with activity.

It was dusk when we got to the beach. We'd walked past streamlined contours of art deco hotels and pastel neighbourhoods studded with royal palms. It may have been a reflection from the salmon-coloured sky, but even the vast stretch of sand took on a Florida pink hue. On Ocean Drive we cut through the Florida humidity and a mess of pedestrians making the latest, greatest, fashion statements. We sat down at a restaurant patio a few blocks from the old Versace mansion, where a tanned waiter with white-blond hair brought us overpriced drinks and snack-sized meals. My attention was divided between Flamenco dancers onstage and fashion drama on the streets. It was a total sensory overload. Vehicles were in the game too, many sporting glitzy rims — an accessory costing up to twenty thousand dollars. Even the license plates had attitude (FQU2, URCRZY).

"Describe yourself in one car or less," read an enormous billboard on a South Beach boulevard. It reminded me of a time at Turi, my old boarding school in the highlands of Kenya, where with little to occupy their spare time, the tenth grade boys undertook a rigorous cataloguing of the girls. The score was not a number out of 10, instead we were assigned vehicles: Jaguar was deemed the highest compliment.

From high school corridors to the drag racing strip, "the automobile is one of the most gendered objects of twentieth century technology."[1] If Automotivism is the state religion of

Homo Automotivis, then autoeroticism is its secular counterpart and seems particularly dominant among the male of our species.

In 2002, the first car designed and developed by women for women was considered a "concept car."[2] Yet, since the inception of widespread car use, women have been driving. Reliant on cars for work and family, two-thirds of all chauffeur trips and nearly half of all car purchases are made by women.[3] This has not altered the masculine dominance of car culture. Car culture prefers women in the role of accessories rather than drivers, with popular media such as *Car and Driver* draping bikini-clad women on every imaginable surface of the automobile, but almost never behind the wheel. Women's bodies have long been used to eroticize cars. Giving new meaning to the word autoeroticism, some designers have used the female form to create vehicles with sex appeal. One resourceful automobile manufacturer dispatched designers to Rio de Janeiro's Carnival with an order to "look at very nice women's breasts" for inspiration. This isn't new. The cone shaped bumper ends of the 1946 Cadillac were the first metallic bust line.

We still live in the era of the muscle car. While the SUV and the pickup truck are wildly popular, cars perceived as "chickmobiles" are often shunned as poison to men, as though somehow emasculating. In a profitable collusion between the male psyche and consumer culture, television shows like *American Hot Rod*, *Monster Garage* and *Overhaulin'* reflect the machismo (and nationalism) of car culture.

Like a trophy wife on the arm, the hot car is a boost to the *Homo Automotivis* ego. As one commentator pointed out: "A healthy dose of horse power is a gift that makes pudgy men see themselves as two belt sizes smaller, balding or graying men as dashing young powerbrokers."

Purchasing a flashy car during a mid-life crisis is standard practice for denying the withering of youth. Classic cars from the mid-60s now fetch up to six figures - in an attempt to buy back youth, baby boomers are purchasing cars they lusted after as teens.

The sexism of car culture is not all fun and games for guys. In Fort Lauderdale, we came across a contest to win a vehicle where the slogan was "You're not living 'till you've got a ride." A young black man, set on impressing the world, makes a huge effort to organize his personal appearance, then hops into his car and hits the town. To his delight he pulls up next to a vehicle full of gorgeous women at the filling station. Then to his horror the women burst into hysterics, peering down onto his pitiful clunker from their mega SUV. He's not man enough for them, and they leave him choking in their dust.

Tunes like Jack Frost's 1915 release, You Can't Afford to Marry Me If You Can't Afford a Ford and Rye Cooder's Every Woman I Know Is Crazy About an Automobile, are a window into the social realities that arose with the emergence of automobile culture.[4] More recently in TLC's "Scrubs," the worthlessness of a man is confirmed when he's seen "hanging out of the passenger side of his best friend's ride."

"The automobile's a credit card on wheels," writes Heathcote Williams. "It's pushy to tell people how much you make, so you tell 'em through your automobile."[5] A luxury vehicle lets the whole world know that you have arrived, both literally and metaphorically. Poring through *Driven* magazine, I paused at a Mercedes Benz ad for the S-Class 2006 that read: "Having nothing to prove is everything."

On the other side of the world in Kenya, East Africa, this sentiment became apparent during a sleepover at a classmate's. Fifteen at the time, we were picked up from school in a posh new Mercedes Benz. When we reached their place, I noted the sharp contrast between a luxury vehicle and the humble furnishings of a house where taps were left to rust and tiles remained broken. After a night crammed into a bedroom shared by three other siblings, it was clear to me that mobile status was the priority.

Since the dawn of the auto age, the car has been a conspicuous symbol of status. The car did not bring about an immediate revolution in mobility, rather a revolution in the "dominant symbols of prestige."[6] Mechanical problems and unpaved roads meant that early automobiles were impractical as a mode of regular transport. They were technological toys for the rich and driving was an elite adventure.[7] By the turn of the 20th century, New York City's Automobile Club had more millionaires than any other social club in the world.[i] [8]

Prior to our modern day acquiescence to the automobile, a car was viewed as an obtrusive and ostentatious display of wealth. Farmers and the American working class were incensed by their presence. A 1904 edition of the farm magazine, *Breeders Gazette*, called automobile drivers, "a reckless, bloodthirsty, villainous lot of purse-proud crazy trespassers."[9] Angry rural citizens often covered roads with broken glass, chains or logs, sometimes digging ditches across thoroughfares to thwart motorists.[10] In 1902 there were "several instances in which rifles were fired at early motorists to frighten them. In one instance a Minnesotan driving a car was shot in the back by locals opposed to the encroachment of the auto."[11] Motorists became fearful of breakdowns and other "compromised" situations that could encourage attacks from pedestrian onlookers.

Cars were also a significant imposition in big cities, where people traded and children played in the streets.[12] In 1901 rioting broke out in a Lower Manhattan Italian neighbourhood after two-year-old Louis Camille was run down and killed.[13] During the next five years, the *New York Times* reported 34 more violent protests sparked by automobiles.[14] By the time the First World War began, motorists had killed over 1,000 New York children.[15]

Animosity towards the automobile was so great that in 1906 Woodrow Wilson, then president of Princeton University,

i *A Monticello, New York, Motor Club costs $125,000 to join.*

declared, "Possession of an auto car is such an ostentatious display of wealth that it will stimulate socialism."[16] Among the wealthy, the automobile was popular partly because it reaffirmed their dominance over mobility, which had been undermined by rail. Prior to the train's ascendance in the mid 1800s the elite traveled by horse and buggy, but the train's technological superiority compromised the usefulness of the horse-drawn carriage. Even for shorter commutes, streetcars became the preferred mode of transport by the early 1900s. More available to various classes of society, the train and streetcar blurred class lines. The automobile, on the other hand, provided an exclusive form of travel.[ii] [17] [18]

...

Back at Nina's Fort Lauderdale bungalow, I channel surfed, pausing to watch an excited fellow in a Che T-shirt crafting clandestine plans. He was not occupied with a socialist revolution, rather the revolution of tires belonging to his pal Antwan's jalopy — a car shot to fame on *Pimp my Ride*. Along with millions of other viewers, I watched, entranced, as Antwan's ramshackle vehicle obtained eighteen-inch chrome wheels, limo tint windows, high style suede interior racing seats, a DVD player (with steering wheel monitor) and a fish tank. $20,000 was pumped into a $900 car. The surprise was unveiled to an emotional Antwan at the show's finale. With tears in eyes he said, "I will not be the butt of jokes, anymore ... Ladies, here I come. I'm going to get respect for what I have."

Antwan is not alone in his desire to command respect for what he has. Spending on after-car parts and accessories has skyrocketed to $30 billion a year.[19] "Pimping" is not confined to

---

ii *Before the car (and train) most people walked from place to place. In a 19th century pedestrian city, For Love of the Automobile asserts, "just about everyone but the lame had the same power over space, because all — with the exception of coach owners [horse and buggy], and even there the discrepancy was not so great — were subject to the standard set by their legs."*

a small minority — it is a national obsession. Nearly four in 10 drivers see their vehicle as an extension of themselves, which may explain why so much time and energy is spent cleaning, fixing or simply thinking about the automobile. Car enthusiasts are some of the most imaginative hobbyists and will often strip the bodies of two or more cars, mixing and matching parts to make a new vehicle. Elvis, the King Pimper, covered the floor of his pink Cadillac in white fur and painted the exterior with "forty coats of special dust made from crushed diamonds and fish scales flown in from Asia."[20]

A glimpse into the lifestyles of the rich and famous on MTV's *Cribs* is never complete without a look round the back at the Lincoln or Rolls Royce. From the "understated cool" of the Prius to the elegance of a Maserati, the backyard is the new runway.[iii] And like a Louis Vuitton monogram bag or a pair of Versace jeans, brand names in the automobile industry are worth a small fortune.

Looking to update my wardrobe, I flipped through an edition of *Vogue* to discover an entire 30-page supplement devoted to automobiles. Photographed in exotic locations, under beautiful light and from the most flattering angles, the automobile was presented as the ultimate accessory. And like haute couture design houses, automotive companies thrive on consumers' desire to set themselves apart. There is always a newer, improved model rolling off the assembly line but the differences are mainly aesthetic. Be it a Ferrari or a Lamborghini, it is no coincidence that many of the trendiest cars come from the most fashionable places in the world.

iii According to the July 4, 2007 New York Times, 57% of Prius buyers said they bought their car because it "makes a statement about me." Only 25% said they bought it because it "lowers emissions." According to the Jan. 7, 2007 Los Angeles Times, Sarah McLean, publisher of Limousine and Chauffeured, describes the "Ecolimo" phenomena among the Hollywood elite: "They may not drive an ecological car on their own time, but when they are seen at an event, they want to be branded as cool."

...

The ideological power of the car has been a force to be reckoned with. For *Homo Automotivis,* it is the embodiment of modernity, representing freedom and progress, technological prowess and control over nature.

Rewinding to the expositions and fairs of 1930s America sheds some light on how the automobile gained its tremendous ideological stature. Far from mere happenstance, the automotive industrial complex carefully cultivated an auto-centric vision of a utopian future. In 1937, Shell Oil spotlighted the model expressways of industrial designer Norman Bel Geddes' "Automotive City of Tomorrow" while Richfield Oil brought a new ride, "Autopia," to Disneyland. Concurrently, GM launched a futuristic caravan of red buses dubbed the "Parade of Progress," an exhibition that toured for nearly fifteen years. The most famous expression of this auto-centric ideal was launched at the New York World's Fair in 1939. GM called it "Futurama." This pavilion attracted a whopping 25 million visitors to its exhibitions and ride, with another 20 million viewing the film *New Horizons* (based on Futurama's contents).[21][22] The pavilion offered a simulated trip along a model of GM's vision of 1960 USA, featuring vast suburbs and a network of automatic seven lane superhighways (with 100 mile an hour speed limits).[23] Finally, at the "Highways and Horizons," exhibit, badges were handed out with the slogan: "I have seen the future."[24]

Futurama was, in part, a response to criticisms leveled at capitalism during the Great Depression.[iv] The fair's theme, "Building the World of Tomorrow" aimed to show that prosperity could follow hard times. And, of course, quality-of-life would be measured by the number of cars in the driveway.[v] This sentiment

---

iv *A 1924 Chevrolet ad read: "How Can Bolshevism Flourish in A Motorized Country?"*

v *Much like President Calvin Coolidge's 1928 election slogan, "a chicken in every pot and a car in every garage."*

was captured in a 1937 San Joaquin Valley, California public service billboard, where a family and their dog are pictured out for a drive under the captions, "There Is No Way Of Life Like the American Way" and "World's Highest Standard of Living."[25]

Over 80 years ago, the *Saturday Evening Post* referred to car sales as "a favourite barometer of our national prosperity."[26] In 1947, Paul Hoffman, president of Studebaker, asserted that, "the motor vehicle, together with the roadway it uses, has become a basic condition of our future progress."[27]

Progress is still measured by the number of automobiles sold and the car continues to symbolize capitalist might. As a Mercedes Benz ad aptly explained: "YOU'RE NOT BUYING A CAR. YOU'RE BUYING A BELIEF."[28]

12. Behind the wheel it's me, myself and I — Portland

As we walked through Portland I remembered Anita from Mobile and her plan to move to Oregon. Although the city seemed pleasant and relatively pedestrian friendly, a few hours wandering downtown were not long enough to assess whether her move was a good idea. It was enough time, however, to grab the local newspaper. An *Oregonian* columnist writing about street youth, shared a reader's letter detailing the lengths he went to avoid the homeless: In the morning he entered work through the underground parking. At lunch he eschewed the nearby restaurants and slipped into his car to avoid panhandlers. Finally, he used the parkade exit to avoid street people on his way home from work. Many of us, myself included," a businessman from Northeast Portland e-mailed into the *Oregonian*, "drive garage (home) to garage (downtown) to garage (home) and never leave the building because of this problem. … It's easier just not to deal with it."[1]

Yves' father recounted a similarly bizarre tale about a poverty-phobic colleague at work who was proudly appalled by the sight of public transit riders. Even though it stopped in front of his workplace, he refused to ride the city's SkyTrain.

Describing an era long before the SkyTrain, *Down the Asphalt Path*'s Clay McShane writes about the elite's disdain for public transit riders: "Trolleys were dirty, noisy, and overcrowded. It was impossible for middle-class riders to isolate themselves from fellow riders whom they perceived as social inferiors. Distancing themselves from blacks, immigrants, blue collar workers, and, in general those stereotyped as the 'great unwashed,' was often precisely why the middle classes had moved to the suburbs."[2]

The automobile's capacity to create social distance en route appealed to early car buyers.[3] Prominent auto historian, James J. Flink remarked that, "the automobile seemed to proponents of the innovation, to afford a simple solution to some of the more formidable problems of American life associated with the emergence of an urban industrial society."[4]

The car is "a system of human dissociation."[5] Behind the wheel of their private mobile spaces, drivers are far less likely to mix and mingle than pedestrians. By isolating drivers from fellow human beings, driving can engender hostility and mistrust. Pedestrians, cyclists and public transit riders are forced into a greater awareness of their environment and as a result are more likely to concern themselves with its wellbeing.

Like a turtle that carries its home on its back, it is possible for *Homo Automotivis* to exist almost entirely within his mobile private spaces: from home to work, the mall, gym or bar and back home again.

...

Homo Automotivis reveres individualism, believing the car is essential to his existence. The car has made it possible to live far from the poor (or anyone else without an automobile). As the wealthy shifted to the suburbs, poverty concentrated in U.S. inner cities and those who remained suffered disproportionately. Under-serviced areas with shattered social networks are not only exposed to poverty, they generate it. "Poor neighbourhoods are poverty machines."[6]

In a U.S. metropolitan area with numerous municipalities, wealthier segments of society rarely share a common local government with the lowest income groups.[7] When wealthier people move into enclaves, they strip inner cities of the tax base required to adequately fund public schools and other social services. In one of the most extreme examples of modern day segregation, people barricade themselves into gated communities.

Across the U.S., especially in the car-dominated Southwest, growing numbers of affluent families have retreated into these exclusive and exclusionary residences.[8] More than eight million Americans are holed up in some kind of gated community.[9] [10]

These communities are rooted in fear. They shield a wealthy minority from "the consequences of economic inequity and resentment outside the gates" insists Rebecca Solnit in *Wanderlust*. "It is the alternative to social justice."[11] Nan Ellin describes this phenomenon as "a dramatic manifestation of the fortress mentality growing in America."[12] Queried about their reason for joining these communities, residents cite security (broadly defined as freedom from crime, mischievous teens, strangers etc.) as the major attraction.[13] There may be a sense of security in high walls, but the social costs tower above them. Walls break down the ability for collective understanding and commitment while reducing people's sense of responsibility for what goes on beyond the gates.[14]

The desired outcome of exclusion is sameness; above all else, the same income. Homogeneity is the raison d'etre for the gated community, which is the most extreme manifestation of the suburban tendency towards cultural uniformity. As in nature, the outcome of this inbreeding can be undesirable. The homogeneity of suburban life lends itself to a base-level "corporate" culture in which the lowest common denominator thrives (think strip malls and Wal-Mart). There are few "scenes", cultural, political or otherwise. Television soaked and debilitated by a vast terrain, social engagement is discouraged.

Conducive to consumerism, disconnected and depoliticized, the suburbs are bastions of conservatism. Surveys indicate that suburbanites are less inclined to support government programs, unless considered directly beneficial — highways and education, for instance. Compared to their counterparts in small towns and urban areas, suburbanites "place little emphasis on such social goals as eliminating discrimination and reducing poverty, and tend to reject initiatives such as park acquisition and mass transit."[15]

Right-wing politics reign supreme, intensifying as suburbs sprawl further outwards. Conversely, according to Robert E. Lang, Director of the Metropolitan Institute at Virginia Tech, "at each greater increment of urban density, democrat John Kerry received a higher proportion of the vote [in the 2004 Presidential election]."[16] Put differently, as the dominance of the car increased, so did votes for George W. Bush.[i]

The suburbs are infertile ground for the social movements necessary to tip back the scale between rich and poor. There is a strong argument to be made that the personal automobile poses a significant obstacle to progressive social change.

Monthly car payments keep indebted fingers to the grindstone. In 1932 the Father of Market Research, Charles Coolidge Parlin, explained that purchasing cars through consumer financing encouraged a "better attitude" from labour and that "the automobile furnished one of the greatest incentives to industry and sobriety labour ever had."[17]

A June 2006 *New York Times* magazine cover story on debt discussed the 1919 launch of the General Motors Acceptance Corporation (GMAC), speculating that "acceptance" implied the borrower was a member of a responsible community.[18] The *Times* explained, "indebtedness could discipline workers, keeping them at routinized jobs in factories and offices, graying but harnessed, meeting payments regularly. Good consumers would be good producers."[19] Prior to 1920, only a few expensive items such as sewing machines were bought with deferred payment. But

---

i *According to American Theocracy, in 2004, drivers polled seven points more favourably for Bush than the overall electorate. Additionally, the thirteen states with 75 MPH speed limits (eight in the mountain west and North Dakota, South Dakota, Nebraska, Oklahoma and Texas) all overwhelmingly voted to re-elect George W. Bush.*

this changed with the automobile. Car purchases commenced widespread consumer installment credit; by 1925, three-fourths of automobiles were bought on credit.[20] [21] In 2006, median U.S. household car debt topped $11,000 and the average new car loan took almost six years (70 months) to pay off.[ii] [22] [23] Remember this next time your colleague says, "Sorry sister, I can't risk a strike, I got car payments to make."

In addition to chaining would-be political actors to their desks with debt, the geography of the car has direct political ramifications.[24] Long commutes are dangerous to democracy, leaving little time for civic engagement. For every 10 additional minutes in daily commuting time, community involvement is cut by an average of 10 percent.[25] In *Bowling Alone*, Robert Putnam goes further in describing this culture of disengagement: "Increased commuting time among the residents of a community lowers average levels of civic involvement even amongst non-commuters. In fact, the civic penalty associated with high-commute communities is almost as great for retired residents and others who are outside the workforce as for full-time workers."[26]

Diffuse suburban landscapes discourage political gatherings. Rebecca Solnit notes that "cars have encouraged the diffusion and privatization of space, as shopping malls replace shopping streets, public buildings become islands in a sea of asphalt, civic design lapses into traffic engineering, and people mingle far less freely and frequently."[27]

How many demonstrations take place in the suburbs? A diffuse geography and population denies a pedestrian scale. This point was driven home on the outskirts of New Orleans where we witnessed a man driving from pole to pole, putting up event posters. It seemed futile. Few walked these streets, and at 30

---

ii According to the May 22, 2007 Wall Street Journal, in 2006 29% of car buyers who traded in a vehicle to buy a new one owed more on their car loans than their cars were worth.

mph these posters would barely register. Signs in the suburbs are enormous and usually too expensive for grassroots groups or small businesses. And there are other obstacles to community organizing. Where does one leaflet in a suburb with no centre? The highway?

...

British historian Eric Hobsbawn's description of "the ideal city for riot and insurrection," stands in stark contrast to the modern day suburb. In an insurrectionary city, the poor majority would live in close proximity to government authorities and the wealthy. The ideal city would also "be densely populated and not too large in area. Essentially it should still be possible to traverse on foot."[28]

In her history of walking, Solnit highlights the vital connection between Paris as a great city of walkers and revolution. She also contrasts walkable San Francisco, with its rich history of progressive political activism, to car-dependent Los Angeles, which has seen less political upheaval. Solnit explains: "Only citizens familiar with their city as both symbolic and practical territory, able to come together on foot and accustomed to walking about their city, can revolt. Few remember that the 'right of the people peaceably to assemble' is listed in the First Amendment of the U.S. Constitution, along with freedom of the press, of speech, and of religion, as critical to a democracy. While other rights are easily recognized, the elimination of the possibility of such assemblies through urban design, automotive dependence, and other factors is hard to trace and seldom framed as a civil rights issue."[29]

13. Fueling the fire — Baton Rouge

On a five-hour Louisiana stopover en route to Houston, we asked about the best way to get downtown.

"Why don't you just take a cab?" responded the convenience store cashier.

"Can't we walk there?" I asked.

"Ooh… it's too far."

A twenty-minute walk later we were in the centre of Baton Rouge. It was a quiet Sunday evening and the only open doors seemed to be the ones leading into a casino. A visitor to some U.S. cities might guess that residents have limited options for socializing: Shop in a mall, attend church, or gamble. That evening we chose the latter. I presented various pieces of identification to the two guards standing at the door; first my health card, then a student card and finally my holographic citizenship card (the latter is so important that for one born outside of Canada, a passport cannot be acquired without it). Puzzled, the female security guard scanned through a catalogue of acceptable identification, then asked:"Do you have your driver's license with you?"

I didn't of course and was denied entrance, one more humiliation for a non-driver. Clearly, I was not a real adult, so I slunk away in shame, making a mental note to dress up a little and lose the specs for Vegas. At least Yves had a passport but even that was eyed suspiciously. In these parts, you couldn't really join the club without a driver's license.

Not all was lost, however. There were rumors of another operation across town and the railway tracks were going that way. It was dusk, the most beautiful time of day; the sky was streaked with orange; tiny animals buzzed and chirped. Crossing the city, we passed a lovers' lane of concrete bleachers, where couples watched steamboats roll down the Mississippi. Their glittering lights shone through the evening, conjuring up nostalgia for a place I'd never been before. As we hopped along the tracks I taught Yves an American folk song I remembered singing in my Kampala elementary school. Although we were far from upstate New York, it seemed a perfect opportunity to burst into a few rounds of Erie Canal:

> *"I've got a mule, her name is Sal,*
> *(Fifteen miles on the Erie Canal!)*
> *She's a good ol' worker and a good ol' pal',*
> *(Fifteen miles on the Erie canal!)"*

There's nothing like a good work song to harden one's resolve and by the time we reached the Casino Rouge, docked on the Mississippi, I had formulated the logistics for a new plan of attack: I would small talk my way in.

"Nice city," I began.

"What, Baton Rouge? It's not that nice," responded the guard.

"Oh, no? What's not to like?" I asked.

"The plants," said the guard.

Dangerous plants?

"Are they poisonous?" I asked, recalling the numerous bush-filled paths that had kept us from an untimely end on Baton Rouge's open roads.

"Yeah, they're killing us out here. We can barely breathe."

"What kind of plants *are* these?" I said.

"There's all kinds. Exxon-Mobil is probably the biggest," he said.

"Right." I said, without missing a beat. That kind of plant.

Despite our compelling poisonous plant conversation he denied my entrance, but not before relaxing a minute to describe the difficulties of living in a town where the air was thick with pollution from a panoply of petrochemical plants. His son went to a largely black school a few blocks from an Exxon-Mobil plant in Wyandotte, which is among the most polluted spots in the country.[1]

There is a direct connection between the automobile and the pollution affecting the casino security guard's son. It's the same story around the globe.

...

Gasoline is like crack cocaine to an auto-addicted *Homo Automotivis*. He must have it, damn the consequences. In August 2010 the *Guardian Weekly* explained that, "the oil industry has been responsible for thousands of fires, explosions and leaks over the last decade across America killing dozens of people and destroying wildlife and the environment."[2] The U.S. energy industry has created "more solid and liquid waste than all other municipal, agricultural, mining, and industrial sources combined."[3] 146 million barrels of drilling waste and 22 million barrels of "associated wastes" were generated by the U.S. energy industry in 1995 alone.[4] "Associated wastes" include water containing high concentrations of toxins (benzene, xylene and ethyl-benzene etc.). In some instances, this water is a hundred times more radioactive than nuclear power plant effluent.[5] Much of this ends up in drinking water systems.

As Africa's biggest petroleum producer, Nigeria ships over 40 percent of its oil directly to the USA. The bulk of this comes from the densely populated Niger delta, a region dependent on fishing and farming, much like Louisiana's Mississippi delta. At once oil rich and impoverished, billions of dollars in crude are siphoned out of the Niger delta every year.[6] [7] With scarcely any social services or paid employment, the region has one doctor for every 150,000 residents.[8] But, oil extraction has caused pollution and disease. Burning natural gas, a waste product of oil production, has contributed to a rise in respiratory illness.[9] Although "flaring" natural gas was officially banned in 1984, Shell (Nigeria's biggest multi-national oil corporation) burned hundreds of millions of cubic feet of natural gas in 2010.[10] On top of wasting a precious resource[i], "flaring" causes acid rain, which has destroyed rooftops and deprived the delta's inhabitants of drinkable rainwater. Confronted with the pollution of their streams and creeks, fishermen have been forced further and further out to sea.[11] Many formerly self-sufficient farming communities now import food because the toxic flares have destroyed their crops and rendered the surrounding farmland barren.[12] [13]

The Niger delta is home to the world's biggest flaring operation. It is here, according to the *Guardian Weekly* in mid 2006, that Shell produced "more carbon emissions than everyone else in sub-Saharan Africa put together."[14]

In 2006 a handful of environmental groups and a Nigerian government representative calculated that up to 1.5 million tons of oil — 175 times the pollution unleashed in the Exxon Valdez disaster — were spilled in the delta over the past half century.[15] Later, in 2009, Amnesty International reported at least nine billion barrels of oil spilled in the delta.[16] Sometimes the spills wreak havoc for those dwelling near oil fields. In 1992 a week-long blowout destroyed a stream in the village of Botem. After seven days of mayhem, the village's source of drinking water was gone, the aquatic life of the stream destroyed and nearby farmlands rendered biological dead zone. Similar devastation unfolded in October 1998 when an oil leak flooded a region of the Delta near the village of Jesse. The spill sparked a blast that left over 700 dead. Two years later, two separate pipelines exploded in southern Nigeria, creating an inferno that claimed another 300 lives.[17]

To avoid paying compensation for the death and suffering, oil companies usually deny responsibility for pipeline explosions. Instead, they claim sabotage. Under Nigerian law, this relieves companies of any obligation to compensate victims or even clean

---

i *Natural gas is difficult to transport so until there is an adequate market near the Niger delta it is nearly worthless.*

up the spills.[18] Of course, in such a poor country, illegal pipeline tapping does occur. In late 2006, oil siphoning caused an explosion that killed 260 people in Lagos, prompting Bodet Kuforiji, a university lecturer, to wonder, "How can this be, that people are so poor in Nigeria that they will risk their lives for a little thing? But boats leave for America every day filled with oil."[19]

The Niger delta is fraught with insecurity. Pipeline explosions and environmental degradation are compounded by oil companies' private security. "Many oil facilities are guarded by Nigerian security forces known as the 'spy police'," writes one journalist familiar with the Delta. "They have been assigned to protect oil facilities but are effectively paid, and sometimes trained, by the oil companies, however, they are disliked by local communities ... oil companies have also brought in their own 'security consultants' — often former soldiers from the U.S., UK and South African militaries."[20]

U.S. based security company Triple Canopy, for instance, opened a Lagos office in mid 2006, its first outside of the Middle East.[21] International private security firms Erinys, ArmorGroup, Aegis and Control Risk all operate in the Delta.[22]

The major reason for the growing security apparatus is political violence. The Movement to Emancipate the Niger Delta (MEND) is the most active guerilla group in the region. By kidnapping foreign workers and attacking pipelines, they have reduced the Delta's oil output by as much as a half.[23] MEND operates in the swamps and creeks of the Delta, and is supported by a significant segment of the local population.[24] MEND has called for an end to the destruction of their land and exploitation of the region's impoverished people.

The battle between MEND and foreign oil producers is reminiscent of the high profile conflict between Shell and the Delta's Movement for the Survival of the Ogoni People (MOSOP) in the mid 1990s. Shell was widely condemned after the state executed nine Ogoni activists, including renowned author, Ken Saro-Wiwa. The oil company allegedly bribed witnesses to testify against Saro-Wiwa for a murder he did not commit.[25] The lawsuit *Wiwa v. Shell* explains, "Shell was involved in the development of the strategy that resulted in the unlawful execution of the Ogoni Nine. Shell told the Nigerian regime they needed to deal with Ken Saro-Wiwa and MOSOP. Shell monitored Ken Saro-Wiwa, and closely followed the tribunal and his detention. Prior to the trial, Shell Nigeria informed its parent companies that Saro-Wiwa would be convicted and told witnesses that Saro-Wiwa was never going free. Shell held meetings with the Nigerian regime to discuss the tribunal, including with the military president Sani Abacha himself. Shell's lawyer attended the trial, which, in Nigeria, is a privilege afforded only to interested parties."

Shell had close ties to the Nigerian military junta, providing them with helicopters and boats. It also paid soldiers field allowances and imported weapons for the police.[26]

Between 1958 and 1988, nine hundred million barrels of oil was extracted from Ogoni land, mostly by Shell.[27] Lamenting the ruin wrought upon the Ogoni by oil exploration, MOSOP leader Garrick Leton charged Shell with "full responsibility for the genocide of the Ogoni."[28] He explained: "We have woken up to find our lands devastated by the agents of death called oil companies. Our atmosphere has been totally polluted, our lands degraded, our waters contaminated, our trees poisoned, so much so that our flora and fauna have virtually disappeared. We are asking for the restoration of our environment. We are asking for the basic necessities of life — water, electricity, roads, education. We are asking, above all for the right to self-determination so that we can be responsible for our resources and our environment."[29]

Across the globe, sprawling auto-dependent development is pushing oil extraction into increasingly sensitive environments. Far from the "light sweet crude" of the Niger delta, the heavy oil trapped in Alberta's tar sands is amongst the filthiest sources in the world. With up to three fourths of the final product destined for the U.S. market, by 2030 oil sands could make up more than a third of U.S. oil imports.[30]

Tar sands oil extraction has been labeled the most destructive process known to humankind.[31] Viewed from above, the tar sands are as picturesque as a pair of dirty lungs and the stench of gasoline can be smelled for miles.[32] Amidst a tangle of pipes, waste pools and smoke, an environmental demolition derby of 50-foot 300-tonne monster trucks roam a wasteland riddled with 200-feet deep open pits. Gauged out with dinosaur-sized claws, Athabascan oil is mostly mined not pumped.

Describing the tar sands as "hideous marvels," *Globe and Mail* columnist, Jeffrey Simpson writes, "they are terrible to look at, from the air or from the ground. They tear the earth, create polluted mini-lakes called tailing ponds that can be seen from space, spew forth air pollutants such as sulfur-dioxide and nitrogen oxide, and emit greenhouse gases such as carbon dioxide. ... They are voracious users of freshwater."[33]

Extracting the bitumen (or crude oil) from the thick and sticky mix of clay, sand, and water is no easy feat. For every barrel of oil extracted, somewhere between two and four-and-a-half times as much water is needed to thin out the mixture and separate the bitumen from the sand.[34] To obtain this staggering volume of water, whole streams and rivers in the region have been drained and diverted.[35] We don't need Erin Brockovich to tell us something is wrong with the water; sucked out for the extraction process and then spat out again, most of it ends up contaminated with acids, mercury and other toxins.[36] [37] This wastewater has left northern Alberta scarred with hundreds of toxic dumping pools, better known as 'tailing ponds.' Not only are the tar sands being blamed for Western Canada's first bout of acid rain, the residues pumped into the Athabasca River have increased cancer rates downstream, particularly among First Nations communities dependent upon the waterway.[38]

The resource intensive process uses two tonnes of sand to produce a single barrel of oil.[39] In 2003, Alberta's environment ministry reported that 430 square kilometres (280 sq. miles) of land had been "disturbed" for the oil sands. By summer 2006, that number had reached 2,000 square kilometres, nearly a five-fold increase in three years (even though only two percent of the oil sands — now hailed as one of the world's largest reserves — had been developed).[40]

Thousands of acres of trees have been clear-cut to make way for tar sands mining and if current plans unfold, a forest the size of Maryland and Virginia will be eliminated.[41] Cutting trees emits CO_2 and it also eliminates a carbon sink. The decline in forests has also led to a major reduction in both the region's grizzly bear and moose populations, with oil exploration also harming prairie birds and other animal life.[42]

The tar sands represent the biggest increase in Canadian carbon emissions. This may explain Ottawa's lead role in efforts to disrupt international negotiations to reduce atmospheric CO_2. Every barrel of synthetic oil produced in the tar sands releases 188 pounds of carbon dioxide equivalent into the atmosphere.[43] Comparing this to a conventional barrel of crude, the *New York Times* noted, "a gallon of gas from oil sands, because of the energy-intensive production methods, releases three times as much carbon overall as conventionally produced gasoline."[44] The oil sands are located in and around Fort McMurray (aka Fort McMoney), a region with a population of 61,000. By 2015 Fort McMurray is expected to emit more greenhouse gases than all of Denmark.[45]

Describing "the rush into the oil sands" a *Wall Street Journal* analyst writes: "For years, environmentalists have argued that higher gasoline prices would be good for the Earth because paying more at the pump would promote conservation. Instead, higher energy prices have unleashed a bevy of heavy oil projects that will increase emissions of carbon dioxide."[46] Rather than curbing use, rising prices have led to increasingly unconventional and hazardous sources of oil, such as deep-sea production or tar sands.

The tremendous energy required to bring the oily sand to the surface and separate it out is largely provided by natural gas. Oil sands consume over 500 million cubic feet of natural gas a day, an amount likely to increase to 1.25 billion cubic feet daily by 2016.[47] The process is so inefficient that the natural gas required to produce one barrel of tar sands oil could heat a family home for two to four days.[48] A relatively clean fuel is used to produce a dirtier one, prompting oil analyst Matt Simmons to describe the process as "making gold into lead."[49]

Not everyone is happy about this increasingly sticky situation. "Don't ruin our land to fuel the U.S. gas tank," demanded Grand Chief of the Deh Cho in response to the proposed $16 billion Mackenzie Valley natural gas pipeline, which would ship Alaskan natural gas southbound almost exclusively for use in northern Alberta oil extraction.[50]

The natural gas pipeline seems almost benign compared to some of the ideas floated by oil companies including "the idea of nuclear power as a source for their massive energy needs."[51] This is not the first time a nuclear option has been proposed to extract oil from the tar sands. In 1959, California's Richfield Oil drew up a plan, approved by the U.S. Atomic Energy Commission, to separate bitumen from the sand by detonating a nine-kiloton atomic bomb.[52] It was argued that the heat and energy created by an underground explosion would free the oil from the sand, but after initial tests in Nevada were successful, the idea was nevertheless shelved when Canadian officials expressed concern about the use of the A-bomb.

Government officials have expressed few reservations about tar sands oil extraction and have heavily subsidized the mega-project. A pro-development royalty structure provided oil companies with an incentive to stay in a perpetual state of expansion to avoid triggering a higher royalty rate.[53] This royalty system has obvious environmental implications. In the ten years after the introduction of the royalty legislation, oil production in Alberta increased 88 percent, while government royalty revenues decreased by 39 percent.[54] Although the price of oil more than doubled between 1996 and 2005, Alberta's take on a barrel of oil went down from $3.39 to $2.29.[55] It was not until 2008 that even modest increases in royalties went into effect and those were reduced two years later.

South of Alberta's tar sands, in the American Rockies, politicians and corporations are looking to mimic the "successful" tar sands royalty structure. An oil shale bill, modeled after Alberta's policy, reduced royalties from the customary 12.5 percent of annual revenue down to one percent.[56]

Former Shell CEO, John Hofmeister, proclaimed there were a trillion barrels of shale oil buried in the Rockies.[57] Releasing three to six times more greenhouse gases than conventional oil production, shale oil is becoming an increasingly important source of fuel.[58] [59]

...

With the rise of the combustion engine, leaked oil has devastated ecosystems around the globe. Although it doesn't make the news, 30 percent of ocean spills are routine, calculated discharges meant to steady ships. Seawater is pumped into empty tankers for stability and the contaminated water is then sent overboard when a tanker refills with oil.[60] [61] In addition to intentional discharges, there are thousands of small accidental oil spills every year in the U.S. alone.[62]

Over the past forty years there have been 35 oil spills larger than the Exxon-Valdez.[63] The following is a list of notable spills since the late 1970s:

March 1978 69 million gallons spill near Portsall, France.

July 1979 90 million gallons spill off the coast of Trinidad and Tobago.

June 1979 140 million gallons spill in the Bay of Campeche off Ciudad del Carmen, Mexico.

August 1983 79 million gallons spill in Saldanha Bay, South Africa.

February 1983 80 million gallons spill in the Persian Gulf, Iran.

November 1988 40.7 million gallons spill off the coast of Nova Scotia, Canada.

March 1989 10.8 million gallons spill off the coast of Alaska.

January 1991 380 million gallons spill in the Persian Gulf, Kuwait.

May 1991 51 million gallons spill 700 miles off the coast of Angola.

April 1991 45 million gallons spill near Genoa, Italy.

September 1994 84 million gallons spill in Kolva River, Russia.

April 2010 185 million gallons spill into the Gulf of Mexico.

...

As the oil-refining hub of the Gulf of Mexico, Louisiana is also the most unequal state in the USA. This sharp divide between a wealthy minority and a poor majority is a common feature among petroleum economies. Across the Atlantic, between 1965 and 2004, Nigerian income per capita fell from $250 to $212.[64] As oil was wrung from the "green sponge" of the Niger delta and shipped to the far corners of the globe, inequality escalated. Between 1970 and 2000, the number of Nigerians living on less than a dollar a day rose from 19 million to 90 million (36 percent of the population to 70 percent).[65] Displaying breathtaking powers of deduction, the International Monetary Fund concluded that oil "did not seem to add to the standard of living" and that it "could have contributed to a decline in the standard of living."[66]

14. Driving global warming — New Orleans

An eerie mood hung in the night air as we returned from the French Quarter. A marvelous collection of eclectic houses lay close to streets lined with wrought iron gates and massive aged trees. We were staying at a guesthouse in New Orleans. Furnished with mahogany, heavy linen and curious artifacts, it was a beautiful, restful place. A giant balcony wound round the old house, overlooking a bohemian burrito eatery and a tapas bar with bright orange walls. The owner of the establishment, a friendly man of South Asian descent with family in Uganda, made time to talk and we discovered a shared fondness for politics, travel and the films of Mira Nair. Across from the guesthouse, Yves and I sat under the drunken circles of a beat-up fan. We were quick to adjust to the New Orleans pace. I admired the bright collage of ceramic tiles adorning our table as I sipped my coffee. Jazz played until someone turned the radio dial. The strains of lively chatter were now audible. It was a show run by women of color that sounded like a community radio program I'd helped with in Montreal. There seemed to be a connection between activism and walk-able cities.

New Orleans was wonderful. I was tempted to abandon the road trip and apply for a job at the guesthouse cafe. It seemed like everything was just around the corner and that you really ought to take a look around. We walked past terraced houses in the French Quarter, took the trolley down St. Charles and had a drink on Bourbon Street.[i] Tightly packed and narrow, these streets

i Shockingly, in the '60s urban planners pushed for a six-lane elevated expressway across the French Quarter's Jackson Square.

were made for walking and talking, for noticing other people as they went about their days and for becoming part of the city. We passed a man in an electric wheelchair zooming down St. Louis Street, who stopped to give us directions to Cemetery No.1. Just about everyone was out and about. In this pedestrian haven, I felt an immediate sense of community and safety. We soon found out, however, this was not always the case. The New Orleans we visited was beautiful, but poor, and contained sharp racial boundaries.

At Cemetery No.1 the gates were locked and with no other plans, we walked around the perimeter and onto a narrow road. A block or so later, we noticed a quiet and empty street with a housing project. The silence was broken by the sudden wail of a siren. A police officer jumped out of his vehicle, rushed forward and threatened arrest. The only person in sight was a petrified little boy standing a few yards ahead of us.

"You're under arrest," repeated the cop, now looking me dead in the eye.

"Us, me, what? What have we done?"

"This is private property, miss," he replied

"The whole street?" said Yves, now clearly pissed off.

Like oil and water, law enforcement and Yves are a bad combination, so to avoid a kafuffle I stepped forward with a smile. As a reward we were personally escorted out of the neighbourhood.

"What the hell just happened?" said Yves, when our escort was finally gone.

We were only blocks away from the über touristy French Quarter yet the very act of walking was forbidden. What was really going on? We spotted another officer on duty a few blocks later and stopped to get the scoop.

"There was a murder there last night," he said. "It's for your own good."

After we questioned further, the police officer warned us that entering the projects was strictly forbidden without an invitation from a resident. He explained that this was a municipal bylaw to keep rival neighbourhood gangs from fighting.

Despite this depressing incident, that night we rode the trolley as far as the line would take us; we followed the tracks through noisy shopping streets, down St. Charles, and into hushed residential neighbourhoods. A sudden downpour literally stopped us in our tracks, knocking the lights out on the trolley. The windows shuddered, lightning slit the clouds and the sky seemed to crash down on New Orleans.

Riding the streetcar and walking through New Orleans, we encountered all sorts of friendly folk. Sometimes when my eyes glazed over, even for a moment, a passerby would ask if I needed help getting to where I was going. And for the most part, the directions were grounded in reality. It was refreshing to have help doled out in walking, rather than driving terms.

New Orleans was definitely one of our favourite places. But, that was some months before Katrina and in hindsight, perhaps we should have realized during our visit that it was too good to be true.

...

While political negligence was largely to blame for the city's devastation, "natural" disasters like Katrina are increasingly common. Ten months after that storm blew through New Orleans several climate change studies linked rising ocean temperatures to increasingly powerful hurricanes.[1] Increased evaporation, precipitation and wind velocity caused by heightening ocean temperatures are shaking up the seas. Paradoxically, the same rising temperatures that lead to hurricanes like Katrina also suck moisture from the ground, giving rise to more droughts. It's a bad scene. More rain and more drought.[2][3]

Global warming is no sunny stroll down Main Street. The World Meteorological Organization believes there are clear links between climate change and the growing number of natural disasters.[4] It is exacerbating summer heat waves and wildfires. Rising temperatures may even be heightening volcanic and earthquake activity.[5] [6]

After three decades of mounting evidence regarding the human impact on global temperature increases, there is no longer any substantive disagreement in the scientific community that it exists. As far back as 2004, a *Science* article summarized 928 peer-reviewed papers on climate change, finding that "none of the papers disagreed with the consensus position."[7] The consensus is further illustrated by the collective position of the UN's inter-governmental panel on climate change, a body made up of thousands of scientists that concluded climate change is occurring and that human activity was the cause. The question is not whether temperatures are increasing, but how much.

Global warming is "the equivalent of a nuclear time bomb," said David Freeman, Energy Advisor to the Carter administration.[8] The earth's temperature is the highest it's been in 12,000 years and may become dramatically warmer.[9] In 2007 the UN inter-governmental climate change panel Fourth Assessment Report predicted an increase of between 1.1 and 6.4 °C (2.0 and 11.5 °F) during the 21st century. More recent evidence suggests the higher end estimate is most likely. According to Environment Canada, 2010 was the hottest year on record and it was particularly warm in the north.[10]

NASA reported that in the space of a year there was a loss of Arctic sea ice "the size of Texas".[11] As a result the Arctic is less able to cool the earth.[12]

For many, the time bomb has already exploded. The World Health Organization estimates that global warming is presently responsible for 150,000 deaths a year.[13] According to a December 2010 study, "by 2030, climate change will indirectly cause nearly 1 million deaths a year."[14] Around the world, global warming threatens food security. If greenhouse gas emissions are not curbed, moderate drought is expected to affect half of the world by the end of the century.[15] Global warming is also predicted to devastate human health. The strong link between the distribution of pathogens and the environment means that climate change could lead to a massive increase in disease. A study released at the end of 2010 found that global warming (rendering many areas uninhabitable) could lead to as many as a billion people losing their homes this century.[16] Greenpeace, Oxfam and 18 other groups warned that global warming is a "phenomenon that threatens to reverse human progress and make unachievable all UN targets to reduce global poverty."[17] The world's poorest people are the chief victims of global warming.[18]

In Grade 6 my class traveled to the west of the country to see the massive salt lakes that provide an income for many. As such it was particularly disturbing to read about the difficulties facing Ugandan salt miners due to recent climatic changes. Dependent on dry weather, they have been devastated by the shorter dry season from December to February.

The great irony is that the countries most responsible for climate change are least affected. A March 2011 McGill University study confirmed that climate change will have the greatest impact on the countries that contribute the least to global warming.[19] While Canada and the U.S., for instance, discharge the most greenhouse gasses per capita, places like Bangladesh and Ethiopia will be hardest hit by climate change.[20]

In *Heat: How to Stop the Planet From Burning* George Monbiot makes the link between global warming, the personal automobile and the consumptive economy it underpins. He questions how "the need to drive a car which can accelerate from 0 to 60 miles an hour in 4.5 seconds (the Audi S4 for example) overrides the Ethiopian's need to avoid recurrent famines."[21]

But, as knowledge of global warming increased so did U.S. oil use. Despite significant reductions in energy consumption among manufacturers, oil consumption as a whole continued to rise. In 1990, manufacturing was the largest source of U.S. greenhouse gas emissions.[22] But the transportation sector increased its emissions by two percent annually throughout the 1990s to become the leading source of U.S. emissions in 2000.[23]

From the number of cars on the road to the type of cars driven, there are many reasons for the increase in transportation emissions. Between 1972 and 1987 new regulations and the price of gasoline forced the industry to improve new vehicle mileage per gallon from 14 to 27.5 miles. From 1987 to 2004, however, average gas mileage decreased from 27.5 to 24 miles.[24] The push for rapid acceleration and heavier vehicles contributed significantly to the reversal in fuel economy standards.[ii] The weight gain has been tremendous. In 2006, the average weight of a new U.S. vehicle was 4,142 pounds, 415 pounds heavier than 1997 models and about a thousand pounds heavier than vehicles produced in the early 1980s.[iii] [25] [26]

The scale busting chubby chomper in question is none other than the SUV. Accounting for less than two percent of vehicles sold in 1982, fifteen years later SUVs made up 17 percent of the market and reached a quarter in the mid 2000s.[27] Its ascent is largely attributable to government policy. In the late 1970s, automakers were granted an exemption from Corporate Average Fuel Economy (CAFE) standards for the production of "workhorse vehicles." The exemption was justified since these vehicles were said to be for farmers, construction workers etc. Yet when the exemption was granted, more than two thirds of "workhorse

ii *According to the May 3, 2006 New York Times, "In 1990, a senate proposal to raise fuel economy standards to 40 miles a gallon over 10 years received 57 votes, but lost to a filibuster."*

iii *According to the July 23, 2007 Globe and Mail, the average mid-sized SUV grew 25 cm in length, 10 cm in width and gained 474 lbs between 1997 and 2007. During the same period, compact sedans grew 5 cm in length, 5 cm in width and 374 lbs.*

vehicles" were used as passenger vehicles.[28] Now, less than one in 20 SUVs go off-road and only one in 10 pick-up drivers use it for work.[29] [30]

The CAFE exemption allowed "workhorse vehicles" carrying the same passenger load as a regular car to release about 40 percent more greenhouse gases. To put this into perspective, the Sierra Club says that driving a full size SUV for a year rather than a midsized car burns as much extra energy as leaving a refrigerator door open for six years.[31]

Rather than focusing on fuel efficiency, the auto industry channeled its efforts into size and speed. "Of the nearly 20 million barrels of oil that America uses everyday", writes Paul Roberts, "more than a sixth represents a direct consequence by the decision of automakers to invest the efficiency dividend in power, not fuel economy."[32] Most new cars can go from zero to 60 mph in 9.9 seconds, a huge increase from 14.4 seconds 25 years ago. Today, everyone drives a sports car. The *Wall Street Journal* summarized: "the 2006 model year vehicles are the heaviest, fastest and most powerful vehicles for any year since the EPA began compiling such data in 1975."[33]

The U.S. consumes 21 million gallons of oil every day — nearly a fourth of the world's production. Fuelling personal vehicles (cars, SUVs and light trucks) guzzles over 40 percent of the total oil consumed in the U.S. and another 20 percent is pumped into heavy trucks and other highway vehicles. Internal combustion engines consume more than 63 percent of U.S. petroleum.[34] Additionally, oil is used to produce tires, seats and manufacture vehicles.[35]

The size and number of vehicles on the road mean that although the U.S. comprised only four percent of the world's population in 2004, it consumed nearly half of all gasoline.[36] "If American automobiles were a separate country," states Keith Bradsher in *High and Mighty*, "their [carbon] emissions would exceed those of every country except the United States, China, Russia and Japan."[37] How is it possible that the average American uses five times the energy for transportation as a person in Japan and three times as much as a person in Western Europe?[38]

Of course, with the rapid rise in gasoline prices in 2007-08 the economic cost of *Homo Automotivis'* petroleum guzzling vehicles became apparent to all but the most obtuse. Sales of SUVs and trucks fell dramatically. But this was an economic phenomenon rather than a sudden awakening of environmental consciousness and in October 2010, with lower oil prices returning, SUVs and minivans reached over half of all U.S. vehicle sales.[39]

...

"Alternative" fuels cannot solve the ecological catastrophe that is the private car.

Between 2005 and 2009 U.S. ethanol production more than tripled.[40] About 10.6 billion gallons of bio-fuel were produced in 2009. This was expected to reach 15 billion gallons in 2012.[41] By 2022 Washington wanted that number to reach 36 billion.[42]

Despite its popularity with decision makers, ethanol's ecological benefits are far from clear. Most studies show that gasoline made from U.S. corn produces about 15 percent less carbon dioxide than conventional gas.[43] Some studies suggest, however, that corn-based ethanol produces more CO_2 than oil-based gasoline if all the energy used in the growth phase is properly account for.

Even if carbon emissions are reduced, ethanol has a variety of drawbacks. It is shipped in energy intensive trucks or trains, takes huge amounts of water to produce and increases air pollutants as well as nitrides and pesticides.[44] [45] By using land to feed cars, bio-fuels have unleashed a battle between automobile owners and the world's two billion poorest people. George Monbiot explains: "the market responds to money, not need. People who own cars by definition have more money than people at risk of starvation: their demand is 'effective', while the groans of the starving are not. In a contest between cars and people, the cars would win."[46]

They are already winning. Partly due to increased ethanol production the price of food rose sharply in 2008, which caused riots in Haiti and protests against tortilla costs in Mexico. As this book goes to press in 2011, another food price spike is occurring, one factor cited in the revolutions in northern Africa and the Middle East.

Growing corn to fuel an average car takes five times more land than what's needed to feed a person and in 2009 "the grain grown to produce fuel in the U.S. was enough to feed 330 million people for one year at average world consumption levels."[47] [48]

Proponents claim that the next generation of ethanol will depend on large plant matter instead of foodstuff, but there are problems with this plan too. Breaking down plant cellulose into fermentable sugars currently requires more energy than it creates. Additionally, tremendous energy is needed to harvest bulky, heavy plant matter and to ship it to ethanol refineries.

Hundreds of millions of dollars have been spent researching more efficient ways of turning plants into cellulose without much success. In October 2010 *Grist* noted, "for decades, boosters deemed cellulosic ethanol 'five years way' from commercial viability. Now its status has been upgraded to 'within reach.' Progress!"[49]

The push for ethanol gas was largely driven by economic considerations, not ecology. In the late 1970s, the *New York Times* noted that Archer Daniels Midland Co. (ADM) "tried to solve a problem with seasonal overcapacity in its corn syrup plants by producing something else from abundant corn supplies: ethanol. That set off a two-decade-long lobbying and public relations effort by the elder Mr. Andreas [ADM president] to win broader acceptance for ethanol as a fuel."[50] Among the world's largest agricultural conglomerates, ADM now does billions of dollars in annual ethanol business.[51]

For their part, U.S. automakers support ethanol because it deflects attention away from improving fuel mileage. In fact, under Corporate Average Fuel Economy regulations, making vehicles that can run on ethanol permits carmakers to sell more fuel intensive cars.[52] A vehicle that can run on petroleum gasoline or 85 percent ethanol (E85) receives "a much higher mileage rating than it really gets" even though most of these cars never fill up with E85.[53]

Ethanol is not the only alternative fuel source where politics trump ecology. The highly vaunted electric car merely relocates tailpipe pollution to the source: power stations. Yet, in the U.S. about 75 percent of electricity comes from fossil fuels.[54] More than half of all this electricity is generated by coal, which produces significantly more carbon emissions and pollutants than conventional oil.[55] If the goal of the electric car is to limit global warming, using carbon-based fuels is puzzling.

Non-carbon emitting energy sources can produce electricity of course. Nuclear energy would be the most feasible source. To switch all U.S. cars to nuclear-energy fuelled electricity would take about 200 new nuclear power plants yet no new nuclear plant has been opened in three decades. Solar or wind probably cannot generate enough power to meet current U.S. electricity demand let alone the requirements of an additional two hundred million electric vehicles. To get a sense of their needs, regularly charging an electric car battery doubles the average household electricity bill.[56]

Even though hydrogen fuel cells were invented in the 19th century, car companies have promoted them as a modern solution to global warming.[57] But, it is just another example of smoke and mirrors. According to *Technology Review*, hydrogen fuel cells are "simply flashy distractions produced by automakers" to avoid "taking stronger immediate action to reduce the greenhouse-gas emissions of their cars."[58] No matter how well they're engineered, noted the magazine in 2007, "hydrogen cars offer no real answer to the imminent threats posed by global warming."[59] Replacing the oil U.S. cars, trucks and buses currently use would require 230,000 tonnes of hydrogen per day. To generate that amount of hydrogen by splitting water molecules, the U.S. would have to nearly double its electricity generating capacity.[60] If the energy used to electrolyze water is coal-based, then hydrogen fuel cells create more greenhouse gas emissions than petroleum based gasoline. To generate this electricity from non-carbon emitting sources would require covering a Massachusetts sized area with solar panels or New York State with windmills or building about 350 new nuclear power plants.[61] [62]

Making gasoline directly from coal may be the most environmentally destructive "alternative" fuel source. The U.S. Department of Defense is studying coal-to-fuel technology and the National Coal Council wants government support to process as much as 2.6 million barrels of liquid coal-based fuel by 2025.[63] A number of prominent U.S. politicians, including Barack Obama, have voiced support for coal-to-fuel technology. (Under oil embargo during the apartheid era, South Africa built infrastructure to transform coal into automotive fuel. On a lesser scale, Germany did the same during WWII.)[64]

Widespread coal-to-fuel use would be an environmental nightmare. Conventional oil based gasoline produces an average of 27.5 pounds of carbon dioxide per gallon in production and use, while fuel from coal emits about 49.5 pounds of carbon dioxide.[65] The *New York Times* summarized: "Unless the factory captures the carbon dioxide created during the process of turning coal into diesel fuel, the global warming impact of driving a mile would double."[66] Even with carbon capture, coal-based gas increases carbon emissions by four percent.[67] (Current carbon-capture technology takes up 25 percent of the power generated by a coal plant.[68])

There is no such thing as a green car. The basic point is this: A model of transportation that relies on individuals hopping into two, four or eight thousand pound metal boxes to get from one place to another is utterly unsustainable.

...

As our bus rolled into the lily-white New Orleans suburb of Metairie, our surroundings started to take on a formulaic sprawl that spelled trouble for two car-less souls. Predictably, just getting to Metairie was a frustrating exercise. It was a petrol-fueled relay race where the bus stopped at the edge of the next municipal boundary and passed the buck. This struck us as inefficient. Imagine a similar scenario for highways, where cars stopped at the border of each municipality, needing to find another road to continue their journey.

After missing the last bus to the edge of New Orleans proper, we stopped at a convenience store where we were urged to "take a cab!"

"Can we walk?" Yves asked.

"It'll take you a night and a day," responded the woman behind the till.

The wild exaggerations had returned. A thirty-minute walk later, we were at the edge of Metairie, where we waited to catch the next district bus into the city. I went to a nearby Wendy's where only the drive-thru remained open. Not sure whether or not to take a place in line among the cars, I decided to go for it.

"Ma'am, you gotta be in a car."

"I can't eat at Wendy's if I don't have a car?"

"Not after 10 o'clock."

"Oh."

15. An insatiable thirst for land — Phoenix

The stretch of highway etched deepest in my memory led us into Phoenix. The earth was red and the sky an endless blue. A chorus line of cacti welcomed us into the city and for the first time I felt far from home. But, the stunning dessert highway soon transformed into the familiar territory of overpasses and scattered neighbourhoods. It was still spring, but hot enough to fry an egg on the street. Scuttling from one sparsely leafed tree to the next, shade was a precious commodity in Phoenix and the sidewalks were understandably deserted. Despite under-populated streets, millions call this desert city home.

Over 2,000 years ago, it was Hohokam irrigation systems that allowed the region to be inhabited at all.[1] Today it is a golfing Mecca. An abundance of front lawns and public gardens thrive with greenery despite hundreds of days without rain. A century ago such profound change to the natural surroundings would have been unimaginable. More than any other U.S. city, Phoenix has been profoundly impacted by the rise of the automobile. According to our *Lonely Planet*, "the city practically defines the concept of urban sprawl." Phoenix covered 17 square miles in 1950 yet by 2007 it spread to 500 square miles.[2] The 2.8 million people living in Phoenix occupy half the area of the Los Angeles region but are only a quarter of its population.[i] [3]

On top of being unruly and unattractive, the sprawling developments that characterize Phoenix (and much of the

---

i *According to the March 2, 2007 Guardian Weekly, every year each person in Phoenix emits 1,400 kilograms of greenhouse gases. People in Hong Kong emit 50 kilograms.*

USA) devour vast amounts of land, water and other resources. During the 1990s U.S. land was consumed at twice the rate of population growth and over the past twenty years the amount of space (including housing, retail, schools and roads) occupied per American increased 20 percent.[ii] [4] [5] [6] In *Outgrowing the Earth*, Lester Russell Brown explains: "In the United States, where 0.07 hectares of paved land is required for each car, every five cars added to the fleet require paving an area the size of a football field. Thus the two million cars added to the U.S. fleet each year require asphalting an area equal to nearly 400,000 football fields."[7]

The land devoted to roads, highways and parking has been approaching the amount devoted to U.S. wheat fields.[8] The development pressure placed on prime farmland has reached a point where farmers quip, "the last crop to be grown on America's farmland is not fruit, vegetables and grain, but houses."[9] Every year since 1970, a Delaware-sized chunk of farm, forest and countryside has been lost to development.[10] The displacement of prime farmland for auto dependent development has seen the conversion of forests and wetlands to crop production. These areas are often less suited to farming and so rely more heavily on fertilizers, pesticides and irrigation.[11]

Roads accompanying new development also pose a threat to local ecosystems. Highway construction regularly disturbs and displaces natural habitats. Plant and animal species that can't or won't cross roads cannot feed or reproduce as effectively in fragmented areas.[12] New highway construction, for instance, has severed Florida's jaguars (the cat, not the car) from significant portions of their living space. Vehicles are also a major threat to Canadian grizzly bears while U.S. sprawl is threatening sparrows, chickadees and meadowlarks.[13] [14]

---

ii Each year 400,000 hectares (1 million acres) of land is paved around the world for parking lots, highways and roads. Much of this was once reserved for agriculture.

Uprooting forests for sprawling development means less protection for water systems. Woodlands enhance the absorption of ground water. Without them storm water is trapped above an impervious surface, instead of gradually percolating into the ground. Now on the loose, this surface water "accumulates and runs off in large amounts into streams, lakes, and estuaries, picking up pollutants along the way."[15]

These pollutants include toxic waste from construction site erosion as well as chemical fertilizers from sprawling suburban lawns.[16] A study of Chicago's outskirts determined that a new low-density development produced 10 times more storm water runoff than a denser inner city redevelopment.[17]

Imperviousness is an even greater problem in car-specific infrastructure (roads, parking lots and driveways).[iii] In addition to the products used to protect cars, such as road salt,[iv] these surfaces accumulate a wide range of chemical contaminants released by the automobile: grit, axle grease, antifreeze leakage, lead particles from wheel balances and other metals such as copper and cadmium.[18] [19]

Whether on the road, or parked in the front yard, the car leaks a variety of chemical contaminants. Washing automobiles at home spews oil and grease, as well as metals from rust and break linings into waterways. Additionally, many of the detergents used to clean the car contain chemicals that harm wildlife.[20] Drivers changing their own oil often dispose of it improperly, creating another hazard for pets and wildlife.[21] With so many deaths by anti freeze, animal rights activists called for a mandatory bitter additive to dissuade unsuspecting pets from lapping up the poison.

---

iii Paved surfaces also contribute to global warming. They convert sunlight to heat.

iv According to the March 5, 2010 Globe and Mail: "One of the most detailed investigations ever conducted in Canada into the fate of road salt has found that it is polluting ground water and causing some streams during winter thaws to have salinity levels just under those found in the ocean."

Of all the toxic chemicals discharged by the automobile, the most significant runoff is oil. One quart of oil flows out of the average vehicle every year.[22] Every eight months 11 million gallons of gasoline are spilled in daily runoff.[23] Affecting 40 percent of surveyed waterways, this 'non-point' or runoff pollution is a leading cause of water pollution in the U.S.[24]

...

The *Consumer's Guide to Effective Environmental Choices* lists the purchase of a personal car or light truck as the single most damaging consumer behavior.[25] Put bluntly, the car is "the ecologist's worst nightmare." According to *Asphalt Nation*'s Jane Holtz Kay, "the automobile's abuse overruns our capacity to record it."[26]

Even before the car leaves the lot it has left a deep ecological footprint. To be precise, a single car uses 120,000 gallons of water, generates 29 tons of solid waste as well as 1,200 million cubic yards of air emissions, all before the first test drive.[27]

A 2007 study titled From Dust to Dust, concluded that more than half the energy a car uses in its life cycle is in the production and destruction phases.[28] Growing awareness of these energy costs prompted Norway to make it nearly impossible for car companies to advertise as "green," "clean" or "environmentally friendly" without proving that this was the case throughout the lifecycle from production to emissions to energy use to recycling.[29]

From steel and aluminum, to paint and rubber production, to automotive assembly, the energy consumption of *Homo Automotivis* is enormous. A study taking into account all aspects of car production (such as shipping parts across the world) determined that a Hummer is actually more energy efficient than a Honda Civic despite consuming three to four times more gas.[30] Made largely out of steel, automobiles are responsible for three million pounds of pollution generated by U.S. steel mills.[31] Because of steel pollution and other auto manufacturing waste, Detroit's River Rouge was "one of the dirtiest waterways in America."[32]

Auto plants are also amongst the nation's leading air polluters.[33] Carmakers produce an average of six pounds of reportable toxins for every car they make.[34] An incalculable number of toxins are released in the production of a finished car, from methylene chloride and trichloroethylene in the paint process to PBDEs, used as fire retardants, and phthalates, used primarily to soften PVC plastics. A 1993 study revealed that each of the top-10 polluting car factories or parts suppliers released over a million pounds of toxins. That year, carmakers produced 79 million pounds of dozens of various toxic chemicals.[35]

The devastation of local communities by auto manufacturing is illustrated by Ford's upper Ringwood New Jersey plant, located in a town of about 350 working class residents in the foothills of the Ramapo mountains. Although the factory closed in 1980, residents of the community blame pollutants left by the plant for a plague of bronchitis, skin rashes and nose bleeds they still suffer. A lawsuit against Ford spearheaded by late civil rights lawyer Johnnie Cochran's firm claimed the waste left by Ford contributed to a host of illnesses among residents such as the diabetes that left Paul Eugene Van Dunk without his leg and the cancer that killed his daughter.

The Environmental Protection Agency found thousands of tonnes of paint sludge and other waste in the community and there is evidence that Ford's waste contaminated a local reservoir that provided drinking water for 2.5 million people in the surrounding area. Lead lawyer Andrew Carboy told the *New York Times*: "Ford's involvement here ended almost 40 years ago, but the community is still dealing with the health consequences of Ford's dumping."[36]

The modern automobile contains roughly 5,000 parts, requiring vast quantities of raw materials.[37] A new car contains about 200 pounds of plastic, a material that generates significant pollution in production and is more difficult to recycle than metal.[38][39] Even eco-technologies sometimes reveal a darker side on investigation. Touted as a means to reduce gasoline consumption, car manufacturers use lightweight aluminum to reduce an automobile's weight. Aluminum production, however, is highly energy intensive and (depending on the source) often generates significantly more CO_2 than steel for the same volume of material. Another example is catalytic converters, used to reduce the emission of smog-producing chemicals. While the benefits are clear, little is said about how they increase production of two other potentially dangerous compounds — hydrogen sulphide and carbon disulphide (a known neurotoxin and a carcinogen).[40] Catalytic converters also reduce fuel economy and require vast amounts of ore to provide platinum, which is only released from the rock after an energy-intensive process.[41][42]

Another supposedly eco-friendly technology with limitations is the hybrid battery. Not only are these large batteries difficult to recycle, one of their major elements, cobalt, is linked to uranium waste extraction in the Congo, where radioactive cobalt ore is transported in open trucks.[43] The dust spreads out along the roadside for any passersby to ingest, wreaking human and environmental devastation.[v][44]

Getting rid of a car can generate up to a third of its lifecycle energy costs and as much as a fifth of a car's total pollution.[45] At the end of their lives, car batteries contain a vast array of toxic chemicals.[46] One of the most obvious remnants of the automobile are rubber tires, which take centuries to decompose. Every year cars create billions of pounds of un-recycled scrap and waste.[47]

...

---

v According to the July 27, 2007 Globe and Mail, a study into the lifecycle of a hybrid battery found that Toyota buys nickel from Ontario, which gets shipped to Wales for refining, then to China for further processing, and then to Toyota's battery plant in Tokyo — a ten thousand mile trip, mostly by fossil fuel driven container ships and locomotives.

Wandering through the Phoenix Museum of History, we paused at a description of the U.S. government's scorched earth policy of 1863. Fed up with indigenous resistance towards European settlement, the U.S. army leveled homesteads and expelled much of the Navajo nation from their homes. They destroyed Navajo crops, orchards and fields. Any livestock they found were confiscated or killed. The nation faced starvation. Navajo refugees were then collected by the army and forced from the sacred Four Corners region to an area known as Fort Sumner. After five years of bloody struggle, some amongst the Navajo survived the extermination campaign and returned home.

The death of millions of Native Americans left the U.S. with an abundance of land. In the century predating the car there was a huge push to settle this open space. By offering geographic and social mobility, the frontier shaped the values and institutions of nineteenth century USA. The frontier mentality was the dream of unlimited opportunity in the unsettled regions of the U.S., an ideal that drove people to move ever further outwards.[vi] [48] Living in small towns or farms, Americans were considerably more dispersed than Western Europeans. It is probable that the frontier and its mentality contributed to the rise of the automobile.

Early auto billboards often played off a disturbing side of the frontier mentality, the vilification and objectification of indigenous people. In the 1910s Associated Gasoline erected over 1,200 billposters along the Pacific coast depicting settlers being rescued from hostile Natives, while Fisk Tire advertised the automobile as "a bucking bronco driving into the wild blue yonder watched by Indians on horseback in traditional dress (one

[vi] *According to Twentieth Century Sprawl, when U.S. Army vehicles traveled from coast to coast in the First Transcontinental Motor Convoy of 1910, they said there was "the necessity for a comprehensive system of National Highways, including transcontinental or through — routes East and West, North and South, is real and urgent as a commercial asset to further colonize and develop the sparsely settled sections of the country."*

121

complete with papoose) who gaped after the touring car from behind the clouds of dust left in its wake."[49]

This was a prophetic ad campaign. In many ways, the car and the quest for oil, continues to push indigenous communities towards the brink of extinction. The Rainforest Action Network explains: "The high correlation between petroleum basins and indigenous communities on every continent tells a story of increasing pressure on indigenous peoples and their homelands to feed the industrial world's growing appetite for oil."[50]

In the Andean region of South America, for instance, oil development has violently disrupted indigenous people's way of life, destroying the natural resources, food and water supplies they rely on. In 2009 Hunt oil disrupted a Peruvian indigenous group that had chosen to live in isolation from outside contact.[51] Similarly, Texaco's oil development in Ecuador nearly wiped out the Tetetes and Cofan people, whose population fell from 15,000 to less than 500 in the 1990s. Another group, the Tagaeri Huaorani, was dislocated from their homeland and remain locked in violent conflict with oil developers.[52] John Perkins' bestseller, *Confessions of an Economic Hitman*, describes Ecuadorian indigenous communities lured from their land in the 1970s by missionaries working on behalf of oil interests.[53] Another author explains: "missionaries contacted and physically removed some 200 Huaorani from the path of Texaco's work crews and took them to live in a distant Christian settlement."[54] Over the 28 years Texaco operated in Ecuador, the company dumped an estimated 16.8 million gallons of crude into the environment and over 19 billion gallons of untreated water waste.[55] Ten years after leaving Ecuador, Texaco (now Chevron) was still tied up in Ecuadorian courts in a multi-billion dollar suit over their environmental practices in the country. In February 2011 an Ecuadorian court ordered Chevron to pay $8.6 billion in damages, which the company was refusing to pay.

The Ecuadorian court ruling came after a lengthy campaign of resistance. The Confederation of Indigenous Nationalities of Ecuadorian Amazon (CONFENIAE), explained: "We the indigenous peoples say that development which destroys our rivers, our land and our lives is not real development."[56] After mounting grassroots pressure, the Ecuadorian government expelled U.S.-based Occidental oil in 2006. At the behest of indigenous groups, in early 2011 the Ecuadorian government looked set to sign a $3.6 billon agreement with the United Nations Development Program to keep in the ground some 850 million barrels of heavy crude in the Yasuni tropical rainforest.

While some indigenous groups have won battles to protect their way of life, the broader threat of global warming looms. For example, the melting polar ice cap threatens the livelihood of 150,000 Inuit. In the words of Sheila Watt-Cloutier, chair of the Inuit Circumpolar Conference, "Inuit hunters falling through the ice are linked to the cars we drive."[57]

16. Tankers, transit and terror — New York

We arrived at the Port Authority bus station, and exited a block from Times Square. The nighttime ruckus was an exhilarating rush of taxis, lights and people. An unspoken message flashed through a network of Haitian vendors selling handbags on the sidewalk. Grabbing the four corners of the sheets below, they turned their wares into giant satchels, tossed them over their backs, and moved into the night. The street was cleared in seconds. The police never stood a chance.

Everything was open late; even the metro was 24/7. The 100-year-old New York subway may be rickety, but it is a marvel nonetheless. Alongside millions of New Yorkers it got us where we were going, fast. An astounding half of all daily train trips in the U.S. take place in New York City (with 55 percent of New Yorkers using public transportation to get to work.)[1] [2] "The New York Metropolitan Transportation Authority carries 7.7 million passengers a day in its subway, bus and train systems", writes the *New York Times*, "more than the combined populations of South Dakota, North Dakota, Wyoming, Alaska, Montana and Nebraska."[i] [3]

The Big Apple's greater reliance on active modes of transit is one reason New Yorkers live a year and four months longer than the rest of their country-mates.[4] It also leaves residents with some pocket change to enjoy their city. Taking up 15.3 percent of their income, New Yorkers spend less on transportation than people in any other U.S. city. (The highest spenders are in Tampa, where 23.2 percent of total household income goes to transport.)[5] Compared to

i *But, New Yorkers still drive three times more than people in Tokyo.*

residents of car-dependent cities, New Yorkers use far less gasoline. A study found that "residents on the sprawling exurban fringe of Denver consumed gasoline at twelve times the rate of residents of dense Manhattan."[6] New Yorkers generate only 29 percent of the per capita carbon emissions that the average American produces.[7] Despite this relatively virtuous behavior, one could argue that NYC residents paid an unjust price for the USA's auto obsession. One can make a plausible argument that the death and destruction of 9/11 can be linked to *Homo Automotivis*.

...

Walking and riding the subway through New York, one of the sites easily accessed is Ground Zero. Standing amidst the ruins of the World Trade Centre felt like staring into the bowels of history. That history includes secret armies, coups and war.

Half a century before 9/11, a fifty-year struggle for democracy was terminated in Iran. The country's first popularly elected prime minister, Mohammad Mossadegh, was overthrown in a CIA-coordinated coup and Iran was handed over to a brutal regime that ruled for 26 years. Mossadegh was a nationalist and wanted Iran to benefit from its huge oil reserves. But, the British had different plans. As one of the earliest sources of Middle Eastern oil, the Anglo-Iranian Oil Company (BP's predecessor) had generated immense wealth for British investors since 1915. Unwilling to yield any of their profits, Anglo-Iranian chairman Sir William Fraser responded to Iran's attempts to gain a greater share of its oil wealth by proclaiming, "one penny more and the company goes broke."[8] Yet a 1952 State Department report showed the company was selling its oil at between ten and thirty times its production cost.[9] Needless to say, Anglo-Iranian Oil was unpopular. Even the U.S. State Department noted the company's "arrogance had made it genuinely hated in Iran."[10]

In the face of Anglo-Iranian intransigence, Mossadegh defied the English and nationalized the country's oil industry.

It was a historic move that made Iran the first former colony to reclaim its oil.[ii] The British government responded with outrage, quickly determining that Mossadegh had to go. President Harry Truman was unsure, however, and refused to support Britain's plan to remove the elected prime minister. It was a short-lived position. Once Dwight Eisenhower took office, U.S. policy towards Iran fell into line with Britain.

During a March 11, 1953, national security council meeting, Eisenhower stated that allowing Iran to nationalize its oil would "have grave effects on United States oil concessions in other parts of the world."[11] Immediately following the national security council meeting, the head of the CIA, Allan Dulles, gave the agency's Tehran bureau a million dollars to be used "in any way that would bring about the fall of Mossadegh."[12]

All the Shah's Men explains: "Through a variety of means, covert agents would manipulate public opinion and turn as many Iranians as possible against Mossadegh. This effort, for which $150,000 was budgeted, would 'create, extend and enhance public hostility and distrust and fear of Mossadegh and his government'. It would portray Mossadegh as corrupt, pro-communist, hostile to Islam, and bent on destroying the morale and readiness of the armed forces. While Iranian agents spread these lies, thugs would be paid to launch staged attacks on religious leaders and make it appear that they were ordered by Mossadegh or his supporters."[13]

The first coup attempt failed, landing the CIA's anointed prime minister, General Zahedi, in jail. Four days later, a second coup attempt was successful. Immediately after taking office, the U.S. gave Zahedi $5 million for his government and an additional $1 million for himself.[14] The coup gave U.S. oil interests a foothold in Iran and paved the way for the formation of the Anglo-American Oil Company.

---

ii *Mexico nationalized its oil in 1938, but it won independence over a hundred years earlier.*

The U.S. took over from Britain to become the dominant foreign power in Iran and by the 1970s nearly 70,000 Americans worked there, mostly in the oil industry, which afforded them lavish lifestyles.[15]

Meanwhile, the previously diminished monarchic authority of the existing Shah (Mohammad Reza Pahlav) began to rise. Months after Mossadegh was overthrown, the Shah re-established and entrenched his power with Washington's backing. During his brutal 26-year reign, the Shah received over $1 billion in U.S. support and hosted up to 6,000 U.S. military advisors.[16] [17] The CIA also trained the Shah's SAVAK (Organization of National Security and Intelligence), which killed tens of thousands of political dissidents.[18]

Relatively secular, the Shah's reign saw the rise of hard-line religious opposition. The Shah's brutality forced political opposition underground and into the confines of staunchly anti-western religious institutions. "Resistance," writes Linda McQuaig, "coalesced in the one place it could find a safe haven: the local mosque."[19] A potent blend of religiosity and anti-American sentiment erupted into the 1979 Iranian revolution.

Led by Ayatollah Khomeini, the religious radicalism espoused in the 1979 revolution spurred fundamentalism throughout the region. Later that year, an uprising challenging Saudi Arabia's ruling family saw militants capture Mecca's Great Mosque. Shaken by the insurrection, the House of Saud feared a domestic equivalent to the Iranian revolution and responded by funding religious extremism outside its borders. [20]

Reflecting on the international ramifications of the U.S.' role in Iran, Stephen Kinzer writes: "It is not far-fetched to draw a line from operation Ajax [to get rid of Mossadegh] through the Shah's repressive regime and the Islamic Revolution to the fireballs that engulfed the World Trade Centre in New York."[21]

. . .

Since WWII, Saudi Arabia's ruling family has enjoyed intimate relations with U.S. powerbrokers. The first U.S. oil concessions were granted in 1933 and twelve years later President Franklin D. Roosevelt and Abdul Aziz Ibn Saud shook hands on a deal designed to secure American oil interests in the country.[22] For pledging to honor U.S. oil concessions Roosevelt gave Ibn Saud $20 million and a private DC-3 plane.[23] Roosevelt declared: "I hereby find that the defense of Saudi Arabia is vital to the defense of the United States."[24]

In 1946, the Department of Defense helped create the modern Saudi army and air force.[25] Washington also supplied arms and other assistance to the National Guard, a paramilitary force charged with defending the royal family against internal revolt.[26] For more than six decades, the U.S. has armed and protected Saudi Arabia's ruling family.

In exchange for this protection, Washington maintained considerable influence over Saudi oil policy. A former U.S. ambassador to Saudi Arabia explained: "One of the major things the Saudis have historically done, in part out of friendship with the United States, is to insist that oil continues to be priced in dollars. Therefore, the U.S. Treasury can print money and buy oil, which is an advantage no other country has."[27] Saudi Arabia has also recycled a good share of its petrodollars into U.S. stocks and arms purchases. Between 1950 and 2000, Saudi Arabia purchased nearly a quarter of all American weapons exports and in September 2010 Washington announced a $60 billion arms deal with the Saudis, the largest U.S. arms deal ever.[28] [29]

Notoriously corrupt and opulent, the despotic regime has been preoccupied with keeping Islamic radicalism under their control. The royal family has funded Islamists on foreign soil to divert domestic religious-political frustration towards external focal points and away from the Saudi-U.S. relationship.[30] [31] *Forbidden Truth* explains that "almost all the Islamist networks in the Near

East, Africa, and the West were financed by the Saudi state, or by way of the international Islamic institutions it controlled."[32] But it is in Pakistan and Afghanistan that it was most influential.

In 1979, the year of the Iranian revolution and the Mecca uprising, Soviet troops invaded Afghanistan to strengthen a pro-Soviet regime. With the primary goal of diverting inward dissent, Saudi Arabia's ruling family supported hard-line Muslim guerillas who fought the Soviet occupation. Saudi Islamists were encouraged to join the Mujahideen in Afghanistan. The royal family could sleep easy now that the fight had been taken outside Saudi borders.

While the Saudi government pumped hundreds of millions of petrodollars into the anti-communist struggle in Afghanistan, it was the CIA that got the ball rolling.[iii] The Saudis agreed to match every dollar Washington donated to arm and train the Mujahideen on the border of Pakistan and Afghanistan. At the high point, Washington channeled $300 million a year into Afghanistan through Pakistan's intelligence agency and as agreed, the Saudis matched U.S. funding dollar for dollar.[33]

...

Thousands of miles from New York and decades before 9/11, Osama Bin Laden was born into a family of road-builders. Close to Saudi Arabia's royal family, King Faisal appointed Bin Laden's father, Mohammed, minister of public works. "The king's patronage," writes Steve Coll in *Ghost Wars*, "crowned the Bin Laden family with open royal support and ensured that their construction fortune would grow into billions of dollars as the Saudi treasury reaped the oil profits." [34]

Osama Bin Laden rose to political notoriety during the fight in Afghanistan. To assist the anti-Soviet struggle, he organized and financed foreign Jihadists. Bin Laden recruited throughout

---

iii Pakistan's intelligence agency, ISI, was essentially created by the CIA as Washington's conduit to the Mujahideen.

the region, paying $300 per month to anyone willing to fight in Afghanistan.[35] Bin Laden even opened a U.S. recruiting office.[36] At its high point, his private army numbered in the thousands.

Bin Laden also served as point person for Saudi intelligence in Afghanistan. Coll writes that CIA officers believed, "Bin Laden operated as a semi-official liaison between the GID [Saudi intelligence], the international Islamist religious networks such as Jamat, and the leading Saudi-backed Afghan commanders."[37] Private Saudi sources sent as much as $25 million a month to hard line groups in Afghanistan, including one led by their own pious young millionaire, Osama bin Laden.[38] This network was later renamed Al Qaeda. "Middle-class, pious Saudis flush with oil wealth embraced the Afghan cause as American churchgoers might respond to an African famine or a Turkish earthquake," writes Coll.

...

After the Iranian revolution, some believe, Washington powerbrokers decided it was necessary to move beyond support for oil-producing dictatorships like the Saudi Royal family and the Shah. The surrogate approach was no longer deemed sufficient; the U.S. would take on a more direct role in the oil rich Gulf.[39] Not long after the Iranian revolution, President Jimmy Carter declared that, "an attempt by any outside force to gain control of the Persian Gulf region will be regarded as an assault to the vital interests of America, and such an assault will be repelled by any means necessary, including military force."[iv 40]

The 1991 Gulf War was partly designed to increase the U.S. military presence in the region. After the war, troops remained in Saudi Arabia and Kuwait, strengthening Washington's grip on this oil-producing region.[41] It should not be controversial to note that the Islamic extremists who perpetrated 9/11 were motivated by

---

iv Ostensibly this statement was directed at the USSR, however, there is as much evidence to suggest it was aimed at the people of the Middle East.

U.S. policy in the region. They were incensed by the U.S. military presence on the Saudi Arabian Peninsula (the birthplace of Islam), Washington's unyielding support for Israel's dispossession of Palestinians and its alliance with the corrupt House of Saud.[42] In 1998 Bin Laden declared, "for over seven years the United States has been occupying the lands of Islam in the holiest of places, the Arabian Peninsula, plundering its riches, dictating to its rulers, humiliating its people, terrorizing its neighbours and turning its bases in the Peninsula into a spearhead through which to fight the neighbouring Muslim peoples."[43]

17. Inefficiency pays — Flagstaff

Flagstaff was the closest city to the Grand Canyon and we were staying at a neat little hostel bustling with travelers from around the world. (Unlike European cities or major Canadian centres, youth hostels were few and far between in the U.S.) With little between Flagstaff and one of the world's most famous sites we assumed the thousands of sightseers traveling from the city to the canyon would have a bus or train option. That was a miscalculation. There was no Greyhound route and no public transit of any sort to the canyon. The only option seemed to be the hostel's overpriced van.

Wandering around town looking for a cheap bus, we distracted ourselves with a box of pizza. Sitting on a concrete bench beside the major roadway out of town, we ate our meal and watched car after car whiz by. We were sure some of them were heading to the canyon and I was damned if I'd twiddle my thumbs in Flagstaff any longer. I fished through my backpack, found a tube of lipstick and in large brown letters scrawled "Grand Canyon" onto the pizza box. Three minutes later a beat-up Porsche came screeching to a halt.

. . .

The lure of technological advancement was part of the car's early appeal. At the turn of the century, scientific magazines overflowed with articles on automotive innovations. Cars will "eliminate a greater part of the nervousness, distraction, and strain of modern metropolitan life," *Scientific American* explained in 1899.[1] So smitten was the magazine, they diverted from their usual fare to publish "Style in Automobiles" in 1901.[2]

Mesmerized by these machines, early enthusiasts channeled their excitement into breaking ever-higher speed records.[3] The Futurist manifesto, written in 1909, read: "WE declare that the world's splendor has been enriched by a new beauty; the beauty of speed. A racing car with its hood adorned with great pipes, like serpents of explosive breath — a roaring car that seems to be operating like a machine gun, is more beautiful than the Winged Victory of Samothrace."[4]

Technological advancement is still very much a part of the automobile's mystique. The Mazda Millenia was advertised as "so advanced, it required a whole factory."[5] Image is everything and for the automobile that means cutting edge. Describing the rivalry between the world's biggest carmakers, the *Financial Times* concluded that GM's electric car, the Volt, was used to counter the "halo effect that Toyota gained from the Prius, which rivals the iPod as an iconic product."[6] In fact, the Volt was originally named the iCar.[7] "I admit," said former vice-chairman of GM Bob Lutz, "that it [the Volt] has a secondary benefit of helping to re-establish credibility in technology."[8]

An irony of the automobile is that it is widely viewed as a technological marvel. But Al Gore points out: "We are content to see hundreds of millions of automobiles using an old technological approach not radically different from the one first used decades ago in the Model A Ford."[9] Popular journals, magazines, and other media regularly portray the automotive sector as a forerunner of innovation even though most cars built today operate on the general principles adopted three quarters of a century ago.[10] "There has been no major innovation in car technology this [20th] century," explains *Car Mania*. "During the same period, the railways developed two completely new forms of traction and, with the advanced high-speed trains of the 1990s, have made a significant qualitative advance. There has also been a technological revolution in aerospace technology. In its basic constructional elements, however, the car of the 1990s is not qualitatively different from the car of 1900."[11]

Few are familiar with the automobile's early achievements. In 1899, an electric car topped a 100 kilometres (62 miles) per hour.[12] By 1907, electric cars could travel up to a 100 miles without a charge.[13] Even fewer are aware that the vaunted hybrid technology was in place a century ago. (In a *Popular Mechanics* column, Jay Leno claimed to own hybrids built in 1909 and 1925.)[14]

The car's basic technology has remained much the same because the internal combustion engine lacks the "stretch" of a technology like video or computer chips. For starters, it is impossible to microminiaturize human transport. "If the automotive industry had done as well as the electronics industry," write Graeme Maxton and John Wormald, "a Rolls Royce would be a centimeter long, cost a thousandth of what it does and run 50,000 kilometres on a liter of petrol."[15]

The fundamentals of automobile technology have remained stagnant because of their inherent limitations, not for lack of effort. "The really big spenders in global research and development are not the white coated scientists of Big Pharma and biotech or the geeks of Campus Microsoft," writes Vijay Vaitheeswaran in *Zoom*. "They are the legions of engineers, chemists, physicists and geologists employed by the oil and auto industries. The automobile manufacturers are the biggest spenders worldwide on R&D."[16] Together Ford and GM spent $15 billion in R&D in 2007.[17] [18]

Some say the internal combustion engine is the most refined device the world has ever known. Two to three billion dollars a year is spent to increase engine efficiency yet the average car still wastes at least two-thirds of the chemical energy of gasoline.[19] "The engine in most automobiles is between 20 and 25 percent efficient," notes Mark Eberhart, "meaning that the remaining 75-80 percent of the input energy is turned to heat before reaching the drive train."[20]

In addition to the car's inefficient use of gasoline, these 3000-pound metal boxes carry on average one and a half people, approximately 300 pounds — a mere 10 percent of the vehicle's weight. Let's do the math: If only 30 percent of the gasoline energy is used by a vehicle carrying 10 percent of its weight, then only three percent of the fuel's energy actually moves what needs to be moved.

"The wastefulness of the automobile is staggering," concludes Don Fitz.[21] Even at a standstill, automobiles remain inefficient. This time it is not energy wasted, rather living space. The average car is parked 95 percent of the time.[22] Buses and trains, on the other hand, transport passengers well after individuals arrive at their destination (and pedestrians hold onto their legs after their journey is done). Buses, trains, streetcars, bikes as well as pedestrians (and just about every other animal, plant or mineral) use space and infrastructure more efficiently than personal cars, whether moving or at a standstill. At approximately four meters across, road lanes are roughly the same width as railroad tracks, yet rail carries 20 times the number of passengers.[23] The table below compares the efficiency of various modes of transport.

Mode of Transport	Carrying capacity/lane/hour [24]
Autos on surface streets	1,575 passengers
Autos on elevated highways	2,625 passengers
Buses on surface streets	9,000 passengers
Streetcars on surface streets	13,500 passengers
Streetcars and subways	20,000 passengers
Local subway trains	40,000 passengers
Express subway trains	60,000 passengers

The most obvious manifestation of the car's inefficient use of space is congestion, a problem unlikely to be overcome with timed lights, High Occupancy Vehicle lanes or new traffic engineering tricks. Not even expansion of the U.S. roadway appears capable of alleviating congestion. (This has not stopped automobilists from calling for a wider path for the car.)

Despite the obvious inefficiency of cars, as early as the 1920s, automobilists became increasingly emboldened in their view that streetcars encumbered their movement.[25] California's Department of Public works opposed trolley routes on state-funded roads, arguing that streetcars were the source of congestion.[26] For its part, Denver's official publication, *Municipal Facts*, decried "interference between street cars and automobiles," laying the lion's share of blame on the streetcar. Despite equal numbers of streetcar commuters and auto riders, *Municipal Facts* called for the removal of streetcar tracks as a solution to congestion.[27]

The irony of blaming the streetcar for congestion is that automobiles occupied 10 to 20 times more street space per passenger than streetcars.[28] It wasn't unusual in the 1920s for a hundred trolley-riding straphangers to wait on a single motorist to make a left turn.[29] By 1915, Chicago trolley lines complained about a dramatic (45 percent) drop in their speed in the downtown loop.[30] The problem became so bad that street railway companies picked up the bill for early red-green lights in a bid to return order to the streets.[31] Ultimately, the automobile's appetite for space contributed to pushing the trolley to the brink of extinction.[i]

Despite losing the battle to the automobile, trolley and light rail are safer, cheaper modes of travel as well as more energy and space efficient. Yet, the car's benefactors portrayed the trolley and train as backwards and the car as progress.[32] As the clash between the trolley and the car came to a head in the 1920s, full-page color car ads littered popular magazines calling on people to get the "the latest thing." The campaign shifted gear with one ad claiming: Riding the trolleys is "wrong. It's not fair to your children — your wife — or yourself." [33]

---

i *The car's spatial requirements molded the landscape to the exclusion of walking and it's been a struggle to acquire space for bike path*.

In *Les Québecois au Volant*, Montreal city councilor, Richard Bergeron, argues that contrary to popular understanding, mass transit was condemned for being too efficient. It gave too much service for too little investment.[34] Writing in *Heat*, George Monbiot explains that spending on "lorries" (UK speak for buses) yields significantly more travel than an equivalent investment in cars. "They are used much more intensively," argues Monbiot. "One piece of equipment costing, say 150,000 pounds can carry people on nearly 100,000 substantial person/journeys a year, while a car costing 15,000 [pounds] would be likely not to clock up 1,000 such journeys. This is a tenfold increase in the efficiency of capital use." [ii] [35]

Huge amounts of U.S. capital are sunk into the automobile. Most developed countries spend much less on transport than the U.S. due to greater reliance on subways, busses, bikes, walking and trains. Automotive reliance has meant massive waste. But, author Daniel Lazare says: "True efficiency is the last thing a waste-addicted economy can tolerate."[36] The logic of corporate profit is conspicuous consumption, a trait embodied by the automobile's endless need for space and resources.

The car's inefficiency may be good for those who profit from it, but it's costly, unhealthy, unsustainable and it makes it damn hard for those of us without one to get around.

…

"Need a ride to the Grand Canyon?" asked the middle-aged fellow in a Red Sox cap driving the Porsche.

"Yeah," I replied

"I'm not going to the Canyon," he said, "but I'll take you to the next town."

We accepted, even though we were pretty sure there was no next town.

---

ii *Walking (shoes, socks and hopefully a path) and biking (bike and paved surface), require still less investment.*

The driver's name was Charlie. He was passing through Flagstaff on his way to see a white buffalo. After a few minutes on the road, Charlie swiveled around to stare directly and unapologetically at me before declaring, "You must like reggae music."

Charlie drove fast and talked faster. I was now thankful to be stuffed into the back of the two-seater and the burden of conversation fell squarely upon Yves. In a few short minutes, we learned the details of Charlie's awful week. He'd been booted out of a bar the night before ("I can't understand why they would do that"), purchased a new set of hiking boots ("The sturdiest money can buy"), and been fired from his job for assault charges ("My wife assaulted *me*. She pulled my *hair* out.") And then he mentioned his boots again.

It wasn't until we reached the Grand Canyon that the significance of his footwear dawned on me. Charlie had forgotten about the albino buffalo, trading that rare experience for an afternoon with Yves, myself and a giant crack in the earth. Charlie was quiet as we peered into the Grand Canyon. Maybe he'd been stunned into silence (or maybe he noticed we were feet away from a mile-deep precipice). A few hours later, Charlie drove us back to Flagstaff and then offered us a ride to Vegas. We declined. The next day we boarded the (sweet, sweet) Greyhound non-stop to Sin City.

PART TWO

Understanding the reproductive process of homo automotivis

We've seen how cars have damaged our planet and living spaces. They kill people and other living creatures. They are noisy, inefficient and crowd us out of cities. They cause us to build spread-out and unsustainable urban areas. They poison the earth and our bodies, promote imperialism and trigger wars. Given their pervasiveness, cars must have positive countervailing qualities. How else could we love the automobile so much? There must a reason for the emergence of *Homo Automotivis*.

Cars offer freedom, they say. Yves often describes the thrill of driving down highways in British Columbia, Alberta, Saskatchewan, North Dakota and Minnesota during his junior hockey years: The open road, speed, traveling wherever and whenever you want. We are drawn toward the unconstrained ideal of the open road, but can this quest for "freedom" really explain the fantastic growth of the North American automobile industry? It turns out that is a small part of the "lure" of the automobile. In fact, the rise of the automobile has been an integral factor in the growth of U.S.-style capitalism. The car created *Homo Automotivis,* but this species owes its remarkable success to the myriad ways the automobile became "essential" to almost every corner of the economy. The more we delved, the clearer it became that the automobile industry was much more than the factories building them. Where does the automotive industry begin and end? Are there any sectors of the economy that are not a part of the auto industrial complex?

The car created *Homo Automotivis,* an invasive species that reproduces rapidly under the right conditions. And it is excellent at creating those conditions. Since early automobile history, manufacturing the need for cars has been as important as manufacturing vehicles. This has included everything from advertising, political lobbying and anti-competitive practices to influence over media, academia and the general promotion of car culture. In keeping with our ecological approach, we must understand the car in its overall system and strive to see the interrelationships and complexities. It is especially important to understand how it reproduces if we want to devise an eradication program.

18. An industry's power

Sprawling and gutted, downtown Detroit was home to more parking spots than people. There were empty buildings with broken walls and rusting gates hung off their hinges. We sat on our backpacks and gazed upon the skyline of industrial ruin, wondering whether it was mere coincidence that a place known as the "Motor City" had ended up in such a state. It was hell on earth. A swift decision was made to escape across the water, over the border and into Windsor, Ontario.

Once one of the country's largest cities, Detroit proper had over 1.8 million residents in the 1950s. Now populated by less than nine hundred thousand people, the city has shrunk to its 1915 proportions. Plagued by empty lots and abandoned buildings 35 percent of Detroit is uninhabited.[1] Poor mass transit, car domination and industrial dispersal produced a city where land is given away. But few take it.

Detroit's most famous resident, Henry Ford, believed in the suburbanization of U.S. industry. As a major proponent of dispersal, the Ford Motor Company chose Detroit's outskirts as the site for their 1908 Highland Park Plant. Twelve years later they built the famed River Rouge complex several miles further out.[i] Ford moved even further from the city in 1941, setting up its Washtenaw County plant 30 miles from downtown Detroit. "Turning farm fields into factories is what Henry Ford used to do," noted the *Wall Street Journal*.[2]

Just shy of the wilderness, Honda took this trend to another level in 2006, setting up in a remote town of 10,000, 47 miles south-east of Indianapolis.

---

i Early carmakers, GM, Hudson and Chalmars all built plants on the outskirts of Detroit in the 1910s.

Auto manufacturing is space intensive and moving outside the city limits often meant cheaper land as well as lower taxes and regulatory costs. But ideology was also at play. Ford expressed his disdain for the city, describing it as a place where "social impurities break out in a festering sore."[3] Ford had a plan. "We shall solve the city problem by leaving the city."[4]

Anti-city ideology of old has acquired a new vocabulary where "urban" is equated with crime, decay and racial tension.[5] Today, Detroit epitomizes urban 'decay.' Congratulations, Henry.

There's a school of thought that rejects the notion of factory relocation driven by economic considerations or advances in transportation. Some say businesses saw dispersal as a means of combating labour organizing and rising radicalism.[6][7]

The labour movement was rooted in workers and their families residing near the factory. Factory dispersal separated work and home, reducing the likelihood that members of a workforce would live in the same community.[8] The demise of cities, wrote Daniel Lazare "was the start of labour's great unraveling — as Ford well understood."[9]

Detroit is no tourist trap, but Henry Ford would be proud of its other strengths. As the *Economist* put it, "the car industry more or less invented modern industrial capitalism."[10] As a universally recognized signifier of an advanced industrial nation, all major world economies have had an automotive sector. The saying goes, "What's good for Fiat is good for Italy."[11] And in the USA, it is clear that automobile production has been a keystone of capital accumulation.[12]

At the dawn of the 20th century, automotive manufacturing barely registered as a source of economic activity. Automotive production was 150th among U.S. industries in 1900.[13] Within 10 years it was the 21st biggest. The automobile industry moved up the list for the next 15 years and in 1925 it led all other economic sectors.[14]

Early auto production was not capital intensive. But, it drew together a diverse group of independent parts manufacturers and assemblers.[15] From engine production to gun making, numerous technologies were utilized in early auto manufacturing. Penned in 1928, *A Financial History of the American Automobile Industry* explains: "A number of manufacturers of bicycles, wagons, and carriages ventured timidly into the [auto] business by turning over portions of their facilities to the automobile: Machine-shop enterprises, after a more or less brief experience with parts manufacture, undertook automobile production proper; associates and employees of successful producers broke away to found independent companies."[16]

Studebaker, once the biggest auto producer, had been the world's largest wagon manufacturer.[17] They were not the only auto company that originated in another sector: Peugeot, Rover and Opel in Europe, as well as Pope, Peerless, Rambler, Winton and Willis in the U.S., all began as bike makers.[ii] [18] [19] These bike makers turned auto manufacturers initiated the Good Roads Movement. Emerging in the 1890s, the movement was led by proponents of the bicycle — not the car. Albert Pope, the world's leading bike magnate, financed the League of American Wheelmen (LAW), which promoted road building for cyclists.[20] LAW had some modest success: It won a court case granting cyclists access to private turnpikes in both New Jersey and Central Park; they secured highway funding with the 1891 New Jersey State Aid Act; and pushed for the federal Office of Road Inquiry, which opened in 1893.[21] But LAW's political clout was limited and change came slowly. The bicycle lobby achieved relatively little as it could not attract a host of associated industries. Unlike the car it was a simple product. Just two skinny tires and a frame. While

---

ii *Detroit became home to U.S. automobile production partly because it was the manufacturing hub of stationary gasoline engines for farm use as well as the carriage and wagon trade hub (due to its excellent hardwood forests).*

some bike companies were highly profitable, they did not generate close to as much economic activity.

The American Automobile Association, which included former bicycle manufacturers, emerged as a successor to LAW. Many lobbyists remained, but they were far more influential lobbying for roads for cars than they had been in the bicycle movement.[22]

"Think of the results to the industrial world of putting upon the market a product that doubles the malleable iron consumption, triples the plate glass production and quadruples the use of rubber!" exclaimed Charles Kettering in 1932. "No other one artifact in history has affected so many people in so many industries."[23]

Ford and GM's early investors demonstrate the importance of the automobile to an assortment of related industries. In 1915, Pierre S. DuPont (head of the company bearing his name) became a director at GM and by 1919 he held a quarter of GM's common stock. He was appointed president of General Motors in 1920.[24] The DuPont company produced chemicals and paints and GM purchased massive quantities of these products. The relationship lasted over 40 years, until the Supreme Court forced DuPont to sell its stake in GM, concluding the company received preferential treatment when buying auto paints and lacquers.[iii] [25]

Ford's early investors included John and Horace Dodge, makers of gasoline engines as well as oil scion, John D. Rockefeller.[26] [27] Henry Ford, however, was a megalomaniac, obsessed with maintaining total control of his company, pushing out these early investors and developing his own resources. By 1920 Ford owned Brazilian rubber plantations, Michigan iron mines and lumber mills, as well as glass plants in Pennsylvania and Minnesota and coal mines in Kentucky and West Virginia. He

---

iii *Making sure to be connected with the growing auto industrial complex, the DuPonts also bought a significant stake in the U.S. Rubber Company.*

also acquired a railroad and a fleet of ships to move these goods to his auto plants.[28]

Describing the firestorm of activity surrounding the early automobile *Dynasties* notes: "In 1913, the [Ford] company required one million lamps, eight hundred thousand wheels, eight hundred thousand tires, ninety thousand tons of steel, the hides of 400,000 cattle, nearly two million square feet of window glass and twelve million hickory billets for wheel spokes. It took thirty-five thousand freight cars to ship the finished autos. Ford also needed continuous flows of coal, iron, nickel, brass, rubber, lubricants and gasoline, among other things, brought in from all over — the Mesabi Range, West Virginia, Canada — and all delivered on time. And that was just Ford Motors. Nothing like the auto industry had ever been seen; a swarm of manufacturing plants, suppliers, shippers, agents, road builders, sellers, and repairers all devoted to supplying and servicing a costly and complex object that everyone wanted."[29]

In all of human history there has never been a more ravenous consumer of raw materials than the automobile.[30] (And North America's abundance of natural resources facilitated its ascent.) Describing the attitude during the 1910s resource boom, author Stephen B. Goddard says that "to the industrialists, who were now selling glass, rubber, steel, concrete and their end products in numbers beyond their wildest dreams, whatever needed to be done to sustain the boom and to build pressure for good roads simply had to [be] accomplished."[31]

An industry with a voracious and varied appetite, the auto sector's momentum was propelled by its spin-offs. By 1926, U.S. automakers consumed 85 percent of U.S. rubber, 14 percent of iron and steel, 63 percent of upholstery leather, 50 percent of plate glass, 28 percent of nickel, 21 percent of tin, 25 percent of aluminum, 11 percent of hardwood and 13 percent of copper. (Additionally, 900,000 railroad carloads transported automobile parts and completed vehicles that year.)[32] As vehicle production increased so did the car's resource consumption. In 1968, automobiles consumed 21 percent of U.S. steel, 10.4 percent of aluminum, 36.5 percent of zinc, 8.2 percent of copper, 54.7 percent of lead, 19.4 percent of ductile iron and 40 percent of malleable iron, 14.3 percent of nickel and 66 percent of rubber.[iv] [33]

Today's car uses an average of 1,840 pounds of steel and 300 pounds of aluminum, contributing $15 and $5 billion respectively to the U.S. steel and aluminum industries.[34] (To add value, aluminum manufacturer Rio Tinto owns a number of automobile part makers.) Also directly dependent on the success of the automobile, the global tire industry is worth roughly $90 billion a year.[35]

The average new vehicle contains more than $1,700 in electronics.[36] Volkswagen and Apple joined forces to develop the "iCar" to compete with "Sync" in-car communication and entertainment systems developed by Ford and Microsoft.[37] For its part, Research In Motion (RIM), maker of the BlackBerry, spent $200 million in April 2010 to buy QNX Co. Software Systems to stream BlackBerry software applications to a screen or dashboard in vehicles. The *Wall Street Journal* reported that growing numbers of accessory ad-ons like security alarms, satellite navigation systems, DVD players, heated cup holders and so on, has put such a great strain on car batteries that it has caused a major spike in replacement battery sales. With almost 70 million replacements sold annually, the battery industry is worth approximately $7 billion.[38]

With a profusion of economic interests dependent on auto sales, the industry is a barometer of the entire economy. The revolutionary Model-T kick-started the nation's prosperity a century ago and automobile sales underpinned the Roaring 20s. Still today, automotive production drives the economy. In the wake of 9/11, GM kept its factories running and launched an enormous

---

iv In the late 1960s, Ford built the world's largest "injection molding plastic plant" employing 2400 workers.

zero financing sales blitz. Their strategy, noted the *Wall Street Journal*, was "widely credited with helping the U.S. economy to avert a deeper slump."[39] The "dealer doldrums indicator" is a term used by economists to note the relationship between car sales and recessions.[v] This indicator predicted all five U.S. recessions between 1968 and 2006.[40] For government statisticians, automobile sales warrant their own category of retail trade. At its high point in 1977, auto dealers accounted for 28.5 percent of all U.S. retail trade, explaining the accuracy of the "dealer doldrums indicator."[41]

Auto manufacturing revenues are simply staggering. Even in today's information age, both Ford and GM individually outsold AT&T, IBM and Microsoft combined (in 2002, GM's sales were seven times greater than Microsoft's).[42] Auto manufacturing also dwarfs other transportation sectors, with both Ford and GM's U.S. operations individually generating greater revenues than the entire American airline industry.[43] Revenues generated by some automotive plants exceed those of major multinational corporations. In 1998, for instance, Ford's Michigan Truck Plant generated almost $11 billion — more than that year's international sales for companies like Nike and CBS.[44]

In 1999 *Fortune* 500 named GM, DaimlerChrysler and Ford the world's three largest corporations.[45] Seven years later, GM, DaimlerChrysler and Toyota all ranked in the top ten (six oil companies and Wal-Mart rounded out the list).[46]

By the late 1930s, GM had become "an industrial empire such as the world had never seen before."[47] In 1953, Secretary of Defense and former GM president, Charles Wilson, stated: "I thought what was good for our country was good for General Motors, and vice versa. The difference did not exist. Our company is too big."[vi][48]

---

v Auto dealerships employed over a million Americans in 2008.

vi When its stock went on the market in 1956, Ford ended its reign as the largest family business in the world.

Automobile production is the world's largest single manufacturing activity. Global automobile sales in 1990 equaled the economies of Italy, France or England.[49] In 2005 the global automotive industry was worth $2,100,000,000,000 and ranked eighth among the world's largest economies.[50] In the U.S. alone, new car sales cars topped $450 billion in 2007, with the used car market generating another $260 billion.[51]

The automobile has been the single most important source of corporate profit for a century. In 1952, the *Journal of Economic Review* sought a contemporary measure of the incredible profits acquired by the founders of the British Empire's East India Company. In the end the *Journal* asserted that the fortunes made by imperialists in Asia were nearly as immense as those of Ford Motor Company's early stockholders.[52] A thousand dollars invested in Ford in 1903 was worth $2.5 million in 1919 (accompanied by accumulated dividends of $250,000).[53] Similarly, GM made a profit every year between 1920 and 1979 and in 1955 was the first company to make $1 billion.[54] [55] More recently, Toyota leads the pack as the world's most profitable automobile manufacturer. It did not lose money in a single quarter between 1938 and 2008 and in 2007 it made $28 billon.[56]

The industry's profitability is a major driving force behind the landscape and lifestyles of a car-dominated society. Capitalism is a system of winners and losers. The big and powerful drive out the weaker and less powerful. For the first eight decades of the last century the U.S. car industry was unrivalled as a profit maker. This profitability gave the industry immense economic, cultural and political clout that continues to this day.

19. The road gang

Our expectations weren't high as we entered Houston. It certainly wasn't a tourist Mecca. But we'd heard things were getting better. For whatever reason, the number of Houstonians interested in moving downtown had risen sharply. Was the addition of a light rail system shaking things up a little? Facilitating downtown movement, promoting street level development and pedestrian culture as well as challenging automotive hegemony — all at a tenth the cost of a subway system. Perhaps a revival was underway.

In stark contrast to the gorgeous family run guesthouse we left behind in New Orleans, we were stuck in a smoky motel next to a loud highway. Spending no unnecessary time amongst the fumes of this Texas smoke pit, we grabbed a bus and began our tour. Did we find ourselves in the midst of a new and improved, city beautiful? No. Houston is, shall we say, architecturally challenged. So much so that the International Olympic Committee initially considered the city for the 2012 Summer Games but allegedly passed, concluding it was "too ugly."

After a few uneventful hours of wandering, we sat down at Pepe's, a Mexican restaurant in the middle of a strip mall parking lot on Macario Garcia Street. Our enchiladas were substandard and the view even more so. Visible from the veranda were a Texaco, Autozone, Firestone, Thunderbolt, Cooper Tires, Minit Man carwash and a Whataburger. It was a mini version of Houston; a street completely devoted to the car.

The automobile appears to inspire devotion, but the plain truth is that it requires devotion. Of all the purchases that require effort after buying, the car may be the most needy. It needs to be fed; it requires a smooth road to move on and a place to rest.

Not unlike the horses the aristocracy left behind with the dawn of the auto age, today's horseless carriages are high maintenance. Motorcars need to be washed, buffed and kept safe; they need constant check-ups, new parts and finally a burial ground.

The automobile may be needy, but it certainly is not weak. If you're thinking about taking on the personal car, beware — it travels with a posse. Tough and loyal, these friends are committed to its survival. When you pick a fight with the car, you take on the whole gang.

The auto gang began to form in 1901, when the Hartford Auto Corporation ran 14 service stations in the Boston area.[1] As the years passed associated industries continued to increase their share of the automotive sector and by 1925 Americans spent more on motor vehicle maintenance and operation than on car, truck and tractor purchases.[2] Today, only one in three automotive dollars is generated by carmakers. The rest comes from repairs, fuelling, finance and insurance, amongst other allied ventures.

Cars need transportation too. With 13 million automobiles moved annually by boat, even shipping magnates benefit from the personal automobile.[3] On land, it is not uncommon to encounter multi-layered car hauling trucks that take up huge chunks of the highway. Hauling cars is a multi-billion dollar industry.

As the saying goes, there ain't no romance without finance. Before being swept off your feet by your brand new vehicle, you will probably need help from JP Morgan Chase, GMAC or some other financial acronym. According to a January 2011 *Economist* article, banks do $700 billion in car loans each year and have been making a killing this way for three quarters of a century.[4]

While auto and oil production conjures up images of Detroit or Houston, cars have many friends among New York's banks and investment funds. Banks have long held major investments in the automotive sector and recently large financial institutions, like the Carlyle Group and Cerberus Capital Management, have become major shareholders. Cerberus owns numerous auto parts suppliers as well as Alamo and National Car Rental and in 2007 it bought Chrysler and took control of GMAC.[5][6]

After spending an arm and a leg on a new car, the owner must keep it safe and that means insurance. At $160 billion annually — nine times Uganda's entire economy — the U.S. auto-insurance industry is one of the most successful offshoots of the automotive sector.[7]

Sweaty brows and calloused hands, blue collar workers in another part of town are charged with the endless task of maintaining the automobile after it hits the road. From fine-tuning to emergency repairs, millions are employed in servicing the motorcar's well-being. Boosted by outrageously expensive new parts, the repairs and parts industry is worth a quarter of a trillion dollars a year.[8]

You don't have to be on Macario Garcia Street to notice that everywhere you look, there are profits to be made from the car. A plethora of companies deal in everything from training new drivers to towing idle vehicles. There are parking operations, snow removal companies and people who salt the streets; More than 50,000 car washes wring out $8.6 billion from automobile dirt while U-Haul pulls in over $2 billion a year.[9][10]

The list of industries that profit from the car is virtually endless. Even in death, the car is a moneymaker. An entire culture has been spawned of weekend adventures and day trips to search out junkyard gems. With recognized chains the six thousand auto scrap yards strewn across the USA do $30 billion a year in sales.[11] But many bits and pieces don't make it to the yards; landfills are the final resting place of a huge amount of material from cars. This is another multi billion-dollar industry.

Despite the car's rugged image, it is rather particular about its environment. Unlike the pedestrian, it needs a smooth surface and a straight path. The automobile is a diva. Endlessly pampered to get its show on the road, the automobile needs bright lights, painted lines, bold signs and plenty of parking. With a spot at home, work and on the town, every car needs approximately 1,400 feet of space. So it comes as no surprise that the U.S. asphalt industry sells $15 billion of the sticky stuff every year.[12] With the pedestrian using 100 times less asphalt than the driver, think of how valuable the car is to owners of that industry. It is no surprise that a forward-thinking asphalt magnate also founded one of the first U.S. automobile companies.[13]

Of all of its various appetites, however, Houston impressed upon us the automobile's insatiable thirst for oil. Leaving aside asphalt, oil is used to produce tires, foam, plastics and to power some automobile manufacturing.[14] About 26 billion liters (seven billion gallons) of oil is used to produce a billion tires every year.[15] With two thirds of U.S. oil sales consumed by motor vehicle transport — forty percent by cars alone — Houston is reliant on the automobile for a lot more than navigating its sprawling terrain.

About 175,000 U.S. gas stations do hundreds of billions of dollars in sales. Paul Roberts explains that the oil industry's business model was planned around the gasoline pump, "from the kind of crude oil it sought to the kind of refineries it built, to its intense focus on retail marketing."[16] During the automobile's embryonic phase, the oil industry was already big business. At that time, oil was mainly used to fuel the kerosene lamp, a business destroyed by the emergence of gas and electrical illumination.[17] [18] The powerful oil interests of the day, led by the Rockefeller family, were bailed out of this crisis and set up for life with the advent of the automobile. And as gallon upon gallon was drained from the earth and pumped into gas tanks, big oil swam in its profits. By 1935, eight of the top 16 U.S. companies had their roots in oil.[19]

Today, the global oil industry is worth $3 trillion annually.[20] In 2006, nine of the world's 10 biggest state owned companies were energy producers.[21] And of the world's 11 largest private companies, six produced oil.[22] In July 2007 the world's 10 leading oil companies were valued at $2 trillion.[23] When PetroChina entered the stock market later that year it became the world's first $1 trillion company.[24]

In October 2007, the *Wall Street Journal* called petrodollars one of "financial globalization's new power sources."[25] Petrodollar assets topped $3.5 trillion in 2006 and were expected to reach $6 trillion by 2012. "The amount of oil shipped around on the world's oceans dwarfs any other single commodity," explains author Sonia Shah. "Of the 5.9 billion tons of goods shipped on the world's oceans every year, over a quarter is crude."[26]

…

In the 1920s one in every eight U.S. employees worked for the automotive industrial complex.[27] By 1982 that number peaked at one in five.[28] [29] In the 1950s, the executive secretary of the American Association of State Highway Officials, Hal Hale, justified road building on the basis of the car's relationship to the economy. "One of every seven jobs in the United States was linked to the automobile industry," he argued. "True, there might be other industries of comparable nature but, certainly, these exist by virtue of the presence of the roads which we have built in this country. Therefore, I submit to you that the highway program in the United States is a basic element of our national economy. As such, it is not subject to the customary conception of public works."[30]

Be it highway lodgings or roadside food, the special relationship between the automobile and economy can only "exist by virtue of the presence of the roads." Wal-Mart, for instance, grew on the back of the highway to become the biggest company in the world. Together with other big box retailers, it's been a powerful promoter of highways and automobiles.

The list of automobile dependents and spin-offs goes on and on. U.S. recreational vehicle sales are worth $15 billion annually and there are thousands of American car rental outlets.[31] [32]

About 1.8 million truck-drivers ship 70 percent of all U.S. goods, generating over $600 billion a year.[33] Truckers need to be serviced as well. A thousand truck stops across the USA do $7.8 billion in annual sales.[34]

The motel (or "motor hotel") business created by and for the car does tens of billions of dollars in sales annually. Similarly, the fast food industry is "a $120 billion motorized American experience."[35] MacDonald's, for instance, does a whopping 60 percent of its business via the drive-thru.[36] As one of the world's largest landowners, McDonald's buys property wherever traffic is headed. A target market moving at high speed, hordes of automobolists rush through "commercial buyways" across the USA.[37] By the 1920s, writes Catherine Gudis in *Buyways*, "business men and politicians had come to 'a full realization that the streets of a city are the most important element in its economic usefulness.'"[38]

Land speculators and developers are often the first to recognize the potential wealth spread along the highway. Massive profits are made by purchasing inexpensive agricultural land on city outskirts after which governments are lobbied to rezone the land. Speculators then make a killing selling new houses or commercial space. Developers then ask officials to extend public amenities and roads to these areas.

Suburban developers usually find friends among resource companies. Brick, cement, ceramic, steel, grass, paint, glass and pipe producers all benefit every time a new house is built. In older homes, former owners are merely paid. In newly built suburban and exurban houses there is a lot more money to be made in freshly bought commodities.[39] Size doesn't matter to everyone, but for the resource industry bigger is better. Despite shrinking families, since the 1950s new U.S. house sizes have more than doubled from 800 sq ft to 2,200 sq ft.[40] Sprawling car infrastructure allows for the massive projects undertaken by suburban home manufacturers.

Appliance manufacturers are the better for it too. It's not easy fitting two fridges, a dishwasher, a freezer, a washer and drier, a pool table and four TVs into a small house or apartment; big houses are a boon to the appliance industry. "Urban areas have less junk than suburbs," said 1-800-GOT-JUNK's Darryl Arnold. "But only because they have less space. My residential jobs in apartments and condos downtown are on average one eighth of a load, compared with closer to half a truck load in the suburbs."[41]

The rise of garage-organizing products and services illustrates the extent to which a large home can accumulate merchandise (and generate still more economic activity). It is increasingly common to hire garage-organizing experts. With homeowners spending $800 million for these services in 2005, it is a thriving new industry.[42] As junk begins to seep out of massive suburban homes and into the garage, the automobile's only exurban challenge may be this encroachment into its personal space.

In October 2005 *Business Week* explained the economic importance of car-based infrastructure: "The exurb's rapid growth has been one of the main engines of U.S. economic expansion in recent years. Consider all the home building plus the malls, box stores, restaurant chains, fire departments and schools that have popped up on cheap farmland beyond the suburbs. The new arrivals provided huge growth for retailers and other service companies, hundreds of thousands of new jobs for teachers, firemen and the like, and entrepreneurial opportunities galore. Indeed, it is unlikely that the U.S. economy could have outperformed every other major industrial country in recent years without the explosion of exurbs and their ripple effects on business."[43]

When all's said and done, cars facilitate an extra large culture, which is grand for business. Propelling the capitalist economic system full speed ahead, the automobile is a vehicle of endless consumption.

20. Self-interest, bullying and a willingness to break the law

From *L.A. Confidential* to *Chinatown*, Hollywood has presented Los Angeles as a city of scandals and secrets. The City of Angels is a great place to learn about some of the automotive industry's dirty secrets. Los Angeles played a leading role in three "scandals" that illustrate how the "self-interest" of cars and its corporations can affect, even overwhelm, other creatures, especially human beings, living in the automotive habitat.

On Christmas day 1993, Patricia Anderson and her four children were waiting at a red light when their 1979 Malibu was rear-ended. The car burst into flames, burning three of her children over 60 percent of their bodies. One lost her hand to the fire. All five were victims of GM's bottom line. Despite an internal GM directive that recommended a minimum distance of 17 inches between the fuel tank and the rear bumper, the 1979 Malibu fuel tank was just 11 inches away (its predecessor, on the other hand, had a 20-inch gap). Something else was suspect about this car. A standard metal brace separating the fuel tank from the rear was also absent.

Anderson took General Motors to court, suing the company for insufficient collision protection. As the case unfolded, troubling evidence surfaced: Anderson was not the first person to sue GM for fuel-fed fire accidents. In fact, the company had been expecting a lawsuit. It was soon revealed that Edward Ivey, an engineer from GM's Advanced Design Department, had submitted a report to GM management entitled "Value Analysis of Auto Fuel Fed Fire Related Fatalities." In the report, Ivey multiplied the expected fatalities by the predicted costs of legal damages for

every expected death. He then divided the number by 41 million
— the number of GM vehicles on U.S. roads.

The Corporation laid out Ivey's analysis, which
concluded that an average fuel fed death would cost GM $2.40
per vehicle. The following calculation appeared in the company
report: 500 fatalities x $200,000/fatality = $ 2.40/ automobile
over 41,000,000 automobiles.[1] Redesigning a safer Malibu would
have cost GM $8.59 per automobile. But the cold hard figures
calculated a saving of $6.19 per vehicle if left unaltered.[2] The
deaths would be worth it. After this calculation became public the
law came down hard on General Motors. Los Angeles Superior
Court Judge Ernest G. Williams concluded: "The court finds that
clear and convincing evidence demonstrated that the defendant's
fuel tank was placed behind the axle on automobiles of the make
and model here in order to maximize profits — to the disregard
of public safety."[3] A jury ordered compensatory damages of $107
million and punitive damages of $4.8 billion (later reduced to $1.2
billion in a settlement).[4]

The court's harsh decision was influenced by a fuel-
fed scandal that took place a decade earlier. Precariously placed
between the bumper and axle, the Ford Pinto's gas tank was in the
rear of the car, and even more prone to explosion than the Malibu.
Predictably, Pinto after Pinto blew up, exacerbated by a light body
frame that tended to crush around the doors, restricting escape.[5]
How many died, nobody knows. Estimates of unnecessary deaths
range from dozens to over 900.[6] As with the Malibu, moving the
fuel tank cost money Ford didn't want to spend. When it came to
light that Ford Motors knew of the Pinto's fiery disposition, public
outrage forced a modification of the design. The problem was
solved by the addition of "a small plastic protective casing to the
gas tank. Cost: one dollar."[7] The Pinto chronicle climaxed in 1978
when a California jury awarded one of the victims $128 million,
then the largest amount ever awarded in a product liability suit.[8]

The California State of Appeals concluded that Ford demonstrated, "conscious disregard of the probability of injury to members of the consuming public."[9] Receiving three counts of reckless homicide, it was the first time a corporation had been charged with murder.[10]

Ten years before the Pinto debacle, information surfaced implicating three of the world's largest auto companies in a conspiracy to keep the population in a toxic haze. The "smog conspiracy" was revealed in 1968 when the Department of Justice filed an anti-trust case against the Big Three. They were accused of colluding to withhold the installation of catalytic converters and other technologies to reduce pollution. "Beginning at least as early as 1953, and continuing thereafter," alleged the Department of Justice, "the defendants and co-conspirators have been engaged in a combination and conspiracy in unreasonable restraint of the aforesaid interstate trade and commerce in motor vehicle air pollution control equipment."[11]

In the early 1950s smog became increasingly common. Los Angeles (the car capital of the world) became the centre of the pollution debate. In a bid to quell mounting criticism of car-generated air pollution, Chrysler, Ford, GM and the Automobile Manufacturers Association (AMA) agreed in 1953 to collectively research pollution-reducing technologies. The automotive manufacturers claimed their alliance was driven by a concern for public health. It was not. As time passed evidence emerged that the Big Three had in fact united to block the installment of anti-pollution devices. Their agreement stipulated they would wait for unanimous agreement to move forward on smog-busting technologies. In *Taken for a Ride*, Jack Doyle writes that "the automobile manufacturers, through AMA, conspired not to compete in research, development, manufacture and installation of [pollution] control devices and collectively did all in their power to delay such research, development, manufacturing and installation."[12] The public had been hoodwinked.

But the biggest scandal in automobile history was neither exploding automobiles, nor the smog alliance. It was a conspiracy that changed the face of cities across the United States.

In 1922, Alfred P. Sloan, head of General Motors, created a working group charged with undermining and replacing the electric trolley.[13] The group's first act was to launch a bus line that arrived a minute before the streetcar and followed the same route. The trolley line soon shutdown.[14] At the time, there were hundreds of trolley lines in Los Angeles so it was not particularly noteworthy when one shut down. But it was a harbinger of things to come.

In the early 1920s the streetcar industry was booming. There were 1,200 tramway and inter urban train companies with 29,000 miles of track.[15] In the best years they topped 15 billion riders.[16] Over a thousand miles of trolley track criss-crossed the Los Angeles area alone, carrying most people to work.[17] The streetcar dominated the transit scene, but the competition was gaining strength. The number of cars on the road reached 20 million in the 1920s.[18] While pressure from the automobile mounted, the trolley remained the major form of urban transportation.

During this crucial period in U.S. transit history, GM was intent on eliminating the competition. As one of the biggest companies in the world, GM offered municipal politicians free Cadillacs to vote the company's way and insisted that railway companies shipping their cars aid their campaign.[19] They also pressured banks in small communities to starve local trolley companies of finance and then made credit available to streetcar companies that replaced their tracks with GM buses.[20] [21]

In 1932, GM established United Cities Motor Transportation (UCMT) to buy electric streetcar companies in urban areas and convert them into bus operations. After purchasing streetcar systems, UCMT ripped up their tracks and tore down the overhead wires. Once the conversion was complete, UCMT resold the new bus systems, on condition they were not reconverted to streetcars. New owners signed contracts with UMCT, stipulating that "new equipment using any fuel or means of propulsion other than gas" could not be used.[22] The contracts also required that GM be the source of all new buses.[i]

In the relative obscurity of Galesburg Illinois, UCMT made its first urban takeover in 1933.[23] Moving swiftly, it had already dismantled trolley systems in three urban centres before being censured by the American Transit Association. After its 1935 censure, GM dissolved UCMT. It was not long, however, before its anti-trolley activities were revived and redoubled.[24]

GM and its co-conspirators developed a network of front organizations. In 1936, GM joined with Greyhound to form National City Lines; in 1938 they collaborated with Standard Oil of California to create Pacific City Lines; in 1939 Phillips Petroleum and Mack Truck joined National City Lines.[25] American City Lines was created in 1943 to focus on the biggest cities.[26]

GM's conversion strategy ran into a major obstacle in many big cities. In the larger urban areas trolley lines were often owned by electricity companies that made money from selling the energy to power the rails. The electrical companies benefited from a tax provision allowing them to absorb trolley deficits through lower taxes paid by the parent company. Frustrated by this trolley-electricity ownership arrangement, in the early 1930s GM produced a number of dossiers for Congress highlighting the loss in tax revenues that resulted.[27] GM's strategy was successful. The 1935 Public Utility Holding Company Act made it extremely difficult for energy companies to own trolley lines.

Companies that had previously refused GM's advances began to sell. Eighteen months later, GM scooped up 90 miles

---

i According to Urban Elites and Mass Transportation, by the early 1970s GM accounted for as much as 75% of bus production. In addition to manufacturing buses, its two major competitors, Motor Coach Industries and Flexible Company, acquired engines and other parts from GM.

of tramway in Manhattan.[28] After successfully converting New York's trolley system, GM and its cronies moved on to Tulsa, Philadelphia, Montgomery, Cedar Rapids, El Paso, Baltimore, Chicago and LA.[29] [30] When all was said and done a hundred electric transit systems in 45 cities were ripped up, converted and resold.[31] By the mid-50s nearly 90 percent of the country's electric streetcar structure was gone.[32]

The auto industry's apologists deny any conspiracy took place. Some even claim GM invigorated public transit. Yet, the facts are overwhelming. As Edwin Black points out in *Internal Combustion*, GM and company were condemned by the Department of Justice, Senate and courts (from the lowest district venue to the Supreme Court) for anti-trust practices that were part of this nationwide conspiracy.[33] In a section of the 1947 indictment labeled "THE CONSPIRACY," prosecutors and the grand jury jointly declared: "Beginning on or about January 1, 1937, the exact date being to the Grand Jury unknown, and continuing to and including the date of the return of this Indictment, the defendants, together with other persons to the Grand Jury unknown, have knowingly and continuously engaged in a wrongful and unlawful combination and conspiracy to acquire or otherwise secure control of or acquire a substantial financial interest in a substantial part of the companies which provide local transportation service in the various cities, towns and counties of several states of the United States, and to eliminate and exclude all competition in the sale of motorbuses, petroleum products, tires and tubes to the local transportation companies owned or controlled by or in which National City Lines ... had a substantial financial interest." [34]

The verdict was guilty. Yet the punishment for conspiring to destroy a mode of mass transit amounted to a fine of five thousand dollars.[35] Not much of a disincentive for a company worth billions of dollars. And just after its 1947 conviction, National City Lines revived its anti-trolley activities.[36]

The only legitimate dispute is the extent to which GM's motivation was to promote private auto use or simply to increase the number of gasoline-powered buses, which GM sold. Some believe GM pushed buses to spur future personal automobile sales.[37] Others think differently. "The conspiracy against mass transit," argues Edwin Black, "was first and foremost a conspiracy to convert cities from electric [streetcars] to petroleum [bus] systems."[38]

A Congressional investigator into the trolley conspiracy, Bradford Snell, stood before a senate committee in 1974 to decry the long-term impacts of GM's actions: "Los Angeles was a beautiful city of lush palm trees, fragrant orange groves, and ocean clean air. It was served then by the world's largest electric railway network. In the late 1930s General Motors and allied highway interests acquired the local transit companies, scrapped their pollution free electric trains, tore down their power transmission lines, ripped up their tracks, and placed GM buses on already congested Los Angeles streets. The noisy, foul-smelling buses turned early patrons of the high speed rail system away from public transit and, in effect, sold millions of private automobiles. Largely as a result, the city is today an ecological wasteland: The palm trees are dying of petrochemical smog; the orange groves have been paved over by 300 miles of freeways; the air is a septic tank into which 4 million cars, half of them built by General Motors, pump 13,000 tons of pollutants daily."[ii] [39]

ii Widely disliked this profit driven industry was not without fault. According to Internal Combustion: "Known for deep seated corruption, hidden ownership practices, and unlimited avarice, transit owners commonly eschewed spending money on new equipment and lines when they could stretch old vehicles and infrastructure yet another day and yet another year." The characters that gained control of Minneapolis and St Paul's Twin City Rapid Transit service were particularly shady. After being brought to court for simply shutting down the St. Paul side of the system, the head of the company, Charles Green, exclaimed, "The public be damned!" "I intend to force a profit out of this company! If necessary, I'll auction off all the streetcars and buses and sell the rails for scrap iron!"

Snell's idyllic (if not naïve) description may have inspired ongoing pressure to rebuild streetcars in LA. "In a sense Los Angeles is returning to its roots," read a December 2006 *Washington Post*. "In the 1920s, the region was home to the most elabourate rail system in the country: almost 1,500 miles of track connecting the eastern desert with the Pacific coast ... the MTA [Metropolitan Transit Association] now finds itself rebuilding the old system — in some places along the same rights-of-way."[40]

And that's exactly what he did - with a little help from General Motors. Green's terrible media made it difficult to secure bank loans. But when Twin City Rapid Transit approached GM to buy 25 buses on credit, they offered 525 — all on favourable credit terms.

21. Creating a market

All we knew about Philadelphia was that Boyz II Men and the Philly Cheese Steak Sandwich called it home. Frankly, I thought it was going to be another de-industrialized, gutted, northeast city. Far from it, downtown was positively thriving, during the day and night. Philly had not completely conceded its streets to the automobile and its pedestrian scale gave us glimpses of a pre-car era.

All across the U.S. we noted semi-abandoned train stations, important transportation hubs in another life. Today traveling across the U.S. by train is not a practical option.

In Philadelphia we stood in the grand hall of a beautiful old train station. Once the transportation centre of the city, it now lay quiet and tertiary, but nearly an entire wall of the great hall was covered with a 50 ft x 30 ft car ad. It seemed more than a little out of place. Would you see a promotion for the train at a car dealership? On the contrary, the automotive industry continues to disparage mass transit.

In the mid 1990s GM ran ads in U.S. subways showing a picture of the Aurora with the headline "Tear Up Your Monthly Pass" while more recently BMW covered bus shelters with the statement: "In the land of the bus shelter the guy with a car is king."[1] [2]

In March 2003, GM dealers ran a full-page ad in a Vancouver weekly paper picturing a bus coming at the reader, identified with a route sign proclaiming WET DOG SMELL (the only dogs allowed on Vancouver buses accompany the blind). The following week the bus in the ad was identified as a carrier of CREEPS and WEIRDOS. Both advertisements urged readers to buy a GM car.[3]

...

Beginning in 1908, with the creation of the mass-produced Model-T, Ford produced every second car in the country. For 15 years Henry's company dominated the automotive market. Until, that is, GM's President Alfred Sloan emphasized a new way of selling cars. Sloan believed GM should "abandon its inherited managerial habit of conceptualizing products mainly in terms of simple physical engineering standards."[4] He hired hip Hollywood style-maker to the stars, Harley Earl, and in 1927 GM introduced colorful paint jobs with the creation of an Art and Color section.

The company's priority shifted from advances in engineering to annual car model changes.[i] Combined with mass advertising, annual model changes generated consumer dissatisfaction with older cars — they quickly became undesirable and even embarrassing.[5] To assuage the shame, a replacement was offered, at a slightly higher price. Sloan was upfront about the strategy. "Many may wonder why the automobile industry brings out a new model every year," he explained. "The reason is simple … we want to make you dissatisfied with your current car so you will buy a new one, you who can afford it."[6] And it worked. By the mid 1930s, GM controlled 40 percent of the market.[7]

We all know happy people make for terrible consumers, that contentedness undermines the bottom line, but Sloan's frankness is unsettling: Take away peace of mind, then sell it back year after year — to those who can afford it.

Eight decades later, automakers produced hundreds of models a year. So it is no surprise that three in 10 people admit to buying a car "because it's a new, better, sexier model."[8]

To live in an ad-driven culture is to live in the culture of the car. The auto industry is by far the biggest advertiser, with as many as one in seven ads relating to the automobile.[9] In 2004,

---

i According to Made to Break, writing in 1955, Earl explained, "our big job is to hasten obsolescence. In 1934 the average car ownership span was 5 years: now it is 2 years. When it is 1 year, we will have a perfect score."

cars were five of the eight best-known brands in the U.S. and auto advertisers spent twice the next industry, retail.[10]

Since the dawn of the auto age, car companies have been major advertisers. "Practically noiseless and impossible to explode" read an 1897 Oldsmobile promotion.[11] "Safe, simple and durable," read another for the 1900 Porter Stanhope steamer.[12] In 1910, car companies purchased an eighth of all advertising in mass circulation magazines and by 1917 that proportion reached a quarter.[13] A third of all advertising in *Saturday Evening Post,* the best selling magazine, was purchased by automotive companies in 1923.[14]

For every new vehicle sold today $630 is spent on advertising.[15] The auto industry spends more than $18 billion in U.S. advertising a year.[16] This does not include the hundreds of millions of dollars spent to advertise motor oil and car wax as well as tires and car rentals. Add to this billions of dollars spent on car insurance, classifieds and gasoline.[17] [18]

You simply cannot get away from them. In magazines and newspapers, on TV and radio, car ads are overwhelming. Moving beyond traditional car-drenched media the *Wall Street Journal* noted that, "car companies have been among the most aggressive marketers in trying out new advertising tactics."[19] Whether you're at a party, online, at the mall, playing videogames, at the movies or even writing checks, there is an endless promotion of both brand names and automobility. Car advertisers have conquered nearly every sphere of human consciousness.

In a much-anticipated *Oprah* premier an audience of 300 overworked and underpaid elementary school teachers were surprised with shiny new Pontiac vans. The great car giveaway wasn't Oprah's idea. It was sheer brilliance on the part of Pontiac, which used the show to advertise its new vehicle to an audience of millions. The media storm from the "Oprah's Favourite Things" giveaway, lasted well beyond any 30-second spot, making front-page news across the nation. It was advertising money just cannot buy.[ii]

Not all successful "living product placements" are done to such a grand scale. Cadillac, for instance, developed a subtle "influencer" campaign where vehicles were loaned to CEOs, doctors and other distinguished individuals.[20] For its part, Honda took a more blue-collar approach to selling cars. The company's PR department dispatched a team to pump gas at service stations, passed out popcorn at movie theatres and offered aid in supermarket parking lots. These individuals all wore the company logo and could usually be found close to a car with the slogan "Helpful Honda".[21] Nissan came up with a more novel strategy. To promote the Altima, they deliberately 'lost' 20,000 key rings in bars, concert halls and sports arenas in seven major U.S. cities. Each ring had three keys and a tag that declared: "If found please do not return." The Altima "has intelligent key with push-button ignition and I no longer need these." A second tag was labeled "gas card" and offered the finder the chance to enter a competition with prizes ranging from free gas to a six-month subscription to *Vibe* magazine.[22] This innovative marketing strategy followed on the heels of a campaign that hired actors to stand up in movie theatres and talk back to Nissan Altima commercials.[23]

Toyota also uses grassroots advertising — also known as "viral marketing". Its Scion brand organized house parties to attract a young urban market.[24] Admission was free but partygoers had to RSVP at Scion.com.[iii]

The computer age is making way for increasingly sophisticated and unorthodox strategies. To create a viral buzz,

---

ii In fact, according to people who calculate these things, Oprah's giveaway generated $110 million in promotional value but only cost $8 million.

iii Associating auto brands with "cutting edge pop culture" is not a new strategy; in 1964 Ford Motor Company promoted its Mustang by sponsoring folk-music concerts. (Yes, folk used to be hip.)

Ford's marketing agency altered one of its own ads before launching it into cyberspace. This intriguing fake, or "evil twin" ad, was meant to look like an underground alteration rather than the work of an ad agency.[25]

In another online campaign, Pontiac, in conjunction with *Maxim* magazine, lured 16,000 people to their website to flirt with a model (a person, not a car) for a chance to win a new vehicle. The men with the best pickup lines were entered into a draw. The prize, of course, was a pickup truck. Everyone's a comedian.

Apparently, the mystery genre can also move sales. An intriguing online game dubbed "Who is Benjamin Stove?" unfolded over 12 weeks with twists and turns, alien appearances and conspiracy theories. Clues were revealed as the game progressed, including a crop circle painting resembling ethanol's molecular makeup. The sponsor remained hidden until late in the game, when the elabourate online mystery trail that attracted millions of hits was revealed as a pre-buzz campaign for a GM ethanol ad blitz.[26]

The automobile's new 30-second spot is definitely the videogame. To promote its 2010 GTI hatchback Volkswagen created an iPhone and iPod Touch game. The game allowed players to send messages to competitors on Twitter and post videos of the game to YouTube.[27] Volvo's S40 model enjoyed so much advertising success from Microsoft's 'Rally Sport Challenge Two' that the company used clips from the game to create a TV ad.[28] Another example is the Dodge Caliber, which made paid appearances in *Ghost Recon*, *Crackdown* and custom made four videogames for its launch.[29] [30] Nissan, too, worked with Sony/EA to release a downloadable video game to coincide with the launch of its GTR racecar.[31] Similarly, Chrysler and Activision executives collabourated on *American Wasteland*, where 3D Jeep vehicles appear an average of 23 times every 20 minutes.[32] "Gaming performs much better than TV" in turning brand awareness into an actual preference, according to Daimler Chrysler's Director of Interactive Communications, Bonita Stewart.[33] "I understand that the TV and film writers in Hollywood see it [product placement] as an invasion of their space, but with gamers, we are treated more like private equity investors."[34]

Never is the car treated more royally than in increasingly elabourate car shows. The 1905 New York Auto Show, the largest industrial exhibit of its time, paled in comparison to the extravagance of the modern auto show.[35] Every year billions of dollars are spent on these glamorous events, with the 2007 Detroit show alone costing $200 million.[36] There are all kinds of ways to burn through a pile of cash that high. While past shows were dry and technical the new carfests are fast, fun and glitzy. Chrysler raised the bar when, to the amazement of the crowd, they dropped a pickup truck from the ceiling at the Detroit auto show. In another spectacular move, they hurled a minivan over the heads of company executives to show that their cars were "a cut above the rest".[37]

Automakers often produce carnival-like atmospheres. To launch the 2011 Jetta, Volkswagen brought in grass, sand as well as a bandshell and seating to Times Square, transforming it into a beer garden for the day. Pop diva, Katy Perry, serenaded the automobile with the song, "I Kissed a Girl and I Liked It."[38] Similarly, Lexus took the Black Eyed Peas on a thirteen city 'Taste of Luxury" tour.[39]

They may tour with some big names, but the automobile is no groupie. Like Jack Bauer's big black SUV, they are A-list screen stars in their own right. Chrysler's 300c sedan, for instance, got parts in an *E.R.* season premiere, Queen Latifah's *Beauty Shop* and a Fifty Cent video.[iv][40]

Sometimes, however, the spotlight just isn't bright enough. In autumn 2006 GM pulled out of CBS' *Survivor* because

---

iv *According to the July 6, 2010 New York Times, Mini Cooper made a paid appearance in a music video for "Billionaire" by Travie McCoy.*

it wanted a more prominent role. "It no longer wants to simply give away its cars and trucks," explained *Advertising Age*. "It wants the vehicles to be central to the plot or serve as characters."[41] Most major auto companies have executives based in Los Angeles because new models increasingly rely on branded entertainment.[42] The *Washington Post* explained: "Movies and TV shows are packed with product placements, from soap to soda, but the tango between car companies and Hollywood is increasingly intimate. Most big films these days, like 'Wanted' (Chrysler) and the 'The Dark Knight' (Lamborghini) have significant car placements, and television shows like 'Weeds' (Toyota) and 'Damages' (General Motors) have built similar arrangements."[43] *Advertising Age* summarized the industry's position: "Automakers: Every car needs a movie."[44]

Released in July 2007, *Transformers* was a dream come true for GM. Bumblebee is a Chevy Camaro, Jazz a Pontiac Solstice, Ratchet a Hummer H2, Ironhide a GMC TopKick truck and Stockade a Cadillac Escalade. A number of other GM "car-actors" swept up supporting roles as well.[45] Bob Kraut, GM's director of brand marketing and advertising, was understandably pleased with the film. "The content is very good," said Kraut. "The cars are integral to the story. They generate attention. It's a story of good vs. evil. Our cars are the good guys."[46]

While bigger and better roles go to the car, the real action takes place behind the scenes. Be it a change in dialogue or camera angle, auto companies have taken an increasingly hands on approach to product placement.

Some changes are subtle. In *The Forgotten*, for instance, Volvo slipped a line into the protagonist's dialogue, identifying the brand as her car of choice.[47] Other changes are less subtle. After a scene with an Audi was cut from *Ironman* the car company's multi-million dollar marketing campaign with the movie was thrown into doubt. "The solution: run a drawn out shot of an Audi

Q7 sports utility vehicle being saved by Ironman, complete with a sustained full frontal of Audi's 4-ring logo."[48]

The depth of automakers involvement in film production can be startling. Jaguar, a Ford subsidiary, charted new territory by establishing a three-member global brand entertainment team, charged with featuring its products on TV and the big screen. "[Jaguar's] team vets scripts to make sure they are appropriate for Ford products," explained the *Financial Times*.[49] Throughout the production of *Catwoman*, the tenacious Jaguar team reviewed daily footage of the film.[50] In the brand's biggest scene, Halle Berri leaps from a building and comes face to face with Jaguar's leaping cat logo.

Car companies are aware of the silver screen's value and part with big bucks for permanent spots. Austin Martin paid $35 million to unseat BMW as the official car of *James Bond*.[51] In a massive agreement with Universal Studios and NBC, Volkswagen spent an estimated $200 million to see its products in Universal Films and on NBC television.[52]

Although increasingly prominent, automobile product placements have been in film and television for most of the last century. In 1929, the *New York Times* explained that, "automobile manufacturers graciously offer the free use of high priced cars to [movie] studios."[53] A decade later a study of a hundred films from 10 major studios, recorded 41 Ford appearances, 26 Buick appearances and 19 appearances for Packard.[v][54]

Today's car ads manipulate nearly every value, emotion and human desire. Be it safety, speed, security, family values, rebellion, the status quo, environmentalism, serenity or the defiance of nature. There is no place the industry won't go.

"My Dream? To go straight to the top."

---

v *According to Product Placement in Hollywood Films, the study also found that Cadillac made 14 appearances; Chevrolet, 10; Rolls Royce, 5; Cord, 4; Plymouth and Chrysler had 3.*

"My dream is to conquer ignorance."

"My dream: to get to the corner office."

"To ditch the corner office."

"My dream is to erase illiteracy."

"My dream is to rocket to No. 1."

"My dream is to slay dragons."

"My dream is to increase laughter output by 30 percent."

"It takes determination."

"Commitment."

"Passion."

"Hard work."

"Fearlessness"

"An open mind."

"Courage."

"It takes guts to make a dream come true."

Whoever you are, whatever you want, a Lincoln will make your dreams come true.[55]

22. Meet the press

From New York City to Tallahassee, El Paso to Seattle, an omnipresent media kept us company. From the edge of the Atlantic to the Pacific coast, it was the same old story. Homogenous television news was devoted to terror, crime and natural disasters. Except for a few details even local newspapers had a stale sameness about them. When ownership of TV, radio, magazines and local papers is concentrated in the office towers of a handful of mega-corporations dependent on advertising dollars, why should we expect variety?

Automobile manufacturers are the biggest advertisers, yet cars are an unusual product category because most consumer information does not come from standard paid advertising. With soft drinks, for instance, 90-95 percent of the information consumers gather is ad generated. (Few people past the age of 10 research the latest pop — or "soda" as it's called in Uganda and the USA.) For cars, on the other hand, only a fifth of consumer information is acquired through formal advertising.[1] The rest is a patchwork of knowledge gathered from auto magazines, consumer reports, movies, TV, radio, newspapers, cyberspace and simple word of mouth.[2] The nature of this relationship to consumers requires auto companies to be endlessly innovative. And, in turn, they have penetrated nearly every known form of communication.

Ever read a book about cars? It was probably financed by the industry. "From Mercedes Benz's new audio book sales pitches to Toyota's comic books and Volvo's author readings it's clear 'carlit' is a trend with horsepower," noted a 2005 newspaper.[3] But 'carlit' is yesterday's news. Henry Ford understood that investments had to be made in literary and cultural currency. After commissioning the Henry Ford Museum in Dearborn, Ford hired

Samuel Crowther to ghost write his bestselling autobiography, *My Life and Work* in 1922.[4] This was followed a few years later with *Today and Tomorrow and My Philosophy of Industry*. A group of Ford-funded journalists later elevated pro-automobile ideology in *Freedom of the American Road*.[5] *From Street Car to Superhighway* was a more sophisticated Ford-funded tome, whitewashing automotive history with statements like: "In marked contrast to trolley industry representatives, automobile executives gave little evidence of concern over competition from mass transit."[6] Glazing over the automobile's role in the downfall of the trolley, *From Street Car to Superhighway* fails to mention the industry's purchase and subsequent destruction of urban rail systems across the USA.[i]

Automakers also funded architects and urban planners. Car companies supported the early designs of influential French architect and urban planner Le Corbusier, who once wrote: "The city of today is dying because it is not constructed geometrically, the needs of traffic also demanded total demolition ... This means that wide avenues must be driven through the centre of our towns."[7] [8] For their part, GM awarded infamous New York City "master builder" Robert Moses $25,000 (about $165,000 in today's money) for an essay on highway planning.[9]

As the nation crossed over into the golden era of film, the auto industry began producing promotional flicks masquerading as entertainment. Ford created a motion picture department in 1914.[10] In 1921, Maxwell Motor Corporation, an early U.S. automaker, produced an action film where a young woman is kidnapped and transported to a remote mountain location. The bad guys ride in on horseback and the captive is taken to a hideout with no road nearby. Yet the hero crosses the rugged landscape in a Maxwell and saves the day.[11] By the end of WWII, General Motors alone

---

i *According to Asphalt Nation, prominent automobile historian, John B. Ray, also received financial support from car manufacturers.*

had produced over 50 films, reaching audiences far and wide.[12] During the politically turbulent Depression, GM's *From Dawn to Sunset* portrayed positive relations between the company, its workers and the community.[13] Other films emerging from the auto industry had more specific aims. A 1934 Ford film, for instance, attacked President Franklin D Roosevelt's new inheritance tax, which threatened the family-owned company's ability to maintain control upon Henry Ford's death.[14] Into the 1950s GM and Ford continued to produce films including *Anatomy of a Road* and *Give Yourself the Green Light*.[15]

Suddenly everybody was a filmmaker. Even tire makers contributed with gems such as *Highway Patrol*, produced by BF Goodrich in 1938.[16] Sticking to the same theme, they later produced *Love, Honor and Obey (the Law)*, a film about the need for drivers to follow traffic rules.[17] Calling for order on the road, BF Goodrich promoted a healthy environment for cars and their tires.

Members of the auto industrial complex continue to produce films. In November 2010 the *New York Times* reported: "BP is commissioning a feature length film about the deep water horizon oil spill."[18] This was a follow up to the 12-minute BP financed film on the recovery of the tourism economy in Florida, Louisiana and Alabama after the disastrous spill. Dubbed a "mini-documentary" by the oil company, *A Community Fights Back* focuses on BP's payments to the states and local officials complaints about negative media coverage.[19]

Some members of the auto industry have found that movies, books and advertising are not enough. For complete mass-market saturation, it doesn't hurt to own your own media. This was Henry Ford's logic in 1915 when he used his wealth to turn the *Dearborn Independent* into a widely circulated paper and pulpit from which to propagate his ideas.[ii] More recently, Mercedes Benz

---

ii *This included the English publication of the anti-Semitic Protocols of the Elders of Zion.*

launched a newsstand magazine in a dozen languages featuring articles subtly designed to boost car sales.[20] BMW has a similar 108-page customer magazine with a worldwide circulation of 3.2 million.[21]

The three-dimensional medium of television is another popular option. BMW, for instance, showcases its wares on a TV channel, which it broadcasts 24/7. For its part, GM once owned the three largest U.S. satellite-broadcasting companies.[22]

Even industry offshoots chant the mantra of direct access to the masses. Goodyear, for instance, branched out from their plant paper, *Tire Tracks*, to broadcast over the airwaves in regions where they manufacture.[23]

It is also worth noting that when tuning into broadcasts from the Radio Corporation of America, we listen courtesy of the same company that brought us Hertz auto rental and Hertz parking lots.[24]

At the other end of the automotive industrial complex, big oil has had its hand in numerous media ventures. In 1980, Getty Oil helped establish the Premiere network.[25] Similarly, a subsidiary of Exxon-Mobil printed Bantam and Random House books as well as *Playboy* and *National Geographic*.[26]

But does the auto industry have to own media to "own" the media? If auto executives sit on the governing boards of media companies and media reps sit on the governing boards of auto companies, where is the line between the news and the carmaker? Ford, for instance, has had numerous directors on the boards of the *New York Times*, *Washington Post* and *Los Angeles Times* to name a few.[27] During the same period Ford held a seat on the *LA Times*, the chairman of Times Mirror Company — owner of the *LA Times* and other media — sat on Ford's board.[28]

The fruits of this industry cross-fertilization were on display during a contentious period of interstate construction in the 1960s. Discussing the media's stance and their ties to the auto sector, author Helen Leavitt writes: "In light of the attitude the newspapers have taken on the freeway issue it is interesting to note that *Washington Star* vice president, John W. Thompson, Jr. and *Washington Post* board vice chairman, John W. Sweeterman and vice president Gerald W. Siegel are members of the [pro-highway] Federal City Council and weekly receive their dose of freeway promotion to crank into their editorials."[29]

The auto industry's reach into the newsroom extends beyond the close relationship between executives and the auto lobby. "The public relations departments of the automakers are immense, dwarfing those of federal agencies in Washington," writes Keith Bradford.[30] To get a sense of scale, Bradford contrasts GM's public relations department to the team that assisted George W. Bush in the 2000 presidential election. Helped by a PR team of four spokespeople, each with a dozen assistants, Bush's media squad was a fraction of GM's 150 global press officers, each with numerous assistants.[31] Apparently the business of the U.S. presidency is less important than the business of running the world's top automaker.

PR departments work to build a favourable corporate image and garner positive attention for the automotive sector. They also ward off unflattering stories. In a particularly overt example Toyota responded to its early 2010 recall crisis by creating a social media response room. It was staffed with six to eight people monitoring online conversation and responding at all times. The automakers staff answered consumers on the company's four Facebook pages; created a Twitter chat with Toyota Motor Sales USA President and Chief Operating Officer and launched "Toyota conversations" on Digg and Tweetmeme "to aggregate online chatter and allow Toyota to respond directly."[32]

Usually PR personnel communicate with the newsroom through press releases and personal contacts. Automotive PR departments also coach company executives on messaging.

Auto executives almost never speak "extemporaneously" writes a former Ford PR employee in *News and the Culture of Lying*: "Encounters with the press were guided by what we called Q and A, for Question and Answer. These were multi-paged catalogues of possible questions followed by suggested responses, often a paragraph or two in length. A journalist might think he was getting spontaneous answers to questions, but almost always the source was reading from or referring to the Q and A's."[33]

Q and A's are good preparation. So is cash in hand to soften up journalists. A carrot held out by the auto industry is the enticing possibility of future employment. Automotive PR departments are in the habit of hiring journalists from a healthy cross-section of the popular press. Keith Bradford, former *New York Times* Detroit correspondent, recalls how week after week, he watched his colleagues move from covering the automotive industry to working in its PR departments. "Ford hired reporters, covering it for the *Wall Street Journal*, *Fortune* and *Reuters*," wrote Bradford, describing the assimilation of journalists during a short period in 2000.[34] Bradford describes the awkwardness of critically interviewing recent colleagues. He also felt that critical reporting among his peers was dampened by the possibility of future employment in the well paying automotive sector.

Sometimes the payoff is more direct.[iii] In 2006, for instance, a GM PR firm "offered money to former Labor Secretary, Robert B. Reich in exchange for public comments supporting the automakers employee buyout program."[35] Needless to say, GM was quick to disassociate itself from the actions of its PR firm when this act came to light.

Yet no one in the auto industry denies the practice of whisking journalists to exotic locales to review new models. To unveil the 2006 Explorer, for instance, Ford took a hundred

iii According to the May 10, 2010 Wall Street Journal, GM and others pay to promote vehicles as Consumer Digest "best buys."

journalists to a resort on Lake Placid.[36] As with many trips of this nature, the digs were luxurious. "In June and early July [2008], Bentley Motors flew 150 journalists from around the world to Boston to drive its new Continental Flying Spur sedan and admire the luxury carmaker's new North American head office. The visitors stayed at the Boston Harbor Hotel, which describes itself as a 'supreme blend of style, setting and service on the waterfront'."[37]

On an all-expenses-paid Arctic expedition to test-drive the new Land Rover, a writer for *Driven* magazine defended his journalistic integrity: "My personal deal with this sort of thing is that I'm willing to sell my attention, but not my opinion. The company went to a lot of trouble to get me there and show me such a good time — even bought me new underwear. It would seem ungrateful to slam the car after all that, don't you think? Luckily there's no reason to."[iv][v]

Currying favour with reviewers is a century-old automotive practice that began when automaker Colonel Albert Pope introduced a new model to the public through a press review in 1897.[38] Industry's relationship with the popular press has always been multilayered. Beyond parading new models for journalists, the automotive sector has made efforts to shape coverage of the car. Over a hundred years ago, *Automobile*, a leading trade journal of the day, called for "a campaign of education among the newspapermen."[39] Appealing to auto clubs, they suggested providing car demonstrations to the press to counter early hostility towards the automobile. They also urged, "furnishing a good news 'copy' to the papers."[40] To counter bad press about the growing number of pedestrian deaths in the 1920s, the National Automobile

iv *According to the Nov. 16, 2007 Los Angeles Times, it's not only automakers. For the 2007 Chicago Auto Show Bridgestone flew more than 100 journalists all expenses paid.*

v *According to the Nov. 15 2010 Wall Street Journal, carmakers also woo social media operators. Ford selected 100 people with large followings on sites such as Twitter to test drive its 2012 Focus.*

Chamber of Commerce (NACC) launched a central accident news service. The goal was to "make sure that the reporter gets and records the essential facts."[41] The NACC furnished newspapers with statistics that purported to show that most crashes were the fault of pedestrians, not drivers. According to Bruce Cobb, magistrate of New York City's Traffic Court, the NACC were successful in shifting media coverage of accidents.[42]

By 1902, nearly every paper of repute had an automobile section.[43] The success of the auto industry's media strategy was praised in *Automobile*: "The unprecedented and well nigh incredible rapidity with which the automobile industry has developed … is largely due to the fact that every detail of the subject has been popularized by the technical and daily press."[44]

In *America Adopts the Automobile*, leading auto historian James J. Fink discusses the media savvy of early automobilists: "A large proportion of the [early] information on the automobile that appeared in newspapers and popular magazines was either written or influenced by ardent automobilists. It is unquestionable that this in no small part accounted for the overwhelmingly favourable image of the motor vehicle in the popular press of the day."[45]

In addition to its many carrots, the auto industry also carries a big stick.

Revealing the most powerful driving force behind the media's allegiance to the automobile, the front page of a March 2006 *Advertising Age* screamed: "AUTO-AD SLUMP CRUSHES MAGS".[46] Not for nothing has it been said that Sunday papers are car advertisements surrounded by casual journalism.[vi] By 1917

---

vi On May 14 2007 Montreal daily La Presse devoted 43 pages entirely to cars: a twenty six page auto section; an eight page Mercedes broad sheet pullout; an eight page Mazda supplement in tabloid format. There were also a full page car ad and a Porsche ad taking up a tenth of a page (in an eight page sports section). In addition to the 43 pages entirely devoted to cars, the front page of the business section had a seventh of a page devoted to a Hyundai dealership ad. Add to this the eight page Actuel section where nearly half a page was dedicated to auto

auto companies already bankrolled a fourth of all advertising in mass-produced U.S. magazines.[47] Today as much as one-in-seven advertising dollars comes from the auto industry.[48]

The auto industrial complex is a powerhouse of colossal proportions in their dealings with the media. "Top auto executives hold frequent, off-the-record meetings with the nation's leading publishers and editors, enjoying a level of access that most politicians can only dream of."[49]

Surveying the mediascape, it is no surprise that newspapers once gave as much attention to a few dozen climate-change skeptics as they did to thousands of independent researchers.[50] The auto lobby's VIP access to the newsroom has been around a lot longer than knowledge of global warming. Roy Chapin, founder and chairman of the Hudson Motor Company, said that in 1910 "the *Chicago Tribune* would not mention the name of any motor car in its columns." As a result, Chapin noted, "the dealers in Chicago simultaneously withdrew their advertising from the Chicago Tribune. In a mighty short space of time that paper woke up and promised to do almost anything if they could get the advertising, and since that time they have been very decent in their attitude."[51]

In the early 1970s, controversy erupted as Congress deliberated on new safety standards. During this debate the *New York Times* ran stories that were, in the words of a former staff member, "more or less put together by the advertisers."[52] *New York Times* publisher Arthur Ochs Sulzberger admitted that if the auto industry's position on safety and auto pollution were not presented, it "would affect the advertising."[53] As the source of nearly a fifth

classifieds. In the sixteen page front section, a fifth of page two was an Accura ad; an eighth of a page five was another Acccura ad; a third of a page nine was a Ford ad; a sixth of page ten was a Lexus ad; more than half of page eleven was a Honda dealership ad; and nearly half of page twelve was a Chevrolet ad. Finally, three quarters of page sixteen was devoted to Subaru.

of newspaper ad revenue, the automakers called in favours to successfully push back against seatbelt and air bag laws.[54]

It's not just targeted political fights where the auto industry cashes in. They have a preferred media climate. "Taming the mediascape for an environment conducive to profit," writes Naomi Klein in *No Logo*, "the auto industry are averse to controversy of any kind. Take Chrysler for instance; up until 1997, when Chrysler placed an ad it demanded that it be 'alerted in advance of any and all editorial content that encompasses sexual, political, social issues or any editorial that might be construed as provocative or offensive."[55] Chrysler also requested advanced notice of negative car editorials.[56]

Similarly, in 2005, British Petroleum requested, "that publishers inform it in advance of any text or pictures that cover BP or even the wider energy industry."[vii] [57] Many monthly magazines admit to giving automakers a heads-up (and the opportunity to pull ads) if an unfavourable article is forthcoming.[58]

So, what happens when the automotive industry is not portrayed in all its shining glory? The *LA Times* knows. After printing a story in April 2005 calling for the dismissal of GM's CEO, Rick Wagoner, the auto company immediately yanked all advertising from the paper. Reflecting on this incident, The *New York Times* wrote that the auto industry "has been embroiled perhaps more than any other in ad controversies."[59] They cited three recent cases where advertising was pulled due to unpopular editorial decisions: GM pulled its ads from all Ziff-Davis magazines after *Car and Driver* printed an unflattering review of the Opel-Kadett model — running a photo of the car in a junkyard; auto dealers organized a four-month boycott after the *San Jose Mercury News* published, *A Car Buyer's Guide to Sanity*, which offered negotiating tips to counter aggressive sales tactics; Chrysler withdrew its ads from *Car and Driver* after it published a photo essay displaying the

vii According to Ad Week, in 2005, BP spent $145 million in U.S. advertising.

carnage when a Dodge hit a cow at 60 miles per hour during a test drive in Mexico.[60] Even *Sierra* magazine suffered the wrath of the auto industry in the mid 1990s. (Why an environmental magazine took ads from a car company is another question altogether.) After failing to block a *Sierra* article criticizing the fuel economy of SUVs, automakers withdrew all SUV ads — seven percent of the magazine's gross revenue.[61] This prompted the head of Sierra's advertisement department to quit in disgust.[viii]

The automotive industrial complex's approach to the media is summed up by GM's executive director of advertising and media operations, Betsy Lazar, who told the Wall Street Journal: "It's clear to us that our ads are less effective in a negative editorial environment. It is as simple as that. We actually have research in the auto magazine category that supports that notion. In some categories, in broadcast news, for example, it is the norm to be notified of a breaking negative story. If time permits, we will be notified by the network 'there is a negative story tonight. Would you like to move your ads out?' And we will say, 'Absolutely.'"[62]

---

viii *Early on SUVs were promoted as a way to return to the countryside, hence the association with Sierra.*

23. Driver's Ed.

For anyone interested in the industry's influence over education, take notes. You won't learn this in class.

Children may be forbidden to drive but the automobile industry has not shied away from the classroom. In schools across the U.S. much time and effort has been devoted to extolling the benefits of the personal automobile yet little is taught of its drawbacks. Auto companies have long shown an interest in young minds. They worked hard to convince children that streets were for cars, not for playing. The image-conscious American Automobile Association responded to the growing number of kids hurt and killed by automobiles with "a major, semi-centralized national drive for safety education. Teachers could receive entire safety curricula drafted at the AAA's Washington headquarters. By the end of the 1928-29 school year, the AAA was supplying 50,000 teachers with monthly instructional materials, thereby reaching two million school children."[1]

Three quarters of a century ago the Highway Education Board (HEB) began promoting the road and automobile. Cloaked as a public department, but funded by the auto industry, the HEB took their show on the road. Moving from class to class, they spoke to half a million children.[2] The HEB drew on a diversity of tactics. They made films and pamphlets on the virtues of good roads and their power to advance the standard of living across the country.[3] The HEB did not give dry lecturers. They encouraged participation. Five million children (and adults) took part in essay contests with topics like "how good roads help the religious life of my community."[4] Winners secured a college education courtesy of a Harvey Firestone funded scholarship.[5] Teachers were targeted as well. Tens of thousands participated in HEB-sponsored road safety lesson competitions with at least one winner feted at the White House.[6]

Today's automotive industrial complex has different priorities, but the tactics remain the same. No longer under the guise of the HEB, carmakers still provide schools with curriculum and teaching materials. Colorful and appealing, these "free" resources carry company logos. Through "imprint conditioning" some believe these materials create fuzzy feelings of brand loyalty that can last a lifetime.[7]

During the late 1990s, GM mailed a videocassette to every public and private parochial elementary school in the country. The film was entitled *I Need the Earth and the Earth Needs Me*. Was it a sea change in the industry's environmental practices? Don't hold your breath. In a climate of rising environmental concern, especially among the young, automakers skillfully ducked blame. "Against a backdrop of happy children swimming in sparkling waters and running in picturesque landscapes", writes David C. Korten, "the GM video promotes such activities as planting trees and recycling. There is no mention of mass transit or the need to redesign cities to reduce transportation needs. GM recommends forming car pools and recycling used motor oil."[8]

In another wing of the auto industrial complex, Exxon and Shell are major sponsors of school science videos.[9] These films make little mention of problems associated with oil spills. According to the Consumer's Union, these videos imply "that fossil fuels pose few environmental problems and that alternative energy is costly and unattainable."[10]

Towards the end of 2006 the National Science Teachers Association (NSTA) rejected 50,000 free copies of Al Gore's Oscar winning, *An Inconvenient Truth*. Representing 53,000 science teachers, the NSTA sparked a firestorm of controversy after stating the DVDs would lead to an "unnecessary risk upon the [NSTA] capital campaign, especially [among] certain targeted supporters."[11] The NSTA did not fear the same "risk" in 2001 when they distributed 20,000 copies of Conoco-Phillip's, *A Search for Solutions*.[12] The NSTA, a regular on the corporate honor roll, received $6 million in funding from Exxon Mobil from 1996 to 2006.[13] "NSTA is such a natural partner for us," explained Edward Ahnert, Exxon-Mobil foundation president. "No other organization has the ability to reach thousands of teachers who share Exxon Mobil's commitment to improving science education." [14] Exxon-Mobil pumped another $125 million into school programs through other channels.[15]

The automobile industry has long had other uses for the school system. Early automobilists were confronted by the problem of poor drivers and a dire lack of repairmen. The YMCA was convinced by the Massachusetts Auto Club (in tandem with White Pope-Waverly and Crest automobile companies) that this training would benefit the community. In 1903 Boston came to house the first YMCA school for chauffeurs and auto mechanics.[16] Similar relationships began developing across the country. Auto clubs provided the impetus and financing; auto manufacturers donated cars; and the YMCA gave their space and organizational capacity. It was a tripartite alliance. The schools spread rapidly and by mid-1905 more than 2000 students were enrolled in YMCA auto programs.[17] A century later, YMCAs' continue to provide auto mechanics training.

The Henry Ford Trade School was founded in 1916. Similar to the YMCA, it was promoted as a charity where poor boys could learn a trade. But the school immediately morphed into a training ground for future Ford workers.[18] The YMCA auto mechanics program, the Henry Ford Trade School and numerous other auto industry sponsored initiatives are the antecedents of today's high school auto-mechanics.

Auto interests also promoted high school driving classes. From the mid 1930s to the mid-60s the Automotive

Safety Foundation, an industry front group, provided grants to state agencies to create courses for high school students.[19] At the same time, manufacturers made special provisions for dealers to donate or loan cars to schools.[20] Auto manufacturers and auto clubs financed and promoted the educational programs necessary to sustain automobility.

...

I was only in Boston for a day. The first attractions I sought out were its famous universities. I wondered whether I'd feel the intelligence radiating from the students at Harvard or maybe bump into Noam Chomsky near MIT. Descending into the subway, I resurfaced in the town of Cambridge. I wandered Harvard's well-tended gardens and sat in on a random literature class. Like dozens of nationally recognized post-secondary institutions, Harvard is prized for its contributions to its state and community.

But it's not only the public that values universities. Picking up where they left off in high school, the automotive industrial complex has long enjoyed influence at the university level. Funding competitions and programs that funnel students towards the automotive sector, the industry has shaped universities. Accessing subsidized university infrastructure and benefiting from joint research initiatives, the industry feeds off the nation's brain.

In 2006, ten University of Akron students and one faculty member received $6,500 from GM to travel to the Challenge X competition at GM's Desert Proving Grounds facility in Arizona. GM engineer, Scott Otterson, explained: "The Challenge X competition brings students and faculty into the real world of vehicle development and helps prepare a future generation of engineers so that they are better equipped to make a faster contribution to the engineering profession and the automotive industry."[21] Seventeen universities competed in the Challenge X program modeled after GM's Global Vehicle Development Process.[22]

For decades the auto industrial complex has financed

academic competitions, leading to a variety of innovations. In 1935, the head of the local chamber of commerce transportation committee asked the Department of Engineering and Management at the Oklahoma Agricultural and Mechanical College (now Oklahoma State University) to create a device to pay for parking. This led to a competition amongst students that produced the earliest design for a coin-operated parking meter.[23] A decade and a half later, Ford provided financing for MIT students to design "a sliding kitchen cabinet for station wagons" and "a lightweight tent made of aluminum and Orlon."[24] Out of these designs, the motor home was born.

The auto industrial complex also financed programs to create a workforce. In Montreal, for instance, McGill University now celebrates "PetroCanada Day." After donating a million dollars to the university, PetroCanada spokesperson Andrew Pelletier explained: "We are giving to McGill to train students in certain areas so they will come back and work with us."[25] Pelletier further explained that the introduction of "PetroCanada Day" to the faculty of engineering would, "expose our students to the range of careers offered at Petro-Canada." The faculty's dean, Christophe Pierre, was quick to echo the sentiment: "It is thus crucial for companies such as Petro-Canada to link with universities such as McGill and have access to our engineering students, who are among the very best in the nation."[i][26]

i Government sometimes spearheaded matchmaking between the auto industrial complex and universities. Recognizing the limitations of the country's rubber reserves (with Asian trade routes disrupted due to World War II), Washington developed The American Synthetic Rubber Research Program. Between 1942 and 1956, fifty-six million dollars in government money was pumped into the program, which brought together Cornell, the University of Chicago, the University of Minnesota in Minneapolis and the University of Illinois at Urbana, alongside Goodyear, Firestone, BF Goodrich and U.S. rubber. The program brought together four representatives "from each company laboratory and three from each university laboratory." While the American Synthetic Rubber Research Program exemplifies governmental efforts to marry academia and the auto industrial

The flow of corporate dollars to universities distorts the progress made by academia. A good example is petroleum geology, "the science of finding and measuring oil" which according to *Crude* author Sonia Shah, "shot at least twenty or thirty years ahead of the rest of geology."[27]Another example of this corporate influence is illustrated by British Petroleum's collaboration with the University of California Berkley. In addition to $40 million in state funding, BP contributed a staggering $500 million for Berkley to establish the world's first bio-fuels research centre.[28] With the launch of the Energy Biosciences Institute, Berkeley effectively created a new discipline.[ii] [29] A March 2007 *LA Times* commentary explained: "With the Energy Biosciences Institute, BP would exert influence over an entire academic research centre (spanning 25 labs at its three public partners), bankrolling and setting the agenda for projects that cut across many departments. What's more, BP would set up shop on campus: 50 scientists employed by the company would work on joint projects with academic scientists at Berkley and the University of Illinois."[30] Opponents of the 10-year partnership have dubbed the project "UCBP". For them the deal bolstered BP's image, allowed the corporation to evade city zoning laws and gave it exclusive control over some of the institute's expected findings.[31] Additionally, under the agreement UC Berkley's resources rest heavily on bio-fuel research at the expense of working towards non-automotive modes of transportation.

---

complex, a more recent example is the Partnership for a New Generation of Vehicles, which strived towards the development of extremely fuel-efficient (up to 80 mpg) vehicles. Established in 1993, the program did little to improve gas mileage despite more than a billion dollars in government money. Created by the automotive industry, government and academic partners, Challenge X pushes university-level engineering students to decrease total cycle emissions and energy consumption in a crossover vehicle, while maintaining or exceeding vehicle utility and performance.

ii Ironically, the collaboration initially focused on developing techniques to access difficult-to-find oil.

Auto industry dollars have ushered in a legion of auto-centric programs. Ford gave the University of Michigan ten million dollars to establish a Highway Safety Research Institute.[32] Similarly, General Motors gave Hamilton, Ontario's McMaster University $60 million to establish the Centres for Engineering Design and Corrosion Engineering Research.[33] Through the Canadian Automotive Innovation Network GM invested in McGill and the University of British Columbia. And as part of its $2.5 billion Beacon Project GM gave money to at least eight universities in 2005, creating research chairs at a number of these institutions in order to train automotive engineers.[34] Seemingly tireless, GM also tried to initiate Canada's first accredited degrees in auto engineering and design.[35]

Referred to as "BMW's Custom-Made University" by the *New York Times*, Clemson provides one of the most comprehensive examples of the auto industry's use of a university. The details of the relationship between the university and automaker only emerged due to the public scrutiny of a lawsuit. In one piece of court evidence the Clemson endowment's chief financial officer penned a handwritten letter to BMW officials stating, "BMW is going to drive the entire campus."[36] Clemson massively expanded its automotive focus by opening an International Centre for Automotive Research. "A network council composed of BMW managers meets monthly to advise Clemson on the curriculum," reported the *New York Times*. Not only did BMW have a hand in developing the curriculum, they also drew up a profile of ideal students for the graduate program (and BMW "review[ed] student papers to ensure that proprietary information is not submitted for publication.")[37] Faculty were handpicked as well, with candidates for two BMW-endowed professorships required to sit through interviews with representatives from the vehicle manufacturer. (Michelin Tires and Timken Ball Bearing — two other members of the automotive industrial complex — have also provided financing for professorships at the new graduate school.) A BMW representative also sits on the advisory board of the automotive school.[38] Today, Clemson offers the world's first doctoral degree in automotive engineering. Graduate students and their professors work side-by-side with BMW engineers, mainly on BMW-related projects. Program-trained engineers with the skills to design, build and market hi-tech vehicles are expected to work for BMW after graduating.

While BMW contributed an initial $10 million to the International Centre for Automotive Research most of the money for the Centre, which could reach $1.5 billion, comes from the state of South Carolina. BMW is one of many automobile manufacturers reaping the rewards of publicly funded education. One reason auto manufacturers develop relationships with universities is to tap into (usually publicly funded) infrastructure and trained researchers.

Akin to BMW's role in establishing the first-ever doctoral degree in automotive engineering, Studebaker financed Harvard's pioneering Albert Russell Erskine Bureau of Street Traffic Research in 1926.[39] In subsequent years similar programs spread to universities across the USA. (The Clemson model is expected to spur a similar boom with doctorates in automotive engineering).[40] [41] Studebaker initially financed two annual $1,000 scholarships, following that with an annual $10,000 grant to the Bureau of Street Traffic Research.[42] As Studebaker began to struggle financially the Automobile Manufacturers Association took charge of raising money for the Erskine Bureau and student stipends.[43] In 1936, the Automobile Manufacturers Association gave the Bureau an extra $54,000 grant.[44] The Bureau was run by Miller McClintock who soon became "the No.1 U.S. authority on traffic control."[45] Dependent on automobile industry funds, McClintock framed his job as helping cities "adjust their physical layout ... to the requirements of an automobile age."[46] Peter D. Norton explains: "In Miller McClintock, the auto industry had, by

1927, an articulate and credible spokesman, the first traffic expert with a doctorate in his field. He was insulated from any obvious affiliation with industry by a Harvard byline. And at the industry's expense, he was turning out more such experts each year."[47]

The same year that Studebaker established the Erskine Bureau of Street Traffic Research GM took over the Flint Institute of Technology, renaming it the General Motors Institution (in 1998 the privately accredited university was renamed Kettering University after GM's former head of research). Through GMI the automaker influenced the budding fields of urban planning and traffic engineering. Many early traffic engineers studied at GMI.[48] Guy Span describes the role GMI-trained engineers played in the trolley's demise: "City planning was a relatively new field in the 1930s and few accredited institutions taught the subject. However, one such accredited institution did and it was GMI. ... And you can imagine what the fledgling city planners learned: traffic engineering (buses are good; railways are bad). Each year a new crop was turned loose on an unsuspecting country."[49]

From traffic engineering to highway aesthetics and the indispensable billboard, the auto industrial complex has ensured its interests are well represented at the university level. "In 1924," writes Catherine Gudis, "the OAAA [Outdoor Association of American Advertisers] decided it needed a national research clearinghouse with the expertise and legitimacy of an academic affiliation and established the Barney Link Poster Advertising Fellowship at the University of Wisconsin."[50] The fellowship sponsored research on landscaping, poster readership and methods to determine traffic. At Notre Dame, the OAAA established an outdoor advertising library that focused on traffic and marketing. They also established the first business course in outdoor advertising. "Later," writes Gudis, "such courses [traffic and marketing] became a part of the curriculum of engineering, planning, and business schools nationwide."[51]

Be it the Henry Ford College, Henry Ford Nursing School, MIT's Sloan Automotive Laboratory or the Alfred P. Sloan School of Management, many institutions of higher learning now bear the names of auto industry giants. More valuable than any name, numerous representatives of the automotive industrial complex have sat on the board of governors of these institutions, giving them the power to elect a university's leadership and ultimate control over its direction. The CEO of Exxon sat on Harvard's board while GM's former head, Roger Smith, sat on the Boston University board. Rick Wagoner, another former head of GM, was chairman of the board of visitors for Duke's business school and several GM executives were executives of the National Academy of Engineering. Conversely, Erskine Boyce Bowles, president of the University of North Carolina, sat on GM's board of directors.

The auto industrial complex is attracted to universities because of their standing as institutions for the public good and their status as "reliable" sources of independent knowledge. While universities are understood to be at arms length, this independence is increasingly compromised by a plethora of relationships to the auto industrial complex.

24. Senator, I'd like to take you for a ride

While advertising, education programs and economic self-interest can be seen as indirect means of influencing the political process, sometimes *Homo Autmotivis* is less subtle. For example, the auto industry spends as much as a hundred million dollars a year directly influencing Washington decision-makers.[1] Asphalt, tire, insurance, trucking and other auto associates also spend briskly. The oil and gas industry has more than 600 registered lobbyists including 18 former members of congress and dozens of former presidential appointees.[2] In July 2010 the *Washington Post* noted, "Three out of every four lobbyists who represent oil and gas companies previously worked in the federal government, a proportion that far exceeds the usual revolving door standards on capital hill."[3] The oil industry spent $72.5 million lobbying Congress in 2006 alone.[4]

Let's just say that this money is not used to promote more efficient vehicles or safer highways. Car lobbyists almost always oppose environmental and safety initiatives, from seatbelts and airbags to catalytic converters and improved fuel efficiency standards.

As far back as 1925, oil and auto industry representatives packed a committee organized by the Surgeon-General concerning the health effects of leaded gas.[5] They successfully argued that lead was harmless despite the fact that companies such as Standard Oil of New Jersey knew leaded gasoline was a health threat. Over the next 60 years lead levels increased a hundred-fold until it was finally banned in 1986.[6][7]

···

Over the past century automotive interests have coordinated their lobbying efforts through a variety of associations. In the early 1900s the Automobile Board of Trade arose.[8] It was supplanted a decade later by the National Automobile Chamber of Commerce. Automobile manufacturers began supporting the American Roadbuilders Association in 1903.[9]

At the start of the Depression, some states reallocated gas tax money away from roadways and towards other needs. In response, "General Motors banded two thousand groups [truckers, road builders, teamsters, oil companies etc.] into the National Highway Users Conference (NHUC) to lobby against the practice."[10] When the Chicago Transit Authority proposed using $30 million in state fuel tax to finance improvements to mass transit, the NHUC sent in two full-time workers to coordinate opposition to the measure. In concert with the Chicago Motor Club and Illinois Highway Users Conference, the NHUC defeated the proposal.[11]

Beginning in the late 1930s, the NHUC handed out 19 million copies of Emily Post's book *Motor Manners* and held film screenings celebrating truckers and extolling the joys of driving to nearly 50 million people.[12] In 1951, the NHUC launched Project Adequate Roads, a million dollar initiative that called for a national highway system.[13] Project Adequate Roads helped win the massive Interstate Highway System.

Another group that lobbied for the Interstate was a secret society known simply as the "Road Gang". Beginning in 1942 this group of men met every Thursday in a private Washington, DC, restaurant. The Road Gang included automobile and truck manufacturers as well as tire makers, gas and oil representatives, highway engineers, top highway bureaucrats, paving contractors, trade association executives and public relations specialists.[14][15] No longer a secret society, the group's website explains, "the Road Gang serves the dual purpose of promoting fellowship and providing for the interchange of ideas among 'Washington's Transportation Fraternity.'"[16]

...

The auto industrial complex defends its interests through close relations with a variety of business lobby groups. GM, Ford and Chrysler magnify their lobbying clout with seats on the Business Roundtable and the National Association of Manufacturers (NAM). In the mid-1990s the NAM spearheaded a battle against legislation to curb deaths from small particle pollution. With money from GM, Ford, Chrysler, Mobil and other businesses, NAM financed the Air Quality Standards Coalition (AQSC), which cast doubt on the science of small particles and their deadly effects on human beings (now understood to kill tens of thousands annually).[17] The AQSC spent several million dollars lobbying decision-makers to curb legislation against small particles.[18]

The auto industrial complex's political clout is expanded through their interlocking directorates. Ford executives sit on the boards of many other companies and so do executives from GM and Chrysler.

In *Urban Elites and Mass Transit*, J. Allen Whitt describes how California's Proposition 18, an initiative to divert a small portion of the state gas tax to public transit, was defeated partly because of the oil companies ties to the State's banks.[19] When Proposition 18 failed in 1970, a Standard Oil of California representative sat on the Board of Directors of Crocker-Citizens and a Getty Oil executive sat on the Bank of America board.[i] [20] These were but two of many such strategic interlocking relationships that the auto industry and its associates enjoyed.

---

i In 2006, oil companies spent an astonishing $100 million to defeat California's proposition 87, which would have taxed oil companies between 1.5% and 6%, depending on the price of oil, and used the money for research into alternative energies.

The structure of the auto industry lends itself to political influence. Communities welcome auto plants, which generate spin-off industries and usually employ many well-paid workers. Located in numerous states, auto companies operate in a geographically diverse cross-section of congressional districts. Despite the higher costs, Toyota spread out its U.S. factories, partly to increase its congressional clout.[21] "By sprinkling manufacturing jobs across many states," reported the *Wall Street Journal*, "Toyota built a network of state and federal politicians friendly toward the company."[22] In early 2007, GM's vice chairman, Bob Lutz, confirmed the success of Toyota's strategy. "Toyota has more clout in Washington than we do...frankly they've got more congressmen and senators than General Motors does."[23]

The presence of car dealerships in all 435 congressional districts further magnifies the political clout of the auto industry.[24] Some believe the combined influence of auto dealerships is greater than automakers and in July 2010 the *Financial Times* called car dealers "one of the most potent lobby groups in Washington."[25] Dealers are often major contributors to their congressional representatives and "tend to be pillars of their communities, joining charity boards and donating to Little League teams, all the while networking with potential buyers."[26] Exactly the type of individual any representative likes to have on side.

...

Beyond the wining and dining of formal political lobbying, auto interests push their agenda through "consumer" and "environmental" groups. When it comes to associations like the Automobile Manufacturers Association or the National Association of Automobile Manufacturers, what you see is what you get. If it sounds like a corporate lobby group, it probably is. This is not the case with "consumer" or "environmental" groups; let's just say the Global Climate Information Project's primary concern is not the environment.

More than a century ago, the auto industry began funding the most important auto consumer group, the American Automobile Association (AAA). Just after its formation in 1902, the AAA received five thousand dollars from the National Association of Automobile Manufacturers in return for three seats on their board.[27] While the AAA has been influenced by the industry, other consumer groups have acted as little more than auto industry fronts.

In 1937, the Automobile Manufacturers Association (AMA) and other auto associates established the Automobile Safety Foundation (ASF).[28] Ninety percent of ASF's income came from the auto industry and its suppliers.[29] In subsequent decades, the ASF was more likely than the AMA to testify at congressional hearings, emphasizing "driver education, ignoring vehicle safety."[30] [31] The efforts of the ASF meant the AMA could take a back seat in the fight against safety regulations.

The auto/oil industry also engaged in a fight against anti-pollution legislation. Under increasing heat for smog in 1950s California, the oil industry got proactive. It financed the Stanford Research Institute (SRI) to contest the findings of Professor Arie J. Haagen-Smit who demonstrated that oil refineries and automobiles were the major sources of smog.[32] The SRI's strategy was diversion ("if you can't dazzle 'em with brilliance, baffle 'em with bull") and they "went about attacking the fundamentals of Hagen-Smit's research."[33] The SRI concluded that smog was a mystery.[ii]

More recently, car companies have been working to block fuel mileage legislation through a variety of groups. A nine-page

---

ii According to *Beyond the Car*, in 1959, GM claimed "smog cannot be produced by the normally tuned automobile." It was one of many denials by the industry that verged on the absurd. According to *Taken For a Ride*, at one point, General Motors' CEO, Roger Smith, argued that decreasing NO_2 "could actually cause smog to get worse instead of better." Richard Klimisch of the Automobile Manufacturers Association remarked in 1996: "The effects of ozone [pollution] are not that serious. I hate to say that. But what we're talking about is a temporary loss in lung function of 20-30%. That's not really a health effect."

memo leaked in July 2006 revealed that GM and Ford sponsored a controversial Competitive Enterprise Institute campaign to discredit the growing consensus on climate change.[34] The Big Three have an inglorious history of funding "climate change skeptics", most notably the Global Climate Information Project and the Global Climate Coalition.

But, the biggest financiers of climate change denial are Big Oil. Exxon alone admits to giving $23 million to dozens of anti-Kyoto groups between 1998 and 2007.[35] In 2009 Exxon Mobile gave another $1.5 million to groups that campaigned against controls on greenhouse gas emissions.[36] Be it the Global Climate Commission or the International Petroleum Industry Environmental Conservation Association, black gold pays the bills for a slew of "eco" groups.[37] Even long-standing environmental organizations are not free from petrodollar influence. The World Wide Fund for Nature accepted $1 million from Chevron and BP while Conservation International took $2 million from BP and partnered with the company on a number of projects.[38] [39] BP gave $10 million in cash and land to the Nature Conservancy and the company holds a seat on its international leadership council.[40] More reputable groups such as the Sierra Club and Environmental Defense Fund also have ties to BP and Shell.[41]

Even many of the "watchdog" groups overseeing Alberta's tar sands receive significant funding via the Pew Foundation, an organization established by oil interests. These groups have come under fire for their mild criticisms of the tar sands.

Business Week remarked on the connection between Toyota and the Sierra Club: "Just before Toyota was about to launch the Prius in 1999, it called Dan Becker, director of Global Warming initiatives at the Sierra Club. The company wanted the group's seal of approval for the Prius. Becker persuaded his superiors to create an award for the best hybrid technology. The idea was controversial and Becker says some Sierra Clubbers called him a 'whore for the auto industry.'"[42] The next year, the Prius won the Sierra Club award for excellence in environmental engineering.[43]

…

The doorsteps of the White House and Congress swarm with lobbyists and think tanks. The city is also home to military institutions such as the Pentagon and CIA and a tourist could spend their days wandering the halls of the Vietnam, Korea and World War II war memorial museums. During our travels we witnessed many odes to U.S. military history and passed hundreds of bumper stickers supporting the troops. Bumper stickers can boost morale, but with Ford and GM among the biggest military contractors, it's their bumpers boosting the war. Auto companies have been an important part of the nation's capacity to wage war for nearly a century. "After 1918", writes Matthew Paterson, "the increasing military utility of motorized transport meant that a strong car industry was connected in governments' minds to preparedness for war."[44]

After train tracks were destroyed in France and Belgium during World War I, trucks carried weapons to the front lines. As an indication of their importance, 2,500 trucks used by the allies at Verdun were given the Croix de Guerre for extraordinary service.[45]

In the decades following the First World War, the mobility acquired through road building was viewed as central to military preparedness.[iii] Likewise, the Interstate highway system came under the portfolio of the Secretary of Defense who named the road network the National System of Interstate and Defense Highways.[46]

The marriage between Washington and the automobile was made official when Howard E. Coffin, vice president of Hudson Motor Company, was appointed to head WWI's Council for National Defense. Auto engineers designed the Liberty Aircraft

iii *The autobahn, for instance, was made partly for Germans to be able to fight.*

in 1917 and nearly 25,000 of them were built by auto firms during the war.[47] "When the war ended Washington and the motor industry locked themselves in an ardent embrace that has continued to the present day."[48]

On both sides of the conflict, the auto industry played an even greater role during WWII. The Nazis named their most famous strategy in honor of GM's Opel Blitz light truck. On the other side of the fight, Washington once again called on an auto bigwig to head the National Defense Advisory Council, appointing GM President William P. Knudson head of military production.[49] The auto industry fulfilled an astonishing 20 percent of all the country's WWII military contracts.[50] During WWII they made 47 percent of the machine guns, 57 percent of the tanks, 85 percent of the army helicopters and 87 percent of the bombs produced.[51] Ford's Willow Run plant built B-24 bombers, becoming the biggest bomber plant in the world.[52]

There was a symbiotic relationship between the car industry and military. The auto industry's might enabled the military, but the war also meant new factories for Ford, GM and Chrysler. It is often said that WWII saved Ford from bankruptcy. More recently, military contracts helped revive Chrysler in the early 80s.[53]

Auto companies' ability to arm the war machine wooed Washington politicians and military strategists. The match made in heaven between the auto industry and military was no summer romance. It was 'til death do us part. In a November 2008 *New York Times* article titled "What's good for GM is good for the army," retired General Wesley Clark argued, "rescuing the auto industry is a matter of national security."[54]

25. Public subsidies for private gain

One irony of U.S. politics is that those who claim to oppose government subsidies and vociferously defend the "free market" often support the private car and suburban sprawl. Yet these two defining characteristics of the *Homo automotivis* habitat rely on massive government welfare payments.

The automobile is like a spoiled child who demands half the family income as allowance. Out of every economic sector, the auto industry receives by far the most public support. In 2001, the world's 30 richest governments spent $1.1 trillion (1,100,000,000,000) on road transport.[1] The costs of auto infrastructure are so great that *Carfree Cities* claims: "The savings on street maintenance in a car free city probably exceed the operating costs of the transport system."[2]

Cars are a unique consumer good. They are produced for profit, owned by private individuals, but completely dependent upon public roads. It is hard to conceive of a large-scale privately financed road network. While there are a good number of toll highways financed and operated by private corporations, it is almost impossible to envision an entire city road system — let alone that of a state or nation — financed and operated privately. Simply put, if the state wants roads it must pay for them.

The private car's ability to offload costs onto the public is at the heart of its rise to dominance. German auto historian Winfried Wolf explains: "In road transport there is a possible separation, based on modern technology, between the transport infrastructure (the motorway or road) and the means of transport (the car, truck etc.) This transport technology can therefore be easily organized according to the principle of private appropriation of profit, socialization of costs and losses. Private profits are appropriated by the vehicle manufacturers, the insurance companies, and the motorway construction firms; costs are socialized by means of public financing of motorway construction, policing, hospitalization of the injured and repairs to the environment."[3]

...

We stayed just off the 16th Street Mall, Denver's main commercial artery. It was a car-less street of boutiques, benches and public art, where a bold walkway took up space once trafficked by a steady stream of steel. A lane in each direction was left for a free shuttle bus — aptly tied into both a bus and train network — that moved to and fro the length of 16th Street and took us within walking distance of the library, stadium and university. Downtown Denver is a great place to get around on foot or bus, yet nearly 90 percent of metropolitan area residents still drive to work. In fact, between 1980 and 1997 the number of cars in the Denver area increased 50 percent.[4] During this period, vehicle miles traveled per capita doubled and four fifths of the increase was outside the city limits.[5] This growth in car travel was spurred by sprawl, in turn creating a culture in which sprawl thrived. While Denver proper grew by 138,000 people between 1940 and 1990, its suburbs grew by 1.2 million.[6] Denver is no anomaly. From 1950 to 2005, 90 percent of U.S. metropolitan area growth occurred in suburbs.[7]

Suburbia's rise hurt city centres across the nation. When Denver's downtown hit rock bottom in the late 1980s, the 16th Street mall was launched to rescue the devastated core. Today, it is a recognized success, but when initially proposed, there was considerable opposition. Denver's suburban competitor, Aurora, was threatened by the 16th Street revitalization efforts and in 1987, Aurora's city manager declared: "If the economic, social, and technological forces shaping our city today don't encourage the creation of a downtown, you would be wasting a lot of effort to build one."[8] Seventy years ago, Aurora was little more than grazing fields. At less than 4,000, its population was a fraction of

Denver's. It was just one-tenth Denver's size in 1960, surging to half of Denver's population by 1990.[9] Dubbed "America's fastest growing mid-sized city", Aurora is now two-thirds Denver's population.[10] There are many reasons for Aurora's population boom.

Located 30 miles northeast of the city centre, the Denver International Airport was built just beyond Aurora's limits in the middle of undeveloped farm country. Another political decision that helped Aurora (and other similarly sprawling suburbs) was the 1947 Colorado statute, which afforded developers quasi-public power over the lands they purchased. With this legislation developers could create districts where they had power over zoning, the right to collect property taxes and eminent domain.[11] Like cities and states, developers received the right to raise funds through bonding (without debt limit) supported by the federal government. It was a winning position for private developers. These publicly supported bonds allowed them to finance infrastructure with tax-exempt loans insured by revenues from as-yet-to-be built homes.[i][12] Government favours in hand, developers chose to create their special districts on the outskirts where land was cheap. In this way, the Colorado statute — like milder versions offered by other states — hastened sprawl.

Like most states, Colorado also facilitated diffuse development by prioritizing rural roads. Formerly rural areas like Aurora received roadway spending while Denver and other cities received next to nothing. In the first quarter of the twentieth century, expenditures on rural highways skyrocketed. In the decade following 1904, total spending on rural highways rose from $3 million to $25 million. By the late 1920s, spending on rural roads totaled a billion dollars.[13] Cementing the rural bias, the 1916 Federal Highway Act barred federal funds for highways with

---

i Each $1 billion in bonds cost the U.S. federal government $30 million annually.

populations exceeding 2,500.[14][15] In the late 1920s only five percent of federal road funds were spent in cities.[16] And of this five percent most funds went towards the extension of routes through relatively unpopulated areas.[17] The rural bias in highway funding led to a 1962 Supreme Court challenge in which the court advocated a decrease in rural domination of state highway planning.[18]

Federal legislation encouraged sprawl in other ways too. A bevy of federal tax breaks designed to expand consumption and production have facilitated diffuse development. Aside from subsidies for roads the two most sprawl inducing tax incentives are accelerated depreciation for commercial property and the federal income tax deductions for home mortgage interest, points and property taxes.[19]

Accelerated depreciation allows companies to write off the costs of newly built commercial projects faster than infrastructure depreciates. Introduced in 1954 this tax break spurred the development of many shopping malls.[20] By favouring investment in new, un-built locations, accelerated depreciation encouraged retail and office development on city outskirts, which undermined existing urban locations.

For individual homebuyers, mortgage interest often climbs to half the cost of a house. Initially created in 1920, the federal income tax deduction allows mortgage interest to be deducted from one's tax bill. This is no small chicken; it is a huge incentive for homebuyers. In 2006, mortgage subsidies cost U.S. taxpayers $443 billion.[ii][21] By favouring housing over apartments

---

ii The federal income tax deduction promotes economic inequality. No such advantages are accorded to renters, discriminating against those who often have a greater need for subsidized shelter. (To get a sense of the subsidy's scale, Washington spends four times as much on homeowner subsidies than it does on low-income housing, according to America's Undeclared War.) The federal income tax deduction has been dubbed the "mansion subsidy" because the wealthiest one percent of taxpayers receive more than 20 percent of the benefits while the bottom half of all taxpayers receive less than two percent of the benefit.

(which are more likely to be rented), the income tax mortgage deduction prioritizes auto-use as apartment dwellers tend to own fewer cars than those living in single-family homes.[22] The mortgage subsidy also promotes the construction of new homes rather than the restoration of older housing in compact historic neighbourhoods.[23]

Additionally, these subsidies increase with the size of the mortgage so there is an incentive to build monster houses, which is one reason today's new homes are twice the size they were in 1950. Big homes translate into small numbers of people spread over large areas, a bad environment for walking, biking or mass transit.

In addition to mortgage subsidies, sprawl benefits from (government mandated) standardized pricing for infrastructure. "In the suburbs it is common to have only two houses per acre — as opposed to thirty units per acre or more downtown. As a result building and operating infrastructure — whether the public sector does it, as with roads and sewers, or the regulated private sector, as with electricity or telephone — is between nine to 20 times greater for low density sprawl than for in town — high density development, on a per house basis."[24] Despite higher production costs in exurbia, the price is usually the same for sewage, water, electricity, natural gas, telephone, cable television, postage and parcel delivery etc. Higher-density areas effectively subsidize diffuse development.[iii][25]

...

Like so many city centres across the country, the exodus from downtown Denver was driven by road building. Both sprawl

iii On April 6, 2007, the Washington Post reported that the Federal Rural development program gave $30.3 billion to metropolitan areas with 50,000 or more people between 2001 and 2007. Electric companies, for instance, were awarded almost $1 billion in low interest loans to serve the booming suburbs of Atlanta and Tampa.

and auto use cannot survive without subsidies to roads. And over the past century, trillions in public funds have been poured into paving these passageways across the USA.

The Good Roads Movement's first major federal victory was the establishment of the Office of Public Roads in 1905.[26] When federal income tax was first introduced eight years later, "one of the first things that national government officials did with the added revenue was to fund highway reconstruction projects."[27] Tens of millions of dollars were doled out over the next few years.[28] The 1921 Federal Highway Act increased annual funding to $75 million, which rose to $200 million by the end of the decade.[29][30]

State governments were even more responsive to automobilists. In 1914, Colorado's road lobbyists won a statewide property tax for highway construction and a prohibition against locally levied user fees.[31] Six years earlier automobilists got New York to set aside $50 million for highways and by 1912 the state had run up $100 million worth of highway debt.[32]

Desperate for roadway, between 1916 and 1931 state issued road-building bonds increased from $124 million to $1.2 billion.[33] By the mid-1920s, nearly half of all state debt was used for automobile infrastructure.[34] In 1930, a quarter of Colorado's budget went to roads — 50 percent more than the amount spent on education.[35] During this period only a third of the state's highway spending came from motorists.[36]

Many local governments also went out of their way to facilitate the car. Chicago, for instance, "drove itself into debt with street improvements quite early in the game," spending $350 million on street widening between 1910 and 1961.[iv][37][38] While Chicago was an extreme case, cities across the USA were pumping cash into street widening and road building.

A 1924 study showed that 71 of 233 cities had already

iv At 1923 prices this was more than twice the estimated cost of a comprehensive subway system.

finished at least one street-widening project and 41 other cities had additional projects under way.[39] To widen streets, municipalities often took private land by exercising the right of imminent domain, running freeways through backyards and displacing residents in their wake.[40]

By the end of the 1920s, cities held $3.5 billion in outstanding road bonds.[41] In Denver's case, motorists didn't pay a penny for local roads, bridges or streets.[42] Denver spent huge sums on roads even though two-thirds of the city's population did not drive, relying on under-funded mass transit.[43]

Municipal, state and federal road spending grew rapidly to become the second largest expenditure by the 1920s.[44] Between 1921 and 1932, various levels of government put $21 billion into roads (less than a quarter of which was paid for by cars).[45] For the first quarter century of the automobile's existence, drivers paid a small percentage of road costs. Yet, once automobiles reached the critical mass required to generate tax revenues, automobilists began arguing that gas taxes were "user fees" and should therefore be utilized solely for roads.[v] "As the highway user taxes gained in relative importance the autocrats began to make the case that fuel licenses, and registration levies were really road user 'charges,' not taxes at all."[46]

In 1920, Minnesota amended its constitution, earmarking gasoline taxes solely for road building.[47] By 1974, 46 states had followed suit.[48] In 1934, Washington passed the Hayden Cartwright Act, which read: "It is unfair and unjust to tax motor vehicle transportation unless the proceeds of such taxation are applied to the construction, improvement, or maintenance of highways."[vi][49] Under the Act, states could not gain access to federal road aid

---

v *Early automobilists won special status for gas taxes, even though gasoline was often exempted from retail taxes.*

vi *If the same logic were applied to cigarette and alcohol taxes, the monies garnered would be used to promote smoking or drinking.*

unless they used gas taxes for roads.[50] The effect was to give road building an advantage over health, education and welfare programs in the competition for government monies.[51]

With this legislation came the implication that car-generated "user fees" covered road costs. "Actually," notes Owen D. Gutfreund, "even though states collect gas taxes and a modest federal levy[vii] was imposed to pay part of the Interstate expenses, the total of these charges never amounted to more than one third of highway costs. ... There is a mistaken notion that American drivers pay for their roads through gas taxes."[52]

As WWII came to a close, the 1944 Federal Highway Act authorized $1.5 billion for three years of highway construction.[53] This gave way to the 1950s where the highway lobby's ambitious efforts were well received. The special Eisenhower administration committee set up to decide on a new highway project was headed by a scion of the billionaire DuPont family, whose main corporation manufactured "the explosives so necessary for road construction" and "owned a substantial portion of General Motors."[54]

In 1956, the most extensive public works project in history was initiated: the U.S. Interstate Highway System. Alleged to be "among the only human creations that can be seen by astronauts from an orbiting spacecraft ... it is the longest engineered structure ever built."[55] By the time this project was completed, thousands of bridges and tunnels were erected and 46,675 miles of highway paved. The interstate cost the government $370 billion, with gas taxes covering about half of that.[56] The Interstate Act increased the proportion of highway costs paid by the federal government from 60 percent (stipulated by the 1944 Federal Aid Highway Act) to 90 percent.[57] The federal government carried an even greater proportion in (mostly western) states with large amounts of federal

vii The 1930s saw the introduction of the first federal gas tax which started at just a penny per gallon. It rose to 4 cents in 1960 and didn't change again until the early 1980s. It's been stuck at 18.4 cents since 1993.

land. Here the federal government covered as much as 95 percent of interstate costs.[58] The high proportion of costs covered by the federal government provided a major incentive for states to build roadway. Highway construction created jobs and with Washington footing the bill, it was hard to resist.

The interstate facilitated movement from downtown centres to the suburbs, driving people from cities. "The lavish new interstate highway grants," Gutfreund explains, "would make it easier for Americans to get from their homes to an urban workplace, marketplace, or cultural attraction, but only if they lived outside of the city and owned a car."[59]

Increased awareness of the social and environmental problems of car-dominated landscapes has not reduced government subsidies. By the early 1980s, motorists paid just over half the cost of new highways and less than 50 percent of maintenance costs.[60]

Today, federal and state gas taxes cover between 50 and 60 percent of highway spending.[61] Since most cities do not charge a gas tax, almost all local roadway is subsidized. In the car-dominated cities of the USA, about \$40 billion a year is spent on roads (a quarter of most municipal budgets).

...

By the time we got to Cleveland our budget was so tight we bypassed the Rock 'n Roll Hall of Fame and headed for Jacob's Field instead. An old-fashioned looking baseball stadium, the view was pretty good from the upper deck in right field. Our tickets were cheap, but the Gateway sports complex — home to Jacob's Field as well as a basketball arena — will cost taxpayers hundreds of millions of dollars. Until three million tickets are sold in a season, the Cleveland Indians play rent-free at The Jake. A new stadium and a superior squad helped draw fans, but a quarter century ago the Indians averaged less than a million tickets a season.

Sports stadiums built with public money probably generate more controversy than any other kind of long-term direct subsidy to private business. In Cleveland, the debate even led to several votes in the 1990s to determine whether or not to fund the stadium. Yet it's safe to say that Indians' tickets were less subsidized by government money than the vehicles delivering fans to The Jake.

In the late 1970s Pennsylvania put up a quarter of a billion dollars to secure a Volkswagen assembly plant while Tennessee gave Nissan tens of millions of dollars.[62] A Detroit GM plant that opened in 1983 received $220 million in federal, state and local funds and a 12-year property tax abatement worth another $130 million.[63]

These subsidies continued to rise in the age of "free market" economics. All the auto plants built over the past quarter century have benefited from public investment. Between 1998 and 2004, Asian automakers received $1.1 billion in government money to build five assembly plants in Alabama, Mississippi, Indiana and Texas.[64] The depths of public support can be astounding. Mercedes received a whopping $167, 000 from Alabama for each job its plant created while Tennessee gave Volkswagen $577 million in financial incentives to build a $1 billion plant.[viii 65 66]

Alarmed at southern states success in luring auto manufacturing, Ontario created a $451 million Auto Investment Strategy Fund in April 2004. The Canadian government added hundreds of millions of dollar to the province's attempts to attract auto investments.

Like a good parent, the government is not only there in the beginning, it stays with the automobile throughout its development. Automakers benefit from public research money

---

viii *Public assistance is not only monetary. According to the June 28, 2008 Wall Street Journal, for its factory in Mississippi Toyota told the state that it didn't want homes within 5,000 feet of the plant's paint shop. The planned site had more than ten homes within that radius, but within 36 hours of Toyota's demand, the state had an option to purchase each house and relocate the occupants.*

channeled through universities and the military. The Department of Defense, for instance, runs a multi-million dollar initiative to develop a robot car. Automakers hope these "intelligent" cars will help drivers and perhaps one day take over the task, heightening safety and comfort.[ix 67]

Government funding is often more direct. In early 2007 the U.S. Department of Energy allocated tens of million of dollars to continue advanced battery research for a hydrogen-powered car.[68] The U.S. push for a hydrogen-powered car was set in motion when the Canadian military provided a fuel cell research contract to Vancouver-based Ballard.[69] Since that time, Ottawa and Washington have allocated hundreds of millions of dollars to develop a hydrogen superhighway. And to get one million plug-in hybrids and electric cars on the road, President Obama planned to spend $5 billion through tax credits to buyers and subsidized loans and grants for automakers.[70]

The government also extends a helping hand when the industry fails. On the cusp of bankruptcy in 2009, GM and Chrysler received more than $75 billion from U.S. and Canadian taxpayers.[71] Similarly, in 1979 a bankrupt Chrysler received $1.2 billion in loan guarantees and other support from Washington. The largest corporate bailout in U.S. history at that time, it helped turn the dying company around.[72]

The government does not neglect the auto industry's offspring and generously supports an assortment of associated industries. Tires, steel and aluminum all receive an allowance, despite being long past their adolescence. Washington has been particularly attentive to the fuel requirements of the automobile.

---

ix According to the June 27, 2008 Associated Press, during the 2008 presidential campaign Republican candidate John McCain said, "I think once we develop that technology [hydrogen-powered, electric and ethanol fuelled cars] with pure research and development then we've got to hand it over to private enterprise and the automotive companies."

Over the past two decades, the U.S. government has spent more than a billion dollars in an unsuccessful attempt to develop a fuel from cellulosic ethanol and in 2010, oil refiners received upwards of $7 billion in federal subsidies for mixing ethanol into gas.[73]

Big Oil has received the most unwavering support. The fossil fuel industry is the second most heavily subsidized economic sector in the USA.[74] The U.S. oil industry has long paid significantly less in taxes than other sectors due to a variety of special deductions.[75] But, this did not deter the Bush administration from handing out another $8 billion in energy tax breaks, mostly to oil and gas companies.[76]

Without a doubt, the primary way the public pays for oil is by soaking up the industry's externalities. These costs include direct pollution, pollution cleanup, and military protection of oil supplies. Depending on how you calculate it, government support for petrol costs tens if not hundreds of billions of dollars annually.[x] If oil's externalities were factored into the price of gas, drivers would easily be paying over ten bucks a gallon. Beyond gasoline, the state foots the bill for a variety of other automobile services. Few factor in indirect subsidies received from services like snow removal, policing and courts. "Depending on exactly how you calculate it you find that the total cost of motor vehicle registration, driver licensing, highway police, and highway-related courtroom and jailhouse activity runs some $20-70 billion per year in the United States and only a small percentage of this cost is covered by fines and fees."[77] Add to this $50 billion in free parking and $55 billion for crash injuries and deaths (the proportion not directly borne by drivers).[78]

...

Even as global warming reared its ugly head, public transit and inter-city rail continued to receive a fraction of the funding

---

[x] *A 2004 New Economics Foundation study put total fossil fuel subsidies in developed countries at $73 billion a year.*

devoted to roads.[xi] When Congress passed a five-year $300 billion dollar transportation bill in 2005, it allocated 20 percent of funds to mass transit and 80 percent to roads.[79]

The situation was much the same in the 1990s under Bill Clinton and his supposedly eco-friendly sidekick, Al Gore. Throughout the 1990s, federal spending on highways increased 50 percent faster than mass transit spending.[80] In 1998, 80 percent of the $220 billion federal transportation bill went to highways and 18 percent to mass transit.[81] The imbalance in funding between road and rail peaked in the decades following the introduction of the interstate highway act of 1956. For two decades after the introduction of the interstate, cities and states could tap into federal transportation coffers for 90 percent of their highway costs. During the same period, federal monies for mass transit projects were virtually non-existent. It wasn't until two decades after the Interstate Act, that Washington passed legislation allowing cities to tap into transportation funds for mass transit projects.[82]

During the early 1960s, *Fortune* noted that, "the American consumer, in deciding between private and mass transportation, has for years and years been presented with a market heavily rigged in favour of using his own car in city traffic."[83]

…

As every economist will tell you, capitalism has booms and busts. During a downturn, corporations foresee grim prospects for profit and reduce their investments. Malaise is heightened as the economy is starved of investments. A vicious cycle often ensues where investments cease because prospects are poor yet prospects stay poor until investment begins. The Great Depression of the 1930s exemplified this downward spiral into a bust. To escape this

---

xi According to Take the Rich off Welfare: "Federal, state and local governments spend over $300 billion a year — nearly a 100 times what they spend on public transportation — on car-related costs... Riders on Amtrak and local mass transit systems pay much more towards their cost than auto users do."

vicious economic cycle, famous English economist, John Maynard Keynes, proposed a counter cyclical (boom and bust) economic theory. He argued that in times of downturn, intervention from government was necessary to kick-start the economy. He asserted that the role of government was to stimulate demand through labour-intensive investments. Then, with their newfound income, workers would be able to purchase products, further generating investment. To combat downturn, Keynes went so far as to advocate that government pay workers to dig ditches and fill them in again, as socially inefficient as this may be. Although surpassed by supply-side theory as the dominant force in most economic departments, nearly every wealthy country in the world practices some form of Keynes's counter cyclical theory.

But what do booms and busts have to do with cars? "When we want to pump-prime the ailing economy we build highways," notes *Autokind vs. Mankind*.[84] The "Asphalt Nation", as another author once put it, helped stabilize capitalism. "Car Keynesianism", if you like. In the 1930s, with eight or nine million unemployed, President Franklin Delano Roosevelt set-up the Works Projects Administration (WPA), which created millions of jobs. Across the USA the WPA advanced automotive infrastructure.

"People were building roads, putting gravel on roads, sometimes asphalt and cement, all over the country" explains Burt Folsom.[85] There were other projects as well, Folsom explains, "but mostly roads." Road building is considered the major "success" story of the depressed 1930s.[86] The WPA doubled paved miles, building or surfacing a million miles of road.[87] By 1939, 900,000 of the WPA's 2.07 million workers were involved in street or highway construction, with relief agencies spending $4 billion on these projects between 1933 and 1942.[xii] [88] [89] [90] Railway tracks, on the other hand, had already been laid and were rarely a candidate for

---

xii Roosevelt's predecessor, Edgar Hoover, also funneled $175 million into highway construction partly to create jobs.

economic stimulus. While 38.3 percent of the WPA's budget was spent on streets, roads and highways, only 2.6 percent of the WPA's budget went to other forms of transportation.[91] Demonstrating a bias for roads over rail, the WPA even hired workers to rip up 600 miles of streetcar track.[92]

"Car Keynesianism" continued after the depression ended. In 1944, President Franklin Roosevelt sent a message to Congress in support of interregional highways. He argued that government should "utilize productively some of the manpower and industrial capacity," which would be freed up after the war.[93] Twenty years later, "Car Keynesianism" was still going strong. During the 1960s, for instance, the impoverished Appalachian region was allocated $1.1 billion for its reinvigoration, 80 percent of which was consumed by highway spending.[94] With road building as its mantra, "Car Keynesianism" has effectively stabilized the capitalist system for three quarters of a century. "Car Keynesian" logic has survived to this day, demonstrated by the Federal Highway Administration's insistence on emphasizing that each billion spent on highway construction creates 42,000 new jobs.[95]

...

It is not by chance or simple individual choice that Aurora, Colorado, and innumerable other suburban and exurban areas exploded onto the scene. They are the product of colossal road subsidies and tax breaks designed to expand consumption and production. It is not by chance either that automotive factories are located where they are. They too rely on the public purse. In fact, the entire automotive industrial complex could be characterized as the planet's biggest ever welfare scam.

To put it another way, this invasive species has been successful because it has become a parasite that sucks resources from pretty much every living creature. But its favourite host is the body politic.

26. Honk if you hate cars

"Only after the automobile is dethroned in the law, economics, city planning, mass media, and education, and especially in the politics of public decisions will we be able to say that the revolution is under way."

— *Autokind vs. Mankind*

It is easy to forget that evolutionary dead ends are more common than successful species. It seems likely that this will be the fate of *Homo Automotivis*. If automobile usage in China and Uganda becomes like that of North America, the social and environmental cost would be horrendous. Earth will not be able to sustain the burden of cars taking over our entire planet in the way they have the USA. But will the end of automobility arrive with a crash or a whimper? Are humans smart enough to see the signs of imminent destruction and change before it is too late?

Despite the car's dominance over space, culture and the economy there are signs that *Homo Automotivis* could evolve into a self-consciously anti-car species that lives in harmony with the planet. For example, during the 2007/08 housing crash prices didn't fall as much in New York, Boston, San Francisco and other relatively pedestrian/public transit oriented cities. Similarly, housing prices near urban rail stations rebounded more quickly.[1] Concerns about global warming and higher oil prices appear to have caused a slight shift in attitude about our dependence on cars and the places we live. Another hopeful sign is the change in young people's relationship to the automobile. People in the 18-34 year old age group seem to be driving less, preferring to live in walk-able and transit-oriented urban areas.[2] In 1978, nearly half of 16 year olds and three quarters of 17 year olds in the U.S. had their drivers' licenses. Three decades later those proportions dropped to 31 percent of 16 year olds and 49 percent of seventeen year olds and since 1998 the decline has accelerated rapidly.[3] The environment was the main reason Gen Y cited for driving less but they are also more hooked on computers and you can work on a train or bus, but not (safely) in a car.

To effect change, instead of simply waiting for environmental collapse that compels it, those of us who want to evolve past *Homo Automotivis* must consciously struggle against the forces that enthrall us. Of course there is already significant opposition to *Homo Automotivis*, but it's largely passive. Reflected in frustration with congestion and driving costs as well as concerns about exercise and the environment this discontent needs to be consciously directed against the private car. It's time to organize an uprising against private automobility.

Bits and pieces of this organized uprising are already happening. Activists are challenging auto hegemony in a variety of creative ways. There's an annual World Naked Bike Ride (1,700 participated in Chicago one year) and in 2005 San Franciscans came up with PARK(ing) DAY when parking spots are turned into public green spaces in dozens of cities. A Portland group, Depave, transforms little used asphalt into more livable and earth-friendly green space. Individuals across North America go out of their way to tell SUV and Hummer drivers that their vehicle "is too big" or ask them to "think about the environment." Some French and Greek activists walk over cars that block the small bit of pathway devoted to pedestrians. Elsewhere, people issue fake tickets to gas guzzling vehicles and paint bike lanes or crosswalks when the city won't act. An Austrian civil engineer created the 'Walkmobile', a lightweight car-size device pedestrians can strap on their shoulders to highlight the automobile's immense space requirements. In downtown Montreal, New York and elsewhere thousands of militant pedestrians and cyclists refuse to obey car rules. They jaywalk, cross on red lights or bike against the flow on one-way streets. They make it less pleasant to drive and challenge the notion that people should be subservient to cars.

But, an important principle to keep in mind is to hate the car, but not the driver. While individuals should feel social pressure to get rid of their vehicle, the problem of private automobility will not be solved through lifestyle choices alone. It will take a multi-faceted political battle and someone who drives regularly yet demonstrates, votes and educates others against cars does more to advance the cause than a non-engaged cyclist.

A 2004 *Wall Street Journal* article denigrating world car-free day was given the headline "Honk if you hate cars". The *Journal* editors were trying to be clever, but there's no contradiction between driving and opposing private automobility. Most North Americans live on a landscape dominated by cars and to change this we need systemic transformations, not individual purity.

Systemic change demands mass political action and in a car-dominated society that must include many regular drivers. A sign of the movement's growth may well be a suburban protest with hundreds of cars rolling slowly along — demonstrating, if you like — to demand greater rail or bus service.

One great thing about protesting the car is that street demos against auto domination make a political statement and simultaneously disrupt automobility. Reclaim the Streets protest-parties, for instance, build political power and demonstrate an alternative urban vision. In July 1996, 10,000 protestors took over London's M41 highway "dancing to a sound-system, holding picnics in the central reservation, turning the fast lane into a sand pit for children, whilst entertainment was provided by fire-eaters and jugglers."[4]

During the mid 1990s London activists organized a number of similar actions. In one instance 500 demonstrated under the banner "RECLAIM THE STREETS — FREE THE CITY/ KILL THE CAR" while a flyer for another protest explained "CARS CANNOT DANCE: When they move they are violent and brutish, they lack sensitivity and rhythm. CARS CANNOT PLAY: When they diverge from the straight and narrow, they kill. CARS CANNOT SOCIALIZE: They privatize, separate, isolate and alienate."[5]

Critical Mass is a highly successful bike version of Reclaim the Streets. Under the banner "we are traffic," cyclists gather the last Friday of every month to ride en masse. Begun in San Francisco, Critical Mass takes place in over three hundred cities and sometimes thousands participate.

Moving from the street to municipal hall, 1,500 cities around the world participate in the annual Car-Free day, an initiative of the World Car Free Network ("the hub of the global car-free movement"). In September 2010 Montreal's Agence Métropolitaine de Transport organized a week's worth of "in town without my car" events. On car-free day a big chunk of downtown was closed to cars, which led to a significant decline in nitric oxide levels as well as sound pollution.[6]

For more than a century the auto-industrial complex has inserted itself throughout society. It's time to challenge their influence wherever it may be found. Think about what you can do. For example, does your child's school organize carwashes, take them to auto museums or promote the car in other ways? High schools should remove auto shop and driving lessons from the curriculum and replace these classes with cycling mechanics or environmental studies (or maybe the kids deserve a longer recess).[i] For their part, university students and professors could demand a campus free of GM, Ford and the rest of the auto-industrial complex.

As with tobacco, car advertising should be steadily eliminated (and immediately appropriated). The dominant media,

i In Copenhagen children attend bike ed in the third and ninth grades.

ad agencies and car-makers will no doubt resist bitterly so let's build momentum towards this end by prodding media outlets with ethical advertising guidelines (campus newspapers, green groups etc.) to get rid of car ads. Public transit agencies should be encouraged to reject auto advertising. In fact, they should be pushed to devote their space to anti-car messages. How about covering light rail and buses with: "Cars Kill. Take the Train." Transit authorities could also give bike makers a discount to put up messages that challenge the cultural dominance of the automobile. Heck, maybe Nike would pay to cover bus stops with "Just Do It. Ditch your car."

Imagine if all the money used to sell cars were put into promoting walking and cycling. To even the playing field, health and environmental agencies could run public education campaigns describing the car's negative consequences. Malmö Sweden, for instance, ran a "No Ridiculous Car Trips" campaign to reduce journeys of less than five kilometres (about three miles).[ii]

As an institutionalized antidote to pro-car messages we would do well to push for a statutory holiday commemorating car crash victims. Of course, for this to become a reality it will take a great deal of organizing by a large number of people. But it only takes a handful of individuals to picket or coordinate political theatre at the local auto show, which often draw significant media interest.

Alongside moves to denigrate private automobility, the anti-car movement should promote alternatives through books, films, music and poetry. For their part, the Swedish public transit network, Planka.nu, calls on supporters to promote egalitarian principles and to "happily affirm the public in public transport."[7]

The most important victories curtail the car's dominance over space. Some municipalities have banned new drive-thru windows while others are implementing pedestrian plazas. In

---

ii *Seventy-two percent of U.S. trips less than three miles are made by car and 20 percent of trips less than one mile.*

Montreal, the city's primary commercial artery, Sainte Catherine, is car-free for a dozen blocks from late May to mid-September. Begun in 2008, this pedestrian takeover has been good for air quality as well as local restaurants and bars. The city's third political party, which garnered a quarter of the vote in 2009, wants to gradually extend the period and distance until about 30 blocks of Sainte Catherine are pedestrianized year-round.

In 2009 five-blocks of Broadway around Times Square were turned into a pedestrian plaza. Building on this success, New York was set to remove vehicle traffic from Fifth Street between Herald Square and the Empire State Building.

On our car-less journey, some of our fondest memories were of Santa Monica's Third Street Promenade, Bourbon Street in New Orleans and Denver's 16th Street Mall. All three were car free. All places where a ban on cars decreased one kind of traffic and increased another. These were vibrant, heavily populated streets. Liberated from the narrow spaces between concrete and moving steel, pedestrians swarmed into the open streets where the sun was brighter and the sky more vast.

As streets are reclaimed we must push to raze highways. Initial targets ought to be the most intrusive freeways, bringing immediate benefits and support for future demolition. A first step in many cities would be to tear down the roadway that slices downtown off from the waterfront. It could be strategic for activists from different cities to coordinate simultaneous campaigns targeting the most harmful highways in their respective communities.

Despite the destruction wrought by roadway, grassroots groups saved many parts of North American cities from planned highways. In New York, San Francisco, Boston, Toronto, New Orleans, San Antonio and elsewhere activists thwarted major thoroughfares. We should draw inspiration and insight from these successes, which usually included massive community participation and civil disobedience.

In the late 1960s community groups in Vancouver blocked a freeway downtown and today it stands out as the only major North American city without a highway built through its core. Not coincidentally, the city is hailed as an urban planning success. Compared to other North American cities built in the automobile era, Vancouver's core is a residential utopia (albeit expensive). From 1997 to 2007 Vancouver's population increased 27 percent and the number of jobs rose by 18 percent yet at the same time 10 percent fewer cars entered the city. There were 44 percent more trips by foot, 180 percent by bike and 50 percent by transit.[8]

Eliminating highways into downtown can reduce urban auto dependence but this will be futile if development continues to creep outwards. Measures are needed to curb sprawl and then to gradually return the exurban fringe to farming or woodlands. Adopted in 1973, Portland has had some success with its urban growth boundary. The area beyond the boundary — known as a greenbelt — will not receive public infrastructure services, which curtails sprawl. In 2008 California took a small, but important, step to curb sprawl. The state legislator agreed to allocate $5 billion in transportation money contingent upon regions adopting a "sustainable community strategy". Projects that are part of a "sustainable" plan get first dibs on state transportation disbursements.[9]

One way to stop highway growth is to gradually phase out federal roadway subsidies. Washington shouldn't subsidize such patently destructive paths and states that want to continue building highways should fund them through their own taxes.

Zoning regulations are another important, though indirect, form of public support for automobiles. Regulations demanding large lot sizes and houses removed from the sidewalk should be eliminated while the number of neighbourhoods zoned for single-family homes will need to be drastically reduced. In the short-run, relaxing rules on lane-way housing and basement suites can heighten density.

The car-less need commercial space intermixed with residential areas so zoning that strictly divides uses must be eliminated. Another way to reduce driving is to offer people jobs close to where they live. Why not do away with tax-breaks for sprawl-inducing accelerated depreciation and shift the money to businesses that locate near transit hubs and residential areas?

It's also important to end zoning requirements for off-street parking, which require commercial and residential buildings to secure a certain number of spots based upon the number of dwellings or square feet of space. These requirements enable driving and make it illegal for developers to build car-less dwellings. During the late 1990s in Vienna a car-free neighbourhood was "held up for a number of years because the city's zoning policy required one parking space for each new apartment."[10]

Municipalities should also steadily increase fees for on-street parking. Concurrently, tax breaks to businesses for parking ought to be eliminated and employees who don't drive should receive the value of a space in cash. One Los Angeles study showed that when given the option of receiving the money employers put into parking, 17 percent of employees choose the cash over the free spot.[11]

From another perspective, a 2007 study found that 35 percent of government workers in Manhattan drive to work compared to 14 percent of those working in the (often better paid) financial sector — largely due to the free parking offered to government employees.[12]

Without the bulk of parking costs socialized or buried in product prices, auto-mania could never have taken hold. Were a law passed requiring an end to all public and private parking subsidies, there would be a dramatic reduction in the number of cars on the road. Would drivers pay six dollars a night to park in front of their home? Another ten dollars at work? Fifty-cents at Wal-Mart or a quarter at 7-11?

In September 2007 a think tank close to Britain's Conservative Party proposed that supermarkets be forced to charge for parking.[13] This would decrease car trips and increase business at shops that don't offer parking. Longer-term it could lead towards a greater intermixing of residential and commercial space.

At rest or on the road, car costs have to increase significantly. In 2003 London began charging $12 to enter the centre of town. Stockholm did the same and in 2008 New York City Mayor Michael Bloomberg pushed for a similar fee, but was thwarted by the state legislature. London's move led to an immediate 20 percent drop in carbon dioxide emissions and a 12 percent reduction in the main components of smog while Stockholm saw a 14 percent reduction in CO_2 emissions.[14 15]

Congestion fees are a relatively blunt instrument to curtail driving. The Netherlands has come up with a less crude method of charging drivers. Beginning in 2012 Dutch drivers will pay 4.7 cents for every kilometre they travel. Tracked through a GPS, the fee is set to rise gradually to 9.4 cents by 2018.[16] The "green" charge is on top of a $3.50 per gallon gas tax, which is just a bit above the European norm. High gas taxes dissuade driving yet the U.S. Federal gas tax has been stuck at 18.3 cents a gallon since 1993. Per hundred miles traveled, in 2010 U.S. drivers paid an average of only $1.90 in gas tax.[17] This needs to rise dramatically and rapidly. We've already seen that if externalities created were calculated into the price of oil, a gallon of gas would cost upwards of $10.

In an auto-dominated landscape user fees are generally a regressive form of taxation, hitting the lowest paid hardest. A car-free landscape will eventually benefit those with less but in the meantime there should be efforts to lessen this unjust financial burden. How about giving free bus passes to students in poorer areas and prioritizing mass transit and bike infrastructure servicing working class communities?

Increasing the cost of driving and restricting car space will fail to get large numbers of people out of their cars if they are not combined with moves to increase other transit options and to vastly alter the urban layout.

Requiring no learning after two years of age and no particular discipline of the eyes or rigor of the spinal cord, walking is the safest, cheapest and most ecologically sustainable form of transport. As such it should be our priority. Studies have shown that a willingness and desire to walk are directly related to the quality of the walking environment.[18] Proper sidewalks and lights facilitate walking but many places need significant changes to the urban layout. The car-less require stores, libraries, gyms and employment close to where they live. Most cities and towns need to become increasingly dense.

Bikes cost more and require more space than walking yet they give individuals significantly more mobility and the energy costs are comparable.[iii] Large investments in bike infrastructure are necessary. Bikes deserve separated lanes, not just painted lines. A September 2010 *Yes* magazine article noted, "that physical separation from motorized traffic on busy streets is the single most effective policy for getting more people to bike."[19]

In 2007 a cement-divided bike path was opened on the major thoroughfare of de Maisonneuve Street in Montreal. The path runs along one of the city's main east-west corridors and is connected to some less significant north-south bike lanes. The de Maisonneuve path's popularity encouraged the city to add a short cement divided bike lane along another major north-south downtown street, which is connected to a painted pathway through a residential neighbourhood. After the success of de Maisonneuve's path the city launched Bixi, North America's biggest bike-sharing initiative. About 5,000 bikes are docked at 400 stations, which are

---

iii *Manufacturing bikes consumes electricity but they use human food calories more efficiently than walking.*

never more than 300 metres (330 yards) from each other. With a pass ($78 annually, $28 a month or $5 for 24 hours in 2010) the first thirty minutes of travel is free. The next half hour is $1.50 with the cost rising steadily to spur turnover. Modeled on Paris' wildly successful "Velib", Bixi was exported to Minneapolis, Boston, Portland, London, Melbourne and Washington D.C.

New York also successfully expanded its biking infrastructure. Cycling increased 50 percent in the three years after the city opened a 17-mile trail in west Manhattan and separated bike paths across two bridges to Brooklyn.[20] In 2009, 236,000 New Yorkers rode daily.[21] As this book went to press Copenhagen, the two-wheeled Mecca, was completing segregated bike highways to the suburbs.[22] With up to 15 routes planned, the network includes service stations (with airpumps and tools for quick fixes) and coordinated traffic lighting so a cyclist who maintains a 20 kilometre (12.5 miles) per hour speed can flow through green lights all the way into the city centre.[23]

Safety must be a priority and the burden of responsibility should be placed on those operating the most dangerous means. In car-bike accidents in Holland, for instance, the driver must prove the cyclist was responsible. If he/she cannot, the driver is deemed at fault.[24] Some places have begun to modify road rules for cyclists. In Idaho cyclists only need to yield in front of stop signs while on many one-way streets in France, Belgium and England it's legal for bikes to travel both ways. A number of U.S. cities such as Chicago, Louisville and Portland have biking departments at City Hall designed to better two-wheeled transport. Every municipality should follow suit and give its bike departments steadily increasing budgets.

Little things matter. New York, for instance, forces buildings to allow bikes in their elevators. How about prodding businesses with more than 20 employees to provide a shower and secure bike rack?

Outside of the legislative realm, bike co-ops can provide useful services. At Concordia University in Montreal "Right to Move", a volunteer-run mechanics shop, helps riders fix their bikes.

For environmental, health, safety, noise and cost reasons walking and cycling should be prioritized wherever possible.[iv] But, to get people out of their cars in most cities it will be necessary to massively expand bus and rail services. Reducing costs can spur demand for mass transit. All Vancouver area college and university students ride public transit for less than half the normal price. Through an agreement with the transit authority every student pays $30 a month and gets to use their ID card as a transit pass. The "U-pass" has increased student transit use and heightened demand for better bus services. A couple dozen mid-sized European cities have developed an even better model. In 1996, Belgium's third biggest city, Hasselt, introduced free public transport under the motto "The city guarantees the right of mobility for everyone." At the same time public transport was given primacy on the city's inner ring road. Over the next decade, bus ridership increased a whopping 1,300 percent.[25] Ockelbo in Sweden took a slightly different tack. It amalgamated its public and semipublic transport (regular buses, school buses and mobility service) and made the system free. Ridership increased 260 percent and nearly half of the new riders were former drivers. The reforms significantly decreased administrative costs so Ockelbo even saved money.[26]

There are various successful forms of mass transit around the world. The historic tram system in Zurich, Switzerland, rolls throughout the city. In one of the world's richest cities, 90 percent of commuters use public transit to travel to and from downtown Zurich.[27] In the 1970s Curitiba Brazil built an extensive network

---

iv Carbusters notes: "Only when compared to the Car City does the Public Transport City look good. Compared to the Walking City, it looks like needless inefficiency and technological dependence."

of dedicated bus lanes, which include a prepaid area to speed up the service. Now most of Curitiba's two million commuters take the bus. More expensive than dedicated bus lanes, massive metro systems in Tokyo, Moscow and New York move millions of people daily.

Over the past 15 years Sacramento, Houston, Charlotte, Phoenix and many other car-dependent U.S. cities have laid light rail lines. Much more is needed. People will ditch their car when they can get to all their regular destinations without one. Light rail is a sensible option in many cities. It's comfortable, costs less than a subway and can move large numbers of people. Tramways also challenge automobility by taking space away from cars. Montreal's third party, Projet Montréal, developed a five-year plan to lay 40 kilometres (25 miles) of tramway on a number of the city's major transportation corridors and then another 100 kilometres of light rail over the longer-term. The plan, which complements Montreal's metro, is designed to make the city more accessible for the car-less rather than building transit to enable suburban living.

Light rail and subway stations can anchor neighbourhoods amenable to car-free living. Since Vancouver opened its SkyTrain in 1986 major residential and commercial developments have sprung up around a dozen stations. Yves' car-less aunt and uncle recently moved from the east side of Vancouver (a 15 minutes bus ride from downtown) to New Westminster, a suburb. They now live 12 minutes by foot from a SkyTrain station, which is a 25-minute ride from the centre of the city. Over the past decade a few thousand people have moved into residential buildings within walking distance of the station and there are a wide variety of commercial and restaurant options nearby.

Other cities have followed this model. In 2004, for instance, Denver rezoned the area around two new train hubs to allow high-density apartment living.[28] In *CarFree Cities* J.H. Crawford maps out a post-car city that includes light rail transport nodes with decreasing residential density as you move away from each station.

Car free neighbourhoods are an exciting development. A German group, Autofrei wohnen (Living without cars), promotes these neighbourhoods. In Cologne, Germany's fourth biggest city, Autofrei wohnen helped launch a car-free development of 450 single-family homes and small apartment buildings. Built on a former railway repair yard, roads are zoned for pedestrians. Completed in 2010, the four-hectare neighbourhood is within 700 metres of tram and bus lines as well as two intercity train lines.

As this book went to print a car-free city designed for up to 50,000 was being built close to Abu Dhabi's international airport in the United Arab Emirates. The town will have narrow streets and all of its energy will be produced from sunlight. This 2.3-square-mile community will be slightly smaller than Venice, which is also car-free. So is the 1,000 year old Moroccan city of Fes el Bali. With no public transport or bikes, 300,000 residents get around this UNESCO heritage site by foot.

Beyond shifting money to mass transit and cycling infrastructure it's important to see things holistically. To slow sprawl (and improve equity) homebuyer tax breaks should be shifted to renters. Building public housing and subsidizing co-ops in areas conducive to car-free living are also part of the solution to the sprawling landscape.

More broadly, the anti-car movement will thrive as more people challenge the logic of a system driven by the endless accumulation of profit. Capitalism promotes the private car in other ways. Based upon the private ownership of production and a socialized labour process, individuals are alienated from their labour, and more likely to search for meaning in conspicuous consumption. Additionally, the class character of capitalism hinders rational social planning since a small minority benefit from the way things are currently structured.

To a large extent the anti-car struggle is against concentrated private power (corporations). Our living spaces and transport systems should enhance the human experience while treading as lightly as possible on the environment. Considering its need for constant expansion, it is highly improbable that this can be accomplished under capitalism. As such it's important to explore post-capitalist economic visions. Ecosocialism, "a society in which production is carried out by freely associated labour and with consciously ecocentric means and ends," is one post-capitalist model that has been put forward.[29] Another alternative is Economic Democracy, which is rooted in social-ownership, workplace democracy and human entitlement.[30]

Many profit driven businesses will suffer as we shift away from the car. They concern us little. But, the same cannot be said for the individuals working in these firms. People need jobs and any movement that is serious about large scale social transformation needs to be cognizant of this. But it is important to remember that each dollar spent operating public transit creates more employment than building highways.[31] Additionally, autoworkers can easily assemble buses and trams while ad designers and car salespeople shift their efforts to selling bikes or buses. Others can drive buses or take on a myriad of tasks that grow along with non-car forms of transport. Ultimately, however, shifting to foot and pedal-powered transit places most of the energy burden on the individuals doing the walking or cycling while (more efficient) bus and rail create fewer jobs than the car. But the move away from the car will be part of a challenge to corporate power and conspicuous consumption that includes a shortened formal workweek.

Some believe peak oil will kill sprawl and the car. This doesn't give capitalism sufficient credit. If it's not stopped, capitalism's endless quest for profit will likely destroy humanity before we run out of carbon emitting energy sources. Rising energy prices have already spurred production of uber destructive fuels such as tar sands, shale oil, genetically modified ethanol, deep-sea oil and liquefied coal. Without some fundamental shift in social relations, a century from now energy companies will produce even more destructive forms of car fuel. From a human survival perspective, the planet has too many fossil fuels, not too few.

While some peak oil proponents and environmentalists frame the fight against the car from a negative perspective (*The Party's Over* is the title of one book), the anti-car movement need not focus on personal sacrifice. Let's emphasize the positive. When we no longer depend on the private automobile we will be healthier and less burdened by debt. Children will safely play in front of their dwellings while young adults will go out with less fear of a fatal accident on their way home at night. Our communities will be more vibrant. *Urban Sprawl and Public Health* concludes that there "is strong evidence that mixed-use, walk-able neighbourhoods, contribute to social capital as measured by knowing one's neighbours, participating in political life, trusting other people, and being socially active."[32]

In *Bury the Chains* Adam Hochschild describes the political climate in England just prior to the abolishment of slavery in 1833: "A latent feeling was in the air, but an intellectual undercurrent disapproving of slavery was something very different from the belief that anything could ever be done about it. An analogy today might be how some people think about automobiles. For reasons of global warming, air quality, traffic, noise and dependence on oil [and the other problems outlined in this book], the world would be better off without cars. And what happens when India and China have as many cars as the United States? Even if you depend on driving to work, it is possible to agree there's a big problem."[33]

We can do something about it. It's time to move beyond private automobility.

Bibliography

A Better Place to Live: Reshaping the American Suburb. Philip Langdon. University of Massachusetts Press, 1994.

A Financial History of the American Automobile Industry: A Study of the Ways in Which the Leading American Producers of Automobiles Have Met Their Capital Requirements. Lawrence H Seltzer. Houghton Mifflin, 1928.

A Field Guide to Sprawl. Dolores Hayden; Jim Wark. W.W. Norton, 2004.

Against Automobility. Steffen Böhm; et al. Blackwell, 2006.

Alleviating Urban Traffic Congestion. Richard Arnott; Tilmann Rave; Ronnie Schöb. MIT Press, 2005.

All the Shah's Men: An American Coup and the Roots of Middle East Terror. Stephen Kinzer. J. Wiley & Sons, 2003.

America Adopts the Automobile, 1895-1910. James J Flink. MIT Press, 1970.

American Theocracy: The Peril and Politics of Radical Religion, Oil, and Borrowed Money in the 21st Century. Kevin Phillips. Viking, 2006.

American Transportation Policy. Robert Jay Dilger. Praeger, 2003.

The Atlantic City Gamble. George Sternlieb; James W Hughes. Harvard University Press, 1983.

The Automobile Age. James J Flink. MIT Press, 1988.

The Automobile: A Chronology of its Antecedents, Development, and Impact. Clay McShane. Greenwood Press, 1997.

Automobile Politics: Ecology and Cultural Political Economy. Matthew Paterson. Cambridge University Press, 2007.

America's Undeclared War: What's Killing our Cities and How We Can Stop It. Daniel Lazare. Harcourt, 2001.

Amazonia at the Crossroads: The Challenge of Sustainable Development. Anthony L Hall. Institute of Latin American Studies, 2000

Architecture of Fear. Nan Ellin; Edward James Blakely; et al. Princeton Architectural Press, 1997.

Asphalt Nation: How the Automobile Took Over America, and How We Can Take It Back. Jane Holtz Kay. Crown Publishers, 1997.

A Thousand Barrels a Second: The Coming Oil Break Point and the Challenges Facing an Energy Dependent World. Peter Tertzakian. McGraw-Hill, 2006.

Autogeddon. Heathcote Williams. Arcade Pub., 1991.

Autokind vs. Mankind: An Analysis of Tyranny, a Proposal for Rebellion, a Plan for Reconstruction. Kenneth R Schneider. Norton, 1971.

Auto Mania: Cars, Consumers, and the Environment. Tom McCarthy. Yale University Press, 2007.

Autopia: Cars and Culture. Peter Wollen; Joe Kerr. Reaktion Books, 2002.

Blood and Oil: The Dangers and Consequences of America's Growing Petroleum Dependency. Michael T Klare. Metropolitan Books/Henry Holt & Co., 2004.

Bowling Alone: The Collapse and Revival of American Community. Robert D Putnam. Simon & Schuster, 2000.

Branded: The Buying and Selling of Teenagers. Alissa Quart. Perseus Pub., 2003.

Born to Buy: The Commercialized Child and the New Consumer Culture. Juliet Schor. Scribner, 2004.

The Bottomless Well: The Twilight of Fuel, the Virtue of Waste, and Why We Will Never Run Out of Energy. Peter W Huber; Mark P Mills. Basic Books, 2005.

Buyways: Billboards, Automobiles, and the American Landscape.

Catherine Gudis. Routledge, 2004.

The Car and the City: The Automobile, the Built Environment, and Daily Urban Life. Martin Wachs; Margaret Crawford. University of Michigan Press, 1992.

Carbon Shift: How the Twin Crises of Oil Depletion and Climate Change Will Define the Future. Thomas Homer-Dixon; Nick Garrison. Random House Canada, 2009.

Carchitecture: When the Car and the City Collide. Jonathan Bell; et al. Birkhäuser, 2001

Carfree Cities. J H Crawford. International Books, 2002.

Carjacked: The Culture of the Automobile and its Effect on Our Lives. Catherine Lutz; Anne Lutz Fernandez. Palgrave Macmillan, 2010.

Car Cultures. Daniel Miller. Oxford, 2001.

Car Mania: A Critical History of Transport. Winfried Wolf. Pluto Press, 1996.

Cars and Culture: The Life Story of a Technology. Rudi Volti. Greenwood Press, 2004.

Car Wars: Battles on the Road to Nowhere. Chris Mosey. Vision, 2000.

Car Sick: Solutions For Our Car-Addicted Culture. Lynn Sloman. Chelsea Green, 2006.

Corporate Power, American Democracy, and the Automobile Industry. Stan Luger. Cambridge University Press, 2000.

The Corporation: The Pathological Pursuit of Profit and Power. Joel Bakan. Free Press, 2004.

Confessions of an Economic Hit Man. John Perkins. Berrett-Koehler, 2004.

The Consumer Trap: Big Business Marketing in American Life. Michael Dawson. University of Illinois Press, 2003.

Crude: The Story of Oil. Sonia Shah. Seven Stories Press, 2004.

Dark Age Ahead. Jane Jacobs. Random House, 2004.

The Decline of Transit: Urban Transportation in German and U.S. Cities, 1900-1970. Glenn Yago. Cambridge University Press, 1984.

Developing Alberta's Oil Sands: From Karl Clark to Kyoto. Paul A Chastko. University of Calgary Press, 2004.

Divorce Your Car! Ending the Love Affair with the Automobile. Katie Alvord. New Society Publishers, 2000

Down the Asphalt Path: The Automobile and the American City. Clay McShane. Columbia University Press, 1994.

Driving Over a Cliff?: Business Lessons From the World's Car Industry. Graeme P Maxton; John Wormald. Economist Intelligence Unit, 1995.

Dynasties: Fortune and Misfortune in the World's Great Family Businesses. David Landes. Penguin Books, 2008

Earth in the Balance: Ecology and the Human Spirit. Albert Gore. Houghton Mifflin, 1992.

Ecology Against Capitalism. John Bellamy Foster. Monthly Review Press, 2002.

Economic Democracy: The Working-Class Alternative to Capitalism. Allan Engler Fernwood Pub., 2010.

Economics at the Wheel: The Costs of Cars and Drivers. Richard C Porter. Academic Press, 1999.

The End of Oil: On the Edge of a Perilous New World. Paul Roberts. Houghton Mifflin, 2004.

The Enemy of Nature: The End of Capitalism or the End of the World?. Joel Kovel. Zed Books, 2007

Fast food Nation: The Dark Side of the All-American Meal. Eric Schlosser. Houghton Mifflin, 2001.

For Love of the Automobile: Looking Back into the History of Our Desires. Wolfgang Sachs. University of California Press, 1992.

From Streetcar to Superhighway. Mark S. Foster. Temple University Press, 1981.

Feeding the Fire: The Lost History and Uncertain Future of Mankind's Energy Addiction. Mark E Eberhart. Harmony Books, 2007.

Fighting Traffic: The Dawn of the Motor Age in the American City. Peter D Norton. MIT Press, 2008.

Forbidden Truth: U.S.-Taliban Secret Oil Diplomacy and the Failed Hunt for Bin Laden. Jean-Charles Brisard; Guillaume Dasquié. Thunder's Mouth Press, 2002.

Gangs of America: The Rise of Corporate Power and the Disabling of Democracy. Ted Nace. Berrett-Koehler, 2003.

Getting There: The Epic Struggle Between Road and Rail in the American Century. Stephen B Goddard. University of Chicago Press, 1996.

Ghost Wars: The Secret History of the CIA, Afghanistan, and Bin Laden, from the Soviet Invasion to September 10, 2001. Steve Coll. Penguin Press, 2004.

Goodyear Invades the Backcountry: The Corporate Takeover of a Rural Town. Bryan D Palmer. Monthly Review Press, 1994.

Green Guerrillas: Environmental Conflicts and Initiatives in Latin America and the Caribbean. Helen Collinson. Black Rose Books, 1997.

Gusher of Lies: The Dangerous Delusions of "Energy Independence". Robert Bryce. Public Affairs, 2009.

Heat: How to Stop the Planet from Burning. George Monbiot. Allen Lane, 2006.

The High Cost of Free Parking. Donald C Shoup. Planners Press American Planning Association, 2005.

High and Mighty: SUVs - The world's Most Dangerous Vehicles and How They Got That Way. Keith Bradsher. Public Affairs, 2002.

Highway Robbery: Transportation Racism & New Routes to Equity. Robert D Bullard; Glenn S Johnson; Angel O Torres. South End Press, 2004

Home on the Road: The Motor Home in America. Roger B White. Smithsonian Institution Press, 2000.

How To Live Well Without Owning a Car. Chris Balish. Ten Speed Press, 2006.

The Hype About Hydrogen: Fact and Fiction in the Race to Save the Climate. Joseph J Romm. Island Press, 2004.

In Praise of Slow: How a Worldwide Movement is Challenging the Cult of Speed. Carl Honoré. HarperSanFrancisco, 2004.

In the Shadow of a Saint. Ken Wiwa. Alfred A. Knopf Canada, 2000.

Internal Combustion: How Corporations and Governments Addicted the World to Oil and Derailed the Alternatives. Edwin Black. St. Martin's Press, 2006.

Interstate: Express Highway Politics, 1941-1956. Mark H. Rose. Lawrence, Regents Press of Kansas, 1979.

Into the Buzzsaw: Leading Journalists Expose the Myth of a Free Press. Kristina Börjesson. Prometheus Books, 2002.

Inventing Reality: The Politics of the Mass Media. Michael Parenti. St. Martin's Press, 1986.

The Iranian Labyrinth: Journeys Through Theocratic Iran and Its Furies. Dilip Hiro. Publishers Group West, 2005.

Le Corbusier: A Life. Nicholas Fox Weber. Alfred A. Knopf, 2008.

Les Québécois au volant, c'est mortel. Richard Bergeron. Les Intouchables, 2005.

Lots of Parking: Land Use in a Car Culture. John A Jakle; Keith A Sculle. University of Virginia Press, 2004.

Life After the Thirty Second Spot: Energize Your Brand With a Bold Mix of Alternatives to Traditional Advertising. Joseph Jaffe. John Wiley & Sons, 2005.

Made to Break: Technology and Obsolescence in America. Giles Slade. Harvard University Press, 2006.

Mass Motorization and Mass Transit: An American History and Policy Analysis. David W Jones. Indiana University Press, 2008.

Making a Killing: How and Why Corporations Use Armed Force to Do Business. Madelaine Drohan. Random House Canada, 2003.

The Media and Entertainment Industries: Readings in Mass Communications. Albert N Greco. Allyn and Bacon, 2000.

The Media Monopoly. Ben H Bagdikian. Beacon Press, 1983.

The Neighborhoods of Queens. Claudia Gryvatz Copquin. Yale University Press, 2007

News and the Culture of Lying. Paul Weaver. Maxwell Macmillan Canada, 1994.

The News at Any Cost: How Journalists Compromise Their Ethics to Shape the News. Tom Goldstein. Simon and Schuster, 1985.

No Logo: Taking Aim at the Brand Bullies. Naomi Klein. Random House of Canada, 2000.

Once There Were Greenfields: How Urban Sprawl is Undermining America's Environment, Economy, and Social Fabric. F Kaid Benfield; Matthew Raimi; Donald D T Chen. Natural Resources Defense Council, 1999.

Outgrowing the Earth: The Food Security Challenge in the Age of Falling Water Tables and Rising Temperatures. Lester Russell Brown; Earth Policy Institute. W.W. Norton & Co., 2004

Perverse Subsidies: How Tax Dollars Can Undercut the Environment and the Economy. Norman Myers; Jennifer Kent. Island Press, 2001.

Petrodollar Warfare: Oil, Iraq and the Future of the Dollar. William R Clark, New Society, 2005.

Product Placement in Hollywood Films: A History. Kerry Segrave. McFarland, 2004.

Recasting the Machine Age: Henry Ford's Village Industries. Howard P Segal. University of Massachusetts Press, 2005.

Reclaiming our Cities and Towns: Better Living with Less Traffic. David Engwicht. New Society, 1993.

Republic of Drivers: A Cultural History of Automobility in America. Cotten Seiler. University of Chicago Press, 2008.

Resource Rebels: Native Challenges to Mining and Oil Corporations. Al Gedicks. South End Press, 2001.

Road Rage and Aggressive Driving: Steering Clear of Highway Warfare. Leon James; Diane Nahl. Prometheus Books, 2000.

Road Rage. Maria L Garase. LFB Scholarly Pub., 2006.

Sprawltown: Looking for the City on its Edges. Richard Ingersoll. Princeton Architectural Press, 2006.

Superhighway--Superhoax. Helen Leavitt. Doubleday, 1970.

Taken for a Ride: Detroit's Big Three and the Politics of Pollution. Jack Doyle. Four Walls Eight Windows, 2000.

Taking the High Road: A Metropolitan Agenda for Transportation Reform. Bruce Katz; Robert Puentes; Brookings Institution Press, 2005.

Traffic: Why We Drive the Way We Do (And What it Says About Us). Tom Vanderbilt. Alfred A. Knopf, 2008.

The True Costs of Road Transport. David Maddison; Centre for Social and Economic Research on the Global Environment.; et al. Earthscan, 1996.

Trust and Power: Consumers, the Modern Corporation, and the Making of the United States Automobile Market. Sally H Clarke. University Press, 2007.

Twentieth Century Sprawl: Highways and the Reshaping of the American Landscape. Owen D Gutfreund. Oxford University Press, 2004.

Urban Sprawl, Global Warming, and the Empire of Capital.
George A Gonzalez. State University of New York Press,
2009.

*Urban Sprawl and Public Health: Designing, Planning, and
Building for Healthy Communities.* Howard Frumkin;
Lawrence D Frank; Richard Jackson. Island Press, 2004.

Urban Sprawl: A Comprehensive Reference Guide. David C
Soule. Greenwood Press, 2006.

Urban Sprawl: Causes, Consequences, & Policy Responses.
Gregory D Squires. Urban Institute Press, 2002.

Urban Elites and Mass Transportation: The Dialectics of Power.
J Allen Whitt. Princeton University Press, 1982.

Wanderlust: A History of Walking. Rebecca Solnit. Penguin,
2001.

*Wheels for the World: Henry Ford, His Company, and a Century
of Progress, 1903-2003.* Douglas Brinkley. Viking, 2003

*Why Your World is About to Get a Whole Lot Smaller: Oil and the
End of Globalization.* Jeff Rubin. Random House, 2009.

It's the Crude, Dude: War, Big oil and the Fight for the Planet.
Linda McQuaig. Anchor Canada, 2006.

When Corporations Rule the World. David C Korten. Berrett-
Koehler Publishers, 1995.

Zoom: The Global Race to Fuel the Car of the Future. Iain
Carson; Vijay V. Vaitheeswaran. Penguin, 2008.

Endnotes

PREFACE

1 Globe and Mail Jan 5 2010

CHAPTER 1

1 Carjacked, 144
2 Wall Street Journal Mar 3 2011
3 High and Mighty, 76
4 Globe and Mail July 5 2006
5 Mass Motorization and Mass Transit, 4
6 http://usgovinfo.about. com/b/2007/06/15/most-americans-still-drive-to-work-alone.htm
7 National Post May 25 2006
8 Washington Post Oct 12 2006
9 American Theocracy, 60
10 Ottawa Citizen Apr 14 2006
11 Wall Street Journal Oct 17 2006
12 New York Times Mar 14 2004
13 National Post May 31 2008
14 Traffic,139
15 The Observer Apr 3 2007
16 Washington Post Apr 9 2007
17 Los Angeles Times Jun 8 2008
18 http://news.bbc.co.uk/2/hi/ health/3761012.stm
19 A Better Place to Live, 11
20 Lots of Parking, 248
21 http://www.wbtv.com/Global/story. asp?S=12283464
22 Highway Robbery, 182
23 Highway Robbery, 167
24 Driving Over a Cliff, 48
25 Highway Robbery, 166
26 http://www.publictransportation.org/ facts/090107_transit_savings.asp
27 The True Costs of Road Transport, 195

28 Asphalt Nation, 130
29 Carjacked, 110
30 Highway Robbery, 166
31 Wall Street Journal July 8 2004
32 Globe and Mail Sept 11 2006
33 http://www.alternet.org/ story/148061/less_work,_more_ life?page=entire
34 Car Sick, 9
35 Driving Over a Cliff?, 45
36 Down the Asphalt Path, 189
37 Globe and Mail Mar 17 2010
38 New York Times July 25 2006
39 Reclaiming Our Cities and Towns, 18

CHAPTER 2

1 USA Today Feb 28 2011
2 New York Times May 26 2004.
3 Asphalt Nation, 105
4 Divorce Your Car, 91
5 Divorce Your Car, 91
6 Health effects caused by noise: evidence in the literature from the past 25 years. Noise & Health 6: 5-13.
7 Wall Street Journal May 5 2005
8 www.horntones.com
9 Driving Over a Cliff?, 56
10 Globe and Mail Nov 25 2004
11 Urban Sprawl and Public Health, 148
12 Urban Sprawl and Public Health, 141
13 Road Rage and Aggressive Driving, 17
14 Urban Sprawl and Public Health, 152
15 Maclean's Feb 27 2006

CHAPTER 3

1 Autogeddon, 40
2 Globe and Mail Sep 12 2007

Stop Signs

3 http://www.autoblog.
   com/2009/02/05/national-safety-
   council-says-2008-traffic-deaths-hit-
   record-low/ounci
4 Urban Sprawl and Public Health, 110
5 Wheels for the World, 114
6 The Automobile, 60
7 Wheels for the World, 335
8 The Automobile, 66 & 101
9 Driving Over a Cliff?, 20
10 Urban Sprawl and Public Health, 113
11 Wall Street Journal May 11, 2006
12 Wall Street Journal Sept 1 2005
13 Sports utility vehicles and older
   pedestrians. A damaging collision.
   BMJ 331: 787-8.
14 Wall Street Journal Aug 16 2007
15 High and Mighty, 188
16 New York Times June 13 2006
17 National Post Jan 22 2005
18 Gazette Oct 29 2007
19 Globe and Mail Nov 18 2004
20 In Praise of Slow, 103
21 The Consumer Trap, 157
22 How To Live Well Without Owning
   a Car, 94
23 Getting There, 255
24 http://www.washingtonmonthly.com/
   features/2003/0304.longman.html
25 Urban Sprawl and Public Health, 122
26 Am J Public Health 93: 1564−1569
27 Urban Sprawl and Public Health, 110
28 Urban Sprawl and Public Health, 113
29 Urban Sprawl and Public Health, 112
30 La Presse May 15 2006
31 Urban Sprawl and Public Health, 120
32 Wall Street Journal May 11 2006
33 Alleviating Urban Traffic
   Congestion, 118
34 Autogeddon, 30
35 New York Times Sept 13 2010
36 http://www.psychologytoday.com/
   blog/animal-emotions/201007/animals-
   and-cars-one-million-animals-are-
   killed-our-roads-every-day
37 Globe and Mail Nov 24 2004
38 Globe and Mail 2007
39 New York Times Sept 13 2010

CHAPTER 4

1 Taken for a Ride, 455
2 Urban Sprawl and Public Health, 88
3 Neighbourhood socioeconomic
status, maternal education and adverse
birth outcomes among mothers
living near highways. J Epidemiol
Community Health 62: 695-700.
4 Effect of prenatal exposure to
airborne polycyclic aromatic
hydrocarbons on neurodevelopment in
the first 3 years of life among inner-
city children. Env Health Persp 114:
1287-92.
5 Montreal Gazette Feb 16 2005
6 Urban Sprawl, 31
7 Urban Sprawl and Public Health, 188
8 Taken for a Ride, 4
9 Personal Exposures to Traffic-
Related Air Pollution and Acute
Respiratory Health Among Bronx
School Children with Asthma. Env
Health Persp Jan 7.
10 Urban Sprawl and Public Health, 84
11 Montreal Gazette Sept 9 2004
12 Effect of exposure to traffic on
lung development from 10 to 18 years
of age: a cohort study. Lancet 369:
571-7.
13 Association of black carbon
with cognition among children in a
prospective birth cohort study. Am J
Epidemiol 167: 280-6.
14 Distance-weighted traffic density in

*proximity to a home is a risk factor for
leukemia and other childhood cancers. J
Air Waste Manag Assoc 50:175-80.*
15 Economics at the Wheel, 174
16 Globe and Mail Aug 20 2004
17 The Ecologist Nov 2005
18 The Ecologist Nov 2005
19 The Ecologist Nov 2005
20 Urban Sprawl and Public Health, 88
*21 http://www.arb.ca.gov/research/
aaqs/pm/pm.htm*
22 Taken for a Ride, 341
23 Urban Sprawl and Public Health, 82
*24 http://www.fas.org/sgp/crs/misc/
R41062.pdf*
25 Vancouver Sun July 17 2007
*26 Residential exposure to traffic
is associated with coronary
atherosclerosis. Circulation 116: 489-
96.*
*27 Exposure to Traffic and the Onset of
Myocardial Infarction. N Engl J Med
2004 351: 1721-30.*
28 Taken for a Ride, 236
29 Once There Were Greenfields, 55
30 New York Times Nov 11 2005
31 Driving Over a Cliff?, 29
32 Urban Sprawl and Public Health, 77

CHAPTER 5

1 Superhighway-Superhoax, 17
2 Le Devoir May 23 2006
*3 Urban sprawl and risk for being
overweight or obese. Am J Pub Health
94: 1574 — 79.*
*4 Obesity relationships with
community design, physical activity,
and time spent in cars. Am J Prev Med
227: 87—96.*
*5 A silver lining? The connection
between gasoline prices and obesity.
Econ Inquiry Mar 11.*

6 Globe and Mail Nov 22 2004
7 Urban Sprawl and Public Health, 94
8 Wall Street Journal Aug 30 2005
*9 Physical activity and colorectal
cancer. Sports Med 34: 239—252.*
*10 Physical activity and
cardiovascular disease risk in
middle-aged and older women. Am J
Epidemiol 150: 408-16.*
*11 Physical activity predicts gray
matter volume in late adulthood:
the Cardiovascular Health Study.
Neurology 75: 1415-22.*
12 Urban Sprawl and Public Health, 94
13 Urban Sprawl and Public Health, 91
14 New York Times Mar 14 2004
15 National Post Feb 19 2005
16 New York Times July 12 2010
17 Urban Sprawl and Public Health, 106
*18 http://www.sfgate.com/cgi-bin/
blogs/sfmoms/category?cat=1583*
19 USA Today Dec 21 2004
*20 http://www.gomdot.com/Divisions/
Highways/Resources/Programs/SRTS/
Home.aspx*
21 Highway Robbery, 189
22 Urban Sprawl and Public Health, 116
23 Dynasties, 125
24 Autokind vs. Mankind, 242
25 The Automobile Age, 117
26 Wheels for the World, 686
27 Road Rage, 29
28 Urban Sprawl and Public Health, 144
29 Urban Sprawl and Public Health, 146
*30 http://www.ncbi.nlm.nih.gov/pmc/
articles/PMC208820/*
*31 hhttp://www.lowcarbfriends.com/
bbs/lean-life/154822-article-about-
stress-comfort-food-obesity.htmlttp://
www.lowcarbfriends.com/bbs/
lean-life/154822-article-about-stress-
comfort-food-obesity.html*

CHAPTER 6

1 *Advertising Age May 31 2010*
2 *Once There Were Greenfields, 41*
3 *Guardian Weekly Feb 9 2007*
4 *New York Times Feb 28 2006*
5 *Globe and Mail June 10 2006*
6 *The Economist June 24 2006*
7 *Getting There, 238*
8 *Shopping for Subsidies: How Wal-Mart Uses Taxpayer Money to Finance Its Never-Ending Growth*
9 *New York Times Oct 10 2007*
10 *Wall Street Journal Oct 23 2007*
11 *Once There Were Greenfields, 43*
12 *Wall Street Journal Sept 15 2004*
13 *Wall Street Journal Sept 15 2004*

CHAPTER 7

1 *Wall Street Journal Oct 1 2007*
2 *Buyways, 47*
3 *Buyways, 68*
4 *Buyways, 146*
5 *Fast Food Nation, 17*
6 *Buyways, 94*
7 *Buyways, 233*
8 *Buyways, 97*
9 *Buyways, 238*
10 *http://scenicflorida.org/index.php/Litter-On-A-Stick-Billboards-Message-Go-Ahead-Trash-America.html*
11 *Buyways, 53*
12 *Buyways, 65*
13 *Buyways, 102*

CHAPTER 8

1 *The High Cost of Free Parking, 443*
2 *The High cost of Free Parking, 624*
3 *The High Cost of Free Parking, 154*
4 *Lots of Parking, 10*
5 *Lots of Parking, 43*
6 *Reclaiming Our Cities and Towns, 44*
7 *The Car and the City, 55*
8 *Perverse Subsidies, 80*
9 *The High Cost of Free Parking, 217*
10 *Lots of Parking, 2*
11 *Lots of Parking, 1*
12 *The High Cost of Free Parking, 135*
13 *Divorce Your Car, 107*
14 *The High Cost of Free Parking, 136*
15 *Lots of Parking, 8*
16 *Lots of Parking, 96*
17 *Lots of Parking, 35*
18 *Lots of Parking, 35*
19 *Lots of Parking, 35*
20 *The High Cost of Free Parking, 131*
21 *The High Cost of Free Parking, 136*
22 *The High Cost of Free Parking, 136*
23 *The High Cost of Free Parking, 102*
24 *The High Cost of Free Parking, 122*
25 *Lots of Parking, 77*
26 *Lots of Parking, 77*
27 *Lots of Parking, 167*
28 *Lots of Parking, 167*
29 *The Car and the City, 54*
30 *The High Cost of Free Parking, 31*
31 *Lots of Parking, 203*
32 *The High Cost of Free Parking, 84*
33 *Divorce Your Car, 204*
34 *The High Cost of Free Parking, 25*
35 *The High Cost of Free Parking, 152*
36 *The High Cost of Free Parking, 97*
37 *Lots of Parking, 182*
38 *The High Cost of Free Parking, 142*
39 *The High Cost of Free Parking, 144*
40 *The High Cost of Free Parking, 153*
41 *The High Cost of Free Parking, 94*
42 *The High Cost of Free Parking, 24*
43 *http://www.emagazine.com/view/?2418*
44 *The High Cost of Free Parking, 295*
45 *America's Undeclared War, 141*
46 *The High Cost of Free Parking, 207*
47 *Lots of Parking, 79*
48 *Lots of Parking, 79*

49 *Lots of Parking, 51*
50 *http://www.urbanhabitat.org/node/314*
51 *Twentieth Century Sprawl, 59*
52 *Urban Sprawl, 148*
53 *Economics at the Wheel, 163*
54 *Lots of Parking, 183*
55 *The High Cost of Free Parking, 591*
56 *The High Cost of Free Parking, 185*
57 *The High Cost of Free Parking, 546*
58 *Lots of Parking, 8*

CHAPTER 9

1 *Once There Were Greenfields, 121*
2 *Once There Were Greenfields, 121*
3 *Getting There, 207*
4 *Once There Were Greenfields, 121*
5 *Sprawltown, 88*
6 *The Automobile, 53*
7 *The Automobile, 91*
8 *Superhighway-Superhoax, 122*
9 *Once There Were Greenfields, 122*
10 *American Transportation Policy, 44*
11 *Getting There, 217*
12 *Superhighway-Superhoax, 5*
13 *Wheels for the World, 642*
14 *National Post Aug 16 2005*
15 *The Automobile, 104*
16 *The Automobile, 75*
17 *The Automobile Age, 135*
18 *The Automobile Age, 148*
19 *The Automobile Age, 135*
20 *Highway Robbery, 167*
21 *Highway Robbery, 168*
22 *Highway Robbery, 168*
23 *Highway Robbery, 168*
24 *Highway Robbery, 191*
25 *Highway Robbery, 4*
26 *The High Cost of Free Parking, 126*
27 *Highway Robbery, 55*
28 *Highway Robbery, 53*
29 *Highway Robbery, 52*

30 *Highways to Nowhere, 105*
31 *Urban Sprawl, 80*
32 *Automobile Politics, 50*
33 *Car Cultures, 93*
34 *http://www.scivee.tv/node/9645*

CHAPTER 10

1 *Globe and Mail Apr 27 2006*
2 *The Automobile, 42*
3 *Urban Sprawl and Public Health, 41*
4 *Getting There, 201*
5 *http://carbusters.org/files/2010/01/Carbusters-11.pdf.*
6 *Times of London Aug 14 2008*
7 *http://www.memphisflyer.com/backissues/issue525/cr525.htm*
8 *http://www.goodreads.com/quotes/show/146533*
9 *Down the Asphalt Path, 142*
10 *Globe and Mail Aug 31 2004*
11 *The Automobile, 27*
12 *New York Times Aug 27 2004*
13 *The Automobile, 105*
14 *USA Today May 27 2005*
15 *New York Times Magazine May 22 2005*
16 *Globe and Mail June 3 2006*
17 *National Post Mar 5 2004*
18 *Without Wheels, 41*

CHAPTER 11

1 *The Car and the City, 38*
2 *http://www.gizmag.com/go/2672/*
3 *http://www.transact.org/report.asp?id=184*
4 *Down the Asphalt Path, 143*
5 *Autogeddon, 51*
6 *For Love of the Automobile, 11*
7 *Cars and Culture, 9*
8 *America Adopts the Automobile, 145*
9 *Wheels for the World, 114*
10 *Wheels for the World, 114*

Stop Signs

11 Wheels for the World, 114
12 Cars and Culture, 18
13 Down the Asphalt Path, 176
14 America's Undeclared War, 139
15 Down the Asphalt Path, 176
16 The Automobile, 34
17 Car Mania, 48
18 Divorce Your Car, 15
19 New York Times Oct 28 2004
20 Autopia, 71
21 The neighborhoods of Queens, 32
22 Sprawltown, 87
23 Carchitecture, 33
24 Twentieth Century Sprawl, 40
25 The Car and the City, 57
26 Buyways, 47
27 Autokind vs. Mankind, 80
28 http://www.beststuff.com/
fromthewire/mercedes-stakes-its-
ground-with-launch-of-new-s-class.
html

CHAPTER 12

1 Oregonian June 7 2004
2 Down the Asphalt Path. 115
3 From Street Car to Superhighway, 62
4 From Street Car to Superhighway, 23
5 Autokind vs. Mankind, 171
6 Urban Sprawl, 63
7 Urban Sprawl, 66
8 Urban Sprawl, 13
9 Wall Street Journal May 25 2007
10 http://www.highbeam.com/
doc/1G1-20836112.html
11 Wanderlust, 255
12 Architecture of Fear, 94
13 Architecture of Fear, 88
14 Architecture of Fear, 97
15 Urban Sprawl and Public Health, 173
16 New York Times June 16 2006
17 Auto Mania, 44
18 New York Times Magazine June 11
2006
19 New York Times June 11 2006
20 Car Culture, 148
21 The Automobile, 64
22 New York Times June 11 2006
23 Wall Street Journal May 22 2007
24 Down the Asphalt Path, 228
25 Urban Sprawl and Public Health, 172
26 Bowling Alone, 213
27 Wanderlust, 255
28 Wanderlust, 218
29 Wanderlust, 218

CHAPTER 13

1 USA Today Dec 22 2008
2 The Guardian Weekly 06.08.10
3 Internal Combustion, 264
4 http://www.atmosp.physics.utoronto.
ca/people/lev/ESSgc2/11469763.pdf
5 Internal Combustion, 264
6 Resource Rebels, 42
7 New York Times Apr 16 2006
8 Monthly Review Sept 2006
9 In the Shadow of a Saint, 63
10 http://www.independent.co.uk/
news/world/africa/visible-from-space-
deadly-on-earth-the-gas-flares-of-
nigeria-1955108.html
11 In the Shadow of a Saint, 63
12 Resource Rebels, 44
13 In the Shadow of a Saint, 64
14 Guardian Weekly June 23 2006
15 Observer May 30 2010
16 Observer May 30 2010
17 Resource Rebels, 45
18 Resource Rebels, 45
19 Ottawa Citizen Dec 27 2006
20 Financial Times Apr 17 2006
21 New York Times Apr 21 2007
22 http://234next.com/csp/cms/
sites/Next/Home/5258469-146/The_
mercenaries_take_over__.csp

23 http://www.businessweek.com/
news/2010-09-06/jonathan-risks-clashes-
in-oil-rich-nigeria-vote-bid.html
24 http://www.janes.com/articles/
Janes-World-Insurgency-and-
Terrorism/Movement-for-the-
Emancipation-of-the-Niger-Delta-
MEND-Nigeria.html
25 http://www.shellguilty.com/learn-
more/human-rights-abuses/
26 Resource Rebels, 49 & 187
27 In the Shadow of a Saint, 62
28 Resource Rebels, 46
29 Resource Rebels, 47
30 New York Times May 19 2010
31 http://www.hour.ca/news/news.
aspx?iIDArticle=9189
32 Globe and Mail Sept 22 2006
33 Globe and Mail Sept 22 2006
34 http://www.ienearth.org/
tarsandsinfo.html
35 Globe and Mail July 5 2006
36 La Presse May 10 2006
37 Globe and Mail July 5 2006
38 National Post June 27 2006
39 http://ostseis.anl.gov/guide/
tarsands/index.cfm
40 Globe and Mail Sept 22 2006
41 Wall Street Journal Mar 27 2006
42 Ottawa Citizen July 27 2006
43 Wall Street Journal Apr 25 2007
44 New York Times June 30 2006
45 Wall Street Journal Mar 27 2006
46 Wall Street Journal Mar 27 2006
47 Financial Post Dec 5 2006
48 Ottawa Citizen July 10 2006
49 Montreal Hour May 18 2006
50 National Post Sept 20 2004
51 National Post Sept 23 2006
52 Developing Alberta's Oil Sands,
97-98
53 Los Angeles Times Oct 15 2006

54 Los Angeles Times Oct 15 2006
55 Globe and Mail Nov 30 2006
56 Los Angeles Times Oct 15 2006
57 http://www.news.cornell.edu/
stories/April07/Hofmeister.mr.html
58 Washington Post Oct 1 2006
59 Crude, xvii
60 Crude, 79
61 Divorce Your Car, 79
62 Divorce Your Car, 78
63 http://www.associatedcontent.com/
article/454782/the_worst_major_oil_
spills_in_history.html?cat=37
64 Making A Killing, 163
65 Monthly Review Sept 2006
66 Monthly Review Sept 2006

CHAPTER 14

1 New York Times May 31 2006
2 An Inconvenient Truth
3 The End of Oil, 118
4 Financial Times Jan 28 2005
5 Montreal Gazette July 21 2006
6 Presse Canadienne July 4 2006
7 New York Times Apr 17 2006
8 Who Killed the Electric Car (movie)
9 Toronto Star Sep 26 2006
10 Montreal Gazette Jan 11 2011
11 Financial Times Sep 15 2006
12 Heat, 5
13 Financial Times Dec 12 2003
14 Vancouver Sun Dec 4 2010
15 Financial Times Oct 4 2006
16 The Guardian Nov 28 2010
17 Guardian Weekly Oct 29 2004
18 Ottawa Citizen May 15 2006
19 Canadian Press March 6, 2011
20 Heat, 21
21 Heat, 154
22 Urban Sprawl and Public Health, 86
23 Urban Sprawl and Public Health, 86
24 New York Times Oct 05 2004

Stop Signs

25 *New York Times Mar 30 2006*

26 *Wall Street Journal July 18 2006*

27 *High and Mighty, xvi*

28 *High and Mighty, 355*

29 *Globe and Mail Sep 16 2004*

30 *End of Oil, 154*

31 *High and Mighty, xvii*

32 *End of Oil, 155*

33 *Wall Street Journal Jul 18 2006*

34 *Internal Combustion, 261*

35 *Highway Robbery, 3*

36 *San Jose Mercury News June 6 2004*

37 *High and Mighty, 248*

38 *http://www.serconline.org/ trafficcongestionrelief/talking.html*

39 *http://www.salon.com/news/ auto_industry/?story=/news/ feature/2010/11/04/us_truck_recovery*

40 *http://www.agmrc.org/ renewable_energy/ethanol/trends_ in_us_fuel_ethanol_production_ capacity_20052009.cfm*

41 *http://www.ethanolrfa.org/page/-/ objects/pdf/outlook/RFAoutlook2010_ fin.pdf?nocdn=1*

42 *New York Times Dec 24 2009*

43 *Financial Times May 30 2006*

44 *Internal Combustion, 286*

45 *Globe and Mail July 18 2005*

46 *Heat, 159*

47 *National Post Aug 12 2006*

48 *Guardian Weekly Jan 2010*

49 *http://www.grist.org/article/food- 2010-10-26-obama-and-cellulosic- ethanol*

50 *New York Times Oct 8 2006*

51 *New York Times Oct 8 2006*

52 *New York Times June 14 2006*

53 *New York Times June 14 2006*

54 *Globe and Mail Dec 13 2010*

55 *Gusher, 211*

56 *Why Your World Is About To Get A Whole Lot Smaller, 165*

57 *The Hype About Hydrogen, 35*

58 *Technology Review Mar 2007*

59 *Technology Review Mar 2007*

60 *Carbon Shift, 207*

61 *Carbon Shift, 207*

62 *A Thousand Barrels a Second, 174*

63 *Wall Street Journal Aug 16 2006*

64 *Carbon Shift, 115*

65 *New York Times July 5 2006*

66 *New York Times July 5 2006*

67 *New York Times May 29 2007*

68 *Technology Review Sept 2010*

CHAPTER 15

1 *Finanacial Times Aug 25 2007*

2 *Guardian Weekly Mar 2 2007*

3 *Finanacial Times Aug 25 2007*

4 *Once There Were Greenfields, 86*

5 *Urban Sprawl, 6*

6 *Globe and Mail Sep 28 2006*

7 *Outgrowing the Earth, 92*

8 *Outgrowing the Earth, 92*

9 *Once There Were Greenfields, 68*

10 *Lots of Parking, 244*

11 *Once There Were Greenfields, 66*

12 *Divorce Your Car, 118*

13 *Globe and Mail June 11 2007*

14 *Vancouver Sun Jun 14 2007*

15 *Once There Were Greenfields, 80*

16 *Urban Sprawl, 24*

17 *Urban Sprawl and Public Health, 129*

18 *Urban Sprawl, 32*

19 *Urban Sprawl and Public Health, 134*

20 *Ottawa Citizen May 21 2006*

21 *Divorce Your Car, 81*

22 *Economics at the Wheel, 176*

23 *Internal Combustion, 264?*

24 *Urban Sprawl, 32*

25 *Divorce Your Car, 63*

26 *Asphalt Nation, 82*

27 *Divorce Your Car, 83/84*

28 La Presse Aug 27 2007
29 Ottawa Citizen Sep 14 2007
30 La Presse Aug 27 2007
31 Divorce Your Car, 83
32 Wheels for the World, 746
33 Divorce Your Car, 69
34 Divorce Your Car, 83
35 Divorce Your Car, 69
36 New York Times Jul 29 2007
37 Divorce Your Car, 84
38 Divorce Your Car, 84
39 The Automobile, 160
40 Times of London Apr 16 2007
41 The Bottomless Well, 145
42 Driving Over a Cliff?, 22
43 National Post Sept 24 2005
44 Toronto Star Nov 21 2004
45 La Presse Aug 27 2007
46 The Environmental Cost of One Car
(report)
47 Divorce Your Car, 84
48 Driving Over a Cliff?, 63
49 Buyways, 62
50 Resource Rebels, 41
51 http://news.mongabay.
com/2009/1025-hance_huntoil.html
52 Resource Rebels, 56 & 71
53 Confessions of an Economic
Hitman, 142
54 Amazonia at the Crossroads, 82
55 Amazonia at the Crossroads, 80/81
56 Resource Rebels, 73
57 http://indigenousrights.info/web/
index.php?odas=276&giella1=eng

CHAPTER 16

1 USA Today Apr 6 2004
2 USA Today Mar 22 2004
3 New York Times May 7 2006
4 New York Times July 12 2010
5 Wall Street Journal July 12 2004
6 Once There Were Greenfields, 60

7 National Post Feb 20 2008
8 All the Shah's Men, 80
9 All the Shah's Men, 80 & 87
10 All the Shah's Men, 87
11 All the Shah's Men, 160
12 All the Shah's Men, 160
13 All the Shah's Men, 163
14 All the Shah's Men, 191
15 Montreal Gazette Sept 24 2006
16 All the Shah's Men, 202
17 Blood and Oil, 44
18 The Iranian Labyrinth, 98
19 It's the Crude, Dude, 294
20 Blood and Oil, 88
21 All the Shah's Men, 204
22 Forbidden Truth, 68/69
23 It's the Crude, Dude, 289
24 Petrodollar Warfare 43
25 Blood and Oil, 40
26 Blood and Oil, 41
27 Petrodollar Warfare, 149
28 Petrodollar Warfare, 45
29 http://news.yahoo.com/s/
afp/20100913/wl_mideast_afp/u
ssaudiweaponstrade_20100913060123
30 Forbidden Truth, 68
31 Ghost Wars, 83
32 Forbidden Truth, 80
33 Ghost Wars, 65
34 Ghost Wars, 85
35 Ghost Wars, 155
36 Ghost Wars, 155
37 Ghost Wars, 87
38 Ghost Wars, 165
39 It's the Crude, Dude, 267
40 It's the Crude, Dude, 267
41 End of Oil, 106
42 Blood and Oil, 55
43 Blood and Oil, 54

CHAPTER 17

1 Divorce your car, 11

Stop Signs

2 *Wheels for the World*, 40
3 *Against Automobility*, 26
4 *Cars and Culture*, 42
5 *Against Automobility*, 223
6 *Financial Times Jan 15 2007*
7 *http://www.businessweek.com/magazine/content/08_21/b4085036665789_page_3.htm*
8 *Financial Times Jan 15 2007*
9 *Earth in the Balance*, 325
10 *America Adopts the Automobile*, 250
11 *Car Mania*, 168
12 *Le Monde Oct 25 2006*
13 *http://news.cnet.com/8301-11128_3-9894597-54.html*
14 *New York Times May 12 2007*
15 *Driving Over a Cliff?*, 55
16 *Zoom*, 16
17 *Financial Times Oct 29 2007*
18 *http://www.businessweek.com/magazine/content/08_21/b4085036665789_page_3.htm*
19 *End of Oil*, 89
20 *Feeding the Fire*, 252
21 *http://www.earthtalktoday.tv/earthtalk-voices/solutions-fossil-fuels-don-fitz.htm*
22 *Traffic*, 148
23 *Carfree Cities*, 39
24 *Urban Elites and Mass Transportation*, 196
25 *Interstate*, 92
26 *The Automobile*, 83
27 *Twentieth Century Sprawl*, 79
28 *From Street Car to Superhighway*, 62
29 *America's Undeclared War*, 141
30 *Down the Asphalt Path*, 194
31 *Down the Asphalt Path*, 201
32 *Getting There*, 122
33 *Getting There*, 122
34 *Les Quebecois au Volant*, 97
35 *Heat*, 152
36 *America's Undeclared War*, 229

CHAPTER 18

1 *Le Monde Diplomatique Jan 2010*
2 *Wall Street Journal July 18 2006*
3 *The Automobile*, 59
4 *Car Culture*, 39
5 *America's Undeclared War*, 197
6 *Urban Sprawl*, 10
7 *Urban Elites and Mass Transportation*, 187
8 *Car Culture*, 157
9 *America's Undeclared War*, 152
10 *Economist Sept 10 2004*
11 *Dynasties*, 167
12 *Ecology Against Capitalism*, 99
13 *The Automobile*, 64
14 *Interstate*, 48
15 *A Financial History of the American Automobile Industry*, 279
16 *A Financial History of the American Automobile Industry*, 22
17 *http://www.cruise-in.com/resource/cismar02.htm*
18 *The Automobile Age*, 5
19 *Cars and Culture*, 15
20 *The Automobile*, 16
21 *The Automobile*, 17
22 *Twentieth Century Sprawl*, 15
23 *Autokind vs. Mankind*, 123
24 *Car Culture*, 123
25 *Interstate*, 205
26 *America Adopts the Automobile*, 299
27 *Automobile Politics*, 73
28 *Car Culture*, 101
29 *Dynasties*, 126
30 *Autokind vs. Mankind*, 123
31 *Getting There*, 58
32 *A Financial History of the American Automobile Industry*, 5
33 *Urban Elites and Mass*

Transportation, 195
34 Wall Street Journal Oct 19 2004
35 Financial Times Feb 28 2006
36 Wall Street Journal June 23 2005
37 Times of London Aug 31 2007
38 Wall Street Journal Mar 14 2007
39 Wall Street Journal Oct 29 2004
40 New York Times Aug 19 2006
41 The Automobile Age, 407
42 High and Mighty, 81
43 High and Mighty, 81
44 High and Mighty, 88
45 Divorce Your Car, 58
46 http://www.articlesbase.com/
automotive-articles/toyota-ranked-6th-
in-fortune-global-500-list-181242.html
47 Interstate, 119
48 Internal Combustion, 249
49 Driving Over a Cliff?, 77/78
50 La Presse June 17 2006
51 Wall Street Journal May 2 2007
52 Wheels for the World, 62
53 Wheels for the World, 572
54 The Automobile, 147
55 Carchitecture, 37
56 http://www.nytimes.
com/2008/12/23/business/
worldbusiness/23toyota.html

CHAPTER 19

1 America Adopts the Automobile, 220
2 The Car and the City, 30
3 Financial Times Mar 27 2007
4 Economist Jan 1 2011
5 Wall Street Journal Mar 29 2007
6 Wall Street Journal Sept 25 2007
7 New York Times May 26 2007
8 La Presse Nov 8 2004
9 New York Times July 12 2008
10 Advertising Age Nov 20 2006
11 www.lowlandmpf.com/overview.htm
12 http://www.accuval.net/insights/
industryinsights/detail.php?ID=6
13 Car Culture, 15
14 Driving Over a Cliff? 127
15 The Economist Apr 24 2010
16 End of Oil, 170
17 Driving Over a Cliff?, 119
18 Interstate, 49
19 American Theocracy, 37
20 Crude, 38
21 http://en.wikipedia.org/wiki/
List_of_corporations_by_market_
capitalization#State-owned_companies
22 http://money.cnn.com/magazines/
fortune/global500/2010/full_list/index.html
23 Financial Times July 26 2007
24 Financial Times Nov 6 2007
25 Wall Street Journal October 4 2007
26 Crude, 80
27 Wheels for the World, 333
28 Wheels for the World, 333
29 The Automobile, 151
30 Twentieth Century Sprawl, 51
31 Wall Street Journal May 18 2008
32 Wall Street Journal May 31 2006
33 http://en.wikipedia.org/wiki/
Trucking_industry_in_the_United_
States#cite_note-52 http://www.atri-
online.org/index.php?option=com_con
tent&view=article&id=65&Itemid=76
34 Wall Street Journal May 1 2007
35 New York Times Nov 27 2006
36 http://thetimes-tribune.com/
news/business/supersized-dunmore-
mcdonald-s-debuts-area-s-first-dual-
drive-thru-1.829675
37 Buyways, 160
38 Buyways, 120
39 The Consumer Trap, 120
40 A Field Guide to Sprawl, 110
41 National Post Jul 5 2008
42 New York Times Feb 20 2006
43 Business Week Oct 17 2005

CHAPTER 20

1 The Corporation, 68
2 The Corporation, 68
3 The Corporation, 68
4 http://findarticles.com/p/articles/
mi_m1355/is_8_96/ai_55398731/
5 Dynasties, 145
6 Dynasties, 145
7 Dynasties, 146
8 Wheels for the World, 672
9 Wheels for the World, 674
10 Wheels for the World, 673
11 Taken for a Ride, 29
12 Taken For a Ride, 29
13 Les Quebecois au Volant, 53
14 Les Quebecois au Volant, 54
15 Les Quebecois au Volant, 53
16 Les Quebecois au Volant, 53
17 LA Times Sept 5 2006
18 http://www.randomhistory.
com/2009/01/21_cadillac.html
19 Les Quebecois au Volant, 57/55
20 Les Quebecois au Volant, 54
21 Mass Motorization and Mass
Transit, 61
22 Urban Elites and Mass
Transportation, 46
23 Internal Combustion, 219
24 Internal Combustion, 210
25 Internal Combustion, 230
26 Internal Combustion, 233
27 Les Quebecois au Volant, 56
28 Les Quebecois au Volant, 56
29 Fast Food Nation, 16
30 Les Quebecois au Volant, 58
31 Urban Elites and Mass
Transportation, 47
32 Gangs of America, 1
33 Internal Combustion, 199
34 Internal Combustion, 223
35 http://www.ejnet.org/rachel/
rehw439.htm
36 Internal Combustion, 246
37 Les Quebecois au Volant, 53
38 Internal Combustion, 227
39 The Bigness Complex, 66
40 Washington Post Dec 17 2006

CHAPTER 21

1 Taken for a Ride, 449
2 Carbusters 33
3 Dark Age Ahead, 40
4 The Consumer Trap, 78
5 Made to Break, 50
6 Autokind vs. Mankind, 179
7 http://hbswk.hbs.edu/item/6229.html
8 Financial Times Oct 20 2004
9 Divorce Your Car, 45
10 Advertising Age July 18 2005
11 New York Times July 19 2003
12 Divorce Your Car, 44
13 Down the Asphalt Path, 135
14 The Automobile, 61
15 Carjacked, 47
16 Advertising Age Feb 27 2006
17 Advertising Age Feb 20 2006
18 Advertising Age Mar 13 2006
19 Wall Street Journal Aug 26 2004
20 Wall Street Journal July 27 2006
21 Los Angeles Times June 1 2007
22 NewYork Times Mar 19 2007
23 NewYork Times Mar 19 2007
24 Wall Street Journal Oct 5 2004
25 Advertising Age Feb 6 2006
26 Advertising Age July 10 2006
27 Wall Street Journal Oct 22 2009
28 Life After the Thirty Second Spot, 135
29 Gazette May 2 2006
30 Advertising Age April 17 2006
31 Wall Street Journal Oct 24 2007
32 Business Week Feb 27 2006
33 Business Week Feb 27 2006
34 Business Week Feb 27 2006

35 *The Automobile, 32*

36 *http://www.msnbc.msn.com/ id/22612760/*

37 *New York Times Jan 10 2006*

38 *National Post June 22 2010*

39 *Advertising Age Nov 13 2006*

40 *Wall Street Journal Oct 5 2004*

41 *Advertising Age Oct 2 2006*

42 *Advertising Age Feb 5 2007*

43 *Washington Post Jun 17 2008*

44 *Advertising Age Dec 11 2006*

45 *Advertising Age Oct 2 2006*

46 *Advertising Age Oct 2 2006*

47 *San Francisco Chronicle Oct 24 2004*

48 *Washington Post Jun 17 2008*

49 *Financial Times Apr 12 2005*

50 *Financial Times Apr 12 2005*

51 *Financial Times Apr 12 2005*

52 *New York Times Jan 13 2005*

53 *Product Placement in Hollywood Films, 46*

54 *Product Placement in Hollywood Films, 81*

55 *Advertising Age Aug 14 2006*

CHAPTER 22

1 *High and Mighty, 277*

2 *High and Mighty, 277*

3 *Montreal Gazette Apr 13 2005*

4 *The Automobile, 59*

5 *Autokind vs. Mankind, 85*

6 *From Street Car to Superhighway, 127*

7 *Le Corbusier, 216*

8 *Car Free Cities, 249*

9 *Dark Age Ahead, 39*

10 *Trust and Power, 114*

11 *Product Placement in Hollywood Films, 14*

12 *Product Placement in Hollywood Films, 85*

13 *Product Placement in Hollywood Films, 59*

14 *Product Placement in Hollywood Films, 59*

15 *Republic of Drivers, 98*

16 *Product Placement in Hollywood Films, 74*

17 *Product Placement in Hollywood Films, 69*

18 *New York Times Nov 9 2010*

19 *New York Times Nov 9 2010*

20 *Financial Times Oct 14 2007*

21 *Financial Times Oct 14 2007*

22 *The Media Monopoly, xii*

23 *Goodyear Invades the Backcountry, 151*

24 *Lots of Parking, 55*

25 *The Media and Entertainment Industries, 109*

26 *The Media Monopoly, 61*

27 *Inventing Reality, 29*

28 *The News at Any Cost, 95*

29 *Superhighway-Superhoax, 107*

30 *High and Mighty, 280*

31 *High and Mighty, 280*

32 *Advertising Age Mar 1 2010*

33 *News and the Culture of Lying, 98*

34 *High and Mighty, 279*

35 *New York Times Apr 28 2006*

36 *Financial Times June 29 2005*

37 *Financial Times Jul 19 2008*

38 *Car Culture, 20*

39 *America Adopts the Automobile, 138*

40 *America Adopts the Automobile, 138*

41 *Fighting Traffic, 210*

42 *Fighting Traffic, 210*

43 *Car Culture, 20*

44 *The Automobile Age, 29*

45 *America Adopts the Automobile, 139*

46 *Advertising Age Mar 27 2006*

47 *Divorce your car, 45*

48 *High and Mighty, 277*

49 *High and Mighty, 277*

Stop Signs

50 *New York Times Apr 17 2006*

51 *Fighting Traffic, 209*

52 *Inventing Reality, 48*

53 *Inventing Reality, 48*

54 *Inventing Reality, 48*

55 *No Logo, 31*

56 *Guardian Weekly June 9 2005*

57 *Guardian Weekly Jun 9 2005*

58 *Advertising Age Oct 16 2006*

59 *New York Times Apr 11 2005*

60 *New York Times Apr 11 2005*

61 *High and Mighty, 278*

62 *Wall Street Journal May 31 2006*

CHAPTER 23

1 *Fighting Traffic, 225*

2 *Getting There, 112*

3 *Twentieth Century Sprawl, 25*

4 *Getting There, 113*

5 *Twentieth Century Sprawl, 25*

6 *Getting There, 112*

7 *Divorce Your Car, 51*

8 *When Corporations Rule the World, 158*

9 *Branded, 12*

10 *Born to Buy, 94*

11 *Washington Post Nov 26 2006*

12 *http://www.loe.org/shows/ segments.htm?programID=06-P13- 00049&segmentID=1*

13 *Washington Post Nov 26 2006*

14 *http://www.commondreams.org/ views06/1127-20.htm*

15 *Wall Street Journal Feb 21 2008*

16 *America Adopts the Automobile, 227*

17 *America Adopts the Automobile, 228*

18 *Recasting the Machine Age, 43*

19 *Trust and Power, 163*

20 *Auto Mania, 58*

21 *http://www.uakron.edu/about_ua/ news_media/news_details.dot?news Id=10878&pageTitle=UA+News&c rumbTitle=Challenge+X+Students+ Receive+Donation+From+General +Motors*

22 *www.uakron.edu*

23 *Lots of Parking, 37*

24 *Home on the Road, 97*

25 *McGill Daily Oct 5 2006*

26 *McGill Daily Oct 5 2006*

27 *Crude, 55*

28 *Los Angeles Times Feb 7 2007*

29 *Los Angeles Times Feb 7 2007*

30 *Los Angeles Times Mar 24 2007*

31 *Los Angeles Times Apr 21 2007*

32 *Corporate Power, American Democracy and the Automobile Industry, 70*

33 *http://dailynews.mcmaster.ca/story. cfm?id=2773*

34 *Globe and Mail Mar 3 2005*

35 *Toronto Star May 7 2007*

36 *New York Times Aug 29 2006*

37 *New York Times Aug 29 2006*

38 *New York Times Aug 29 2006*

39 *http://en.wikipedia.org/wiki/Albert_ Russel_Erskine*

40 *From Street Car to Superhighway, 111*

41 *The Automobile, 65*

42 *Fighting Traffic, 165*

43 *Fighting Traffic, 234*

44 *Fighting Traffic, 247*

45 *Fighting Traffic, 166*

46 *Fighting Traffic, 168*

47 *Fighting Traffic, 168*

48 *http://www.lovearth.net/ gmdeliberatelydestroyed.htm*

49 *http://www.baycrossings.com/ Archives/2003/04_May/paving_ the_way_for_buses_the_great_gm_ streetcar_conspiracy.htm*

50 *Buyways, 121*

51 *Buyways, 121*

CHAPTER 24

1 *Automotive News Dec 1997*

2 *Washington Post July 22 2010*

3 *Washington Post, July 22 2010*

4 *USA Today Apr 5 2007*

5 *The Automobile, 65 They*

6 *Divorce Your Car, 27*

7 *Into the Buzzsaw, 344*

8 *Getting There, 107*

9 *Urban Sprawl, Global Warming and the Empire of Capital, 60*

10 *Asphalt Nation, 205*

11 *The Decline of Transit, 170*

12 *Getting There, 179*

13 *The Automobile Age, 371*

14 *A Field Guide to Sprawl, 20*

15 *Getting There, 171*

16 *roadgang.org*

17 *Taken for a Ride, 349*

18 *Taken for a Ride, 349*

19 *Urban Elites and Mass Transportation, 151*

20 *Urban Elites and Mass Transportation, 114*

21 *Fortune Mar 19 2006*

22 *Wall Street Journal June 20 2007*

23 *New York Times Aug 29 2006*

24 *Financial Times July 15 2010*

25 *Financial Times July 15 2010*

26 *High and Mighty, 66*

27 *Divorce Your Car, 33*

28 *Twentieth Century Sprawl, 31*

29 *Corporate Power, American Democracy and the Automobile Industry, 58*

30 *The Automobile Age, 371*

31 *Autokind vs. Mankind, 89*

32 *Taken for a Ride, 19*

33 *Taken for a Ride, 19*

34 *Washington Post July 27 2006*

35 *Montreal Gazette May 18 2007*

36 *http://www.theglobeandmail.com/ news/politics/second-reading/spector-vision/some-news-you-may-have-missed/article1644648/*

37 *It's the Crude, Dude, 126*

38 *http://carbusters.org/files/2009/11/ Carbusters-14.pdf*

39 *Washington Post May 24 2010*

40 *Washington Post May 24 2010*

41 *Washington Post May 24 2010*

42 *Business Week Mar 5 2007*

43 *Business Week Mar 5 2007*

44 *Automobile Politics, 119*

45 *Fortune Mar 1931*

46 *Internal Combustion, 248*

47 *Cars and Culture, 45*

48 *Getting There, 115*

49 *Cars and Culture, 84*

50 *Cars and Culture, 85*

51 *Cars and Culture, 85*

52 *New York Times Nov 16 2008*

53 *http://www.thirdworldtraveler. com/Foreign_Policy/RulingElites_ MoveRight.html*

54 *New York Times Nov 16 2008*

CHAPTER 25

1 *Heat, 55*

2 *Carfree Cities, 178*

3 *Car Mania, 89*

4 *Twentieth Century Sprawl, 126*

5 *Twentieth Century Sprawl, 126*

6 *Twentieth Century Sprawl 118*

7 *La Presse Feb 20 2005*

8 *Twentieth Century Sprawl, 118*

9 *Twentieth Century Sprawl, 112*

10 *Twentieth Century Sprawl, 112*

11 *Twentieth Century Sprawl, 113*

12 *Twentieth Century Sprawl, 113*

13 *A Financial History of the American Automobile Industry, 10*

14 *The Automobile, 58*

15 *American Transportation Policy, 13*

16 *Twentieth Century Sprawl, 28*

17 *Twentieth Century, 28*

18 *The Automobile, 118*
19 *A Field Guide to Sprawl, 11*
20 *A Field Guide to Sprawl, 66*
21 *USA Today Oct 9 2008*
22 *The High Cost of Free Parking, 165*
23 *Urban Sprawl, 77*
24 *National Post Apr 28 2005*
25 *Once There Were Greenfields, 111*
26 *America Adopts the Automobile, 210*
27 *American Transportation Policy, 12*
28 *New York Times Sept 4 2004*
29 *American Transportation Policy, 14*
30 *Twentieth Century Sprawl, 27*
31 *Twentieth Century Sprawl, 68*
32 *The Automobile, 40 & 44*
33 *Twentieth Century Sprawl, 36*
34 *Twentieth Century Sprawl, 36*
35 *Twentieth Century Sprawl, 80*
36 *Twentieth Century Sprawl, 80*
37 *The Decline of Transit, 166*
38 *The Automobile, 117*
39 *Lots of Parking, 25*
40 *Lots of Parking, 25*
41 *Twentieth Century Sprawl, 36*
42 *Twentieth Century Sprawl, 70*
43 *Twentieth Century Sprawl, 70*
44 *Automobile Politics, 97*
45 *Twentieth Century Sprawl, 29*
46 *Autokind vs. Mankind, 92*
47 *The Automobile, 57*
48 *The Automobile Age, 375*
49 *Twentieth Century Sprawl, 32*
50 *Getting There, 156*
51 *Twentieth Century Sprawl, 34*
52 *New York Times Sept 4 2004*
53 *Cars and Culture, 80*
54 *The Consumer Trap, 119*
55 *The Consumer Trap, 119*
56 *A Field Guide to Sprawl, 52*
57 *The Automobile Age, 371*
58 *Twentieth Century Sprawl, 56*
59 *Twentieth Century Sprawl, 57*

60 *Twentieth Century Sprawl, 106*
61 *Taking the High Road, 58*
62 *The Atlantic City Gamble, 4*
63 *Corporate Power, American Democracy and the Automobile Industry, 109*
64 *Globe and Mail July 1 2005*
65 *Automobile Politics, 100*
66 *Globe and Mail Aug 30 3008*
67 *Montreal Gazette Nov 5 2007*
68 *Wall Street Journal Apr 13 2007*
69 *Automobile Politics, 198*
70 *Globe and Mail Oct 18 2010*
71 *Globe and Mail Jan 11 2010*
72 *The Bigness Complex, 260*
73 *Business Week Oct 1 2007*
74 *Perverse Subsidies, 56*
75 *Take the Rich Off Welfare, 100*
76 *New York Times April 20 2005*
77 *Economics at the Wheel, 184*
78 *Perverse Subsidies, 87*
79 *http://www.inthesetimes.com/ article/4262/the_future_of_transit/*
80 *American Transportation Policy, 71*
81 *Urban Sprawl, 154*
82 *Urban Sprawl, 154*
83 *Divorce Your Car, 104*
84 *Autokind vs. Mankind, 104*
85 *http://rightvoices.com*
86 *Getting There, 157*
87 *Divorce Your Car, 35*
88 *From Street Car to Superhighway, 166*
89 *The Automobile, 91*
90 *Car Culture, 187*
91 *From Street Car to Superhighway, 166*
92 *Lots of Parking, 44*
93 *Twentieth Century Sprawl, 44*
94 *Autokind vs. Mankind, 104*
95 *American Transportation Policy, 36*

CHAPTER 26

1 Advertising Age May 31 2010
2 http://www.treehugger.com/ files/2010/10/new-study-apartments-cars.php
3 Advertising Age May 31 2010
4 Car Wars, 149
5 Car Wars, 148-149
6 Concordia Link Sept 21 2010
7 Carbusters #42
8 Maclean's Sept 27 2010
9 Los Angeles Times Aug 21 2008
10 Car Free Cities, 234
11 Los Angeles Times Oct 10 2006
12 New York Times Jan 12 2007
13 Times of London Sept 11 2007
14 New York Times Nov 11 2005
15 La Presse Aug 14 2006
16 Toronto Star Nov 21 2009
17 USA Today July 2 2010
18 Autokind vs. Mankind, 135
19 http://www.yesmagazine.org/planet/ how-to-make-biking-mainstream-lessons-from-the-dutch
20 Wall Street Journal May 11 2006
21 http://cityroom.blogs.nytimes. com/2010/04/26/more-than-200000-a-day-now-cycling/
22 Maclean's Sept 27 2010
23 Maclean's Sept 27 2010
24 Alleviating Urban Traffic Congestion, 111
25 Carbusters #40
26 Carbusters #40
27 Car Free Cities, 228
28 New York Times Nov 11 2004
29 Enemy of Nature, 243
30 Economic Democracy
31 http://planetgreen.discovery. com/tech-transport/investing-in-transit-creates-more-jobs-than-road-investments.html
32 Urban Sprawl and Public Health, 179
33 Bury the Chains, 86

Acknowledgements

There are so many who helped directly and indirectly bring *Stop Signs* into being, raising an idea until it grew into this book. Many thanks go to Bernadette Stringer, Gary Engler, Jean Rands and Al Engler for their support, encouragement, patience and love. We are so grateful for their help and guidance on this manuscript. Thanks to Mary Mugyenyi for being a role model and inspiration. Thanks to Olga Mugyenyi for her editorial advice and hilarity as well as Nunu Mugyenyi and Benji Mugyenyi for their stories, love and encouragement. Thanks to Pete Garden and Rachel Engler-Stringer for their insight and support. Thanks to Elaine Littman for her beautiful cover designs. We'd also like to thank Maya Rolbin-Ghanie, Dru Oja Jay, Avina Gupta, Veronique Allard and Stefan Christoff for their wisdom and friendship. Thanks to Nadia Hausfather for graciously facilitating our library addiction. Thanks to Ky'okusinga Kanyangyeyo and Esther Kemigisha Tayebwa for their kindness and enthusiasm. Thanks to Jessica Haber, Dan Rosen, Nirina Kiplagat, Tamara Extian-Babiuk, Lisbeth Junge, Aly Stillman-Greene, Mabel Reyes and Sarah Armstrong for sharing their ideas, hearts and homes. Thanks to Katie Earle, Lorraine Harrilal and Laura Ellyn Robbins for their vision, courage and street smarts. We are indebted to a host of writers, journalists and activists — too many to name — from whom we gleaned a wealth of knowledge into the world of the automobile. Thanks to all those who let us crash and to the many beautiful souls we met on our journey across the USA. Thanks to Fernwood Publishers.

Praise for Stop Signs

"In Stop Signs, Mugyenyi and Engler take readers on an insightful, fact-filled journey through the primary habitat of the car-dominated species they call Homo automotivis. With wit and originality, they weave travel tales into a convincing argument against the auto economy, culminating with a fresh call to leave car culture behind."

Katie Alvord, Author, Divorce Your Car! Ending the Love Affair with the Automobile

"Stop Signs is at one and the same time an entertaining, fact-filled anthropological tour of the land of *Homo Automotivis,* and the first all-out global ecological critique of the American automobile addiction. Not since Jane Holtz Kay's *Asphalt Nation* has a book appeared that so clearly exposed the auto-irrationality of the most car-dependent country on earth."

John Bellamy Foster, editor Monthly Review and co-author, The Ecological Rift

"This book is a must read for anyone who wants to understand the impact of the private automobile on our urban transportation options. Think about a future with expensive gas, many areas with poor public transit and sprawl. Ask yourself what is the future of cities that are not today developing compact public transit oriented cities that are walking and cycling friendly. Where will you want to be living?"

David Cadman, Vancouver City Councillor, International President ICLEI-Local Governments for Sustainability